MW00446222

"*Awakening the Avatar Within* is a phenomenal guidebook on how to live on the leading edge of consciousness and awaken your latent superpowers. It is indispensable reading for those wishing to claim their power to live an extraordinary life of deep love and fulfillment of their highest purpose."

—**Christy Whitman,**
author of *The Desire Factor* and
the *New York Times* bestseller *The Art of Having It All*

"*Awakening the Avatar Within* guides you through the essential actions and practices you can do to fulfill the higher potential that you always knew was possible but may have had a hard time actualizing. Avatars are human beings going through a process of re-wiring the energy circuitry of their bodies so they can embody higher light more of the time. This is required reading for anyone ready for awakening to their true self and learning to practice energy healing at a high level of expression."

—**David T. Kyle, Ph.D.,**
bestselling author of *Energy Teachings of The Three*

"*Awakening the Avatar Within* is one of those books you will want to keep around for years. It can help you gain insights for self-transformation. This book is a treasure of workable insight and approaches."

—**Richard Gordon,**
Founder of Quantum-Touch,
author of *Quantum-Touch and The Secret Nature of Matter*

"Darren Starwynn's book, *Awakening the Avatar Within*, is both inspirational and practical. It is a treasure map of how to heal, grow and embody the Divine Self. Anyone with the willingness to follow this motivational guide and apply the simple and grounded processes can accelerate their awakening journey. This book is a spiritual gift, for it shows us how to be a part of the Second Coming of Christ, which is a group event. I highly recommend it for all who want to live their True Nature and manifest a creative and transformative purpose."

—**Karen La Puma,**
author of the *A Toolkit for Awakening book* series

"*Awakening the Avatar Within* is a sophisticated yet accessible guidebook for healing and spiritual awakening that brilliantly incorporates wisdom from many streams, including Darren Starwynn's own direct connection with Source. Fresh, inspired, and heart-based, it's filled with mind-expanding concepts, moving stories, compelling testimonies, and powerful exercises that will totally uplift your entire being, from body, to mind, to spirit. It's also an illuminating resource for healing practitioners who want to go deeper with their clients. Thank you, Darren, for using your superpowers to bring this gift forth. It should become required reading for anyone incarnated on planet Earth."

— **Marguerite Rigoglioso, Ph.D,**
Author, *The Mystery Tradition of Miraculous Conception:*
Mary and the Lineage of Virgin Births

"These days, there seems to be an endless stream of books and Internet sites about healing and consciousness, Darren's book *Invoke the Avatar Within* stands out like a bright beacon of light. Darren has done something new and different, very necessary in these destructive times on our planet Earth. He has provided a practical roadmap for evolving both our minds and physical bodies to a higher level of consciousness and vitality through the principles of epigenetics and spiritual alchemy. He has convincingly shown a way that people can become Avatars, and how awakened Avatars can join forces to literally change this world. Today, in the compromised political and public domains, it is truly difficult to name any heroes, Darren's work is indeed champion."

—**Jon Whale. PhD.,**
author of The Catalyst of Power, scientist and inventor

"In his latest book, *Awakening the Avatar Within*, Darren Starwynn manages to describe the current problems, and the solutions for all of humanity in clear and easy prose, and makes it easy to follow his guidance in how to recognize and develop the Avatar you already are. In addition, you can feel an energy transmission that emanates from the very pages of the book. This book is chock-full of intriguing information along with easy-to-follow guided practices, all designed to awaken your remembrance of who you really are."

—**Vidya Frazier**,
author of *The Ascension Lightworker Guide*
and *Awakening to the Fifth Dimension*

"In *Awakening the Avatar Within*, Darren Starwynn, O.M.D., offers a practical and pertinent guide to how to be a "practicing evolutionary", and help heal our own lives, along with humanity's traumas. As the boundaries between the physical and metaphysical become more porous, Darren helps awakening souls guide others through this evolutionary passage – so that heaven becomes a practice instead of a destination."

— **Steve Bhaerman**,
aka Swami Beyondananda, Comedian,
Uncommontator and co-author of *Spontaneous Evolution* with Bruce Lipton

"*Awakening the Avatar Within* guides the reader through practical steps of a deep inner awakening of their highest self, helping tap into pure consciousness, your own healing transmission and the ability to transcend old habits and patterns that have kept us stuck as mind/limiting self."

—**Shannon Kassoff**,
Yoga Teacher, Master Reiki Teacher

"This very inspiring, spiritual book got me thinking on a deep level, and had transformative practices and exercises that brought me to renewed levels of inner peace, greater understanding, and greater oneness with the Universe."

—**Betsy Schenk**, Psychotherapist

"Darren Starwynn offers great insight and inspiration, as well as practical exercises and suggestions for navigating the trajectory of your life, no matter what age. *Awakening the Avatar Within* teaches you how to nurture your authenticity while maintaining your integrity with your relationship to yourself and to others."

—**Debra Bentley**, Acupuncturist

"*Awakening the Avatar Within* offers invaluable coaching on self-development and practices which will enhance mental and spiritual health. It shows a pathway from struggling to survive toward blossoming into the kind of culture and humanity which will put human values before corporate greed."

—**Diana Bickford**, Holistic Healer

"Each time I took up your book, I noticed I needed to adjust my vantage point and relax into a state of openness and exploration— distinctly different from predominant paradigm/consensus reality. Additionally, I experienced this material as <u>living</u>. It resonated throughout my days when I wasn't reading. Concepts would arise or I would experience situations in a new light, which I could feel!"

—**Jacob Barnett**, Tai Chi instructor

"This is an excellent, in-depth, very accessible offering for anyone wanting to explore the true nature of the self, especially in the context of this time of consciousness and evolution, as well as processes for healing the self and others—written by a highly regarded, long-time healer and teacher to many."

—**Marjorie Bair**, spiritual teacher

"This book is about how to tap into who you really are. We are all special, and Darren Starwynn will help you see your own personal power, lift your self-confidence, and get you on the right track to achieving everything you ever wanted. Achieving your dreams is often for the greater good too!"

—**Michele Arnold**, Acupuncturist

"*Awakening the Avatar Within* has the potential to shift one's perception from limited belief systems to understanding that the field of all possibilities exists at your fingertips."

—**Paul Bando**,
Holistic Health Practitioner

AWAKENING
THE
AVATAR WITHIN

AWAKENING
THE
AVATAR WITHIN

**A Roadmap to Uncover Your Superpowers,
Upgrade Your Body and Uplift Humanity**

DARREN STARWYNN, O.M.D.

Copyright © 2022
Darren Starwynn, O.M.D.
All rights reserved. No parts of this book may be reproduced or transmitted in any form or by any means, mechanical or electronic, including photocopying, recording, or by any information storage and retrieval system, without permission in writing from the author, except short excerpts for review purposes.

This book is also available in e-book and audiobook versions, as well as hardcover collector's edition containing full-color original artwork and photographs.

Purchase of this book entitles you to access free audio & video guided meditation course. Access it at: www.drstarwynn.com/practices

ISBN: 978-0-578-25142-4 (Paperback)
ISBN: 978-0-578-25321-3 (Hardback)
ISBN: 978-0-578-25143-1 (eBook)

Library of Congress Control Number: 2021912289

Publishing Consulting: Geoff Affleck, AuthorPreneur Publishing Inc., geoffaffleck.com
Cover artwork by: Zizi Iryaspraha Subiyarta, Pagatana.com
Editing and proofreading: Susan Nunn, Laura Davis and many other highly appreciated volunteers
Typesetting: Amit Dey, amitdey2528@gmail.com
Original artwork: Kate Bakkila, kleandesignbykate@gmail.com
Photography: Jane Richey Photography
Modeling: Jackie Teele

Published by Desert Heart Press, Tiburon, California
Email contact: info@drstarwynn.com

OCC014000 BODY, MIND & SPIRIT / New Thought
OCC011010 BODY, MIND & SPIRIT / Healing / Energy (Qigong, Reiki, Polarity)
OCC019000 BODY, MIND & SPIRIT / Inspiration & Personal Growth

Contents

Avatar Roadmaps

Original Artwork Illustrations

Illustrations are by Kate Bakkila unless otherwise noted.

Foreword

by
Dr. Sue Morter

At this unique moment in our collective history, humankind is emerging in an evolutionary uprising toward higher consciousness, bringing an ever-increasing clarity of what is ours to claim. Quantum Science is providing a pathway for the logical mind to embrace versions of ourselves previously left only to the esoteric and spiritual conversation. Historical sciences (and many of their limited perspectives based in linear thinking) are now being surpassed by discoveries in the disciplines of human biology, neuro and cellular plasticity, and the undisputable power of the mind that, when coupled with the energies of heart coherence, has the ability to transform our health, our happiness, and even our world.

In this world where science and spirituality are drawing ever nearer, Darren's message joins the ranks of those awakening humanity to the fact that we are so much more than we've been conditioned to believe. *Awakening the Avatar Within* aligns with the energies emerging during this important time on our planet, calling us to step into our magnificence and embody our Truth as the Soulful Self, or the Avatar we are.

As evidence of our ability to restructure ourselves both neurologically and bio-chemically become increasingly obvious, it is time for us to embrace this new truth of our being. Research is showing us, beyond the shadow of a doubt, that we generate our reality and are either *surviving* or *thriving* within it. What we think, feel, and believe has an impact on every experience of life itself, including the activation of our very own genetic inheritance and the reconstruction of it. Now more than ever, we are being shown that we are a complete and creative force on earth with the power to change our own chemistry as well as our own cellular structure, even regenerating injured and damaged tissues previously thought to be permanently altered.

We are "youth-ing" ourselves, healing ourselves and others with remote communications, and tapping into our source with greater potency, more now than at any other time in recorded history.

We are learning that *everything* is energy, *including us,* and that energy can be altered but never destroyed. We are changing our identity, realizing our pain and suffering is a by-product of assuming we are a separate and distinct entity, rather than a constant stream of energetic consciousness. We are now aware there is a foundational field of energy – of which we are each an expression – that allows us to access a never-ending abundance of resource to live the life that we can imagine. We need only remember how.

In my book *The Energy Codes: The Seven Step System to Awaken Your Spirit, Heal Your Body and Live Your Best Life,* I show people how to access that essence of our true Self, while offering the science behind the principles and practices therein. The book is not only a collection of theories and concepts compiled from cutting edge science. Rather, it is based on my personal experience of higher states of consciousness that ignited for me during a life changing moment in deep-state meditation. In that moment, I awakened, not only as having a profound revelation of human possibility, but having the direct experience of it – an initial moment of felt contact inside a new reality. In that state I recognized who and what we truly are through an actualization.

Witnessing the complete bandwidth of consciousness from this space I realized that heaven and earth are a continuum, not two separate and distinct realms. There is no dividing line. I also realized the truth of what we are: A compression of light that, as it embodies all the way to the physical end of the spectrum, becomes another vibrational frequency - One that we call Love. The degree to which we allow this to move through us with each breath and without distortion is the degree to which we experience our true selves – Love in a body.

Since my moment of awakening, I've spent my life in experimentation of the processes it would take to return to this sacred space on command. I spent 10 years codifying this process into what has become "The Energy Codes" which I now teach in more than 95 countries around the world.

A blending of science and spirituality was needed to be able to speak to the comprehensiveness of the topic. Fortunately, I had experience and a rapidly rising expertise in both. As a scientist, I was interested in reproducing this state and understanding what was happening as I did. As a doctor, I wanted it to matter for humankind. The process has taken me to a space of Avatar in my own awareness, and my life has changed because of this. Each of us has this capacity. We need only find the guidance to help us remember how.

I share this information with you to offer additional perspectives to the point that Darren Starwynn is making for us in his new book *Awakening the Avatar Within: A Roadmap for Uncovering Your Superpowers, Upgrading Your Body and Uplifting the Human Race.* Darren is interested, as am I, in demystifying the mystery and walking the awakening path with practical feet.

Once we realize how natural it is for us to rise into our own Christed consciousness, as he will explain to you here, a critical mass can occur for humanity which will facilitate the process for others to awaken as well, to not only the life but the reality we were meant to have and share. This book will help you change your life into an empowered expression of the Avatar that you truly are. Enjoy the ride!

Dr. Sue Morter is an internationally known authority on bridging science, spirit, and human possibility. She is a master of Bioenergetic Medicine, a Quantum Field visionary, and a best-selling author.

www.drsuemorter.com.

Introduction

There is now a rapidly growing movement of people who recognize that awakening of human consciousness is the ultimate solution to our personal and planetary problems. They recognize the truth that there is one common denominator to all the environmental, social, political, economic and health crises facing the human race now. That common denominator is the part of the human mind denying our true, divine self – the universal consciousness of Love and oneness.

This book is a roadmap to an extraordinary transformative process few people even believe is possible. Each of its chapters contains consciousness-awakening messages combined with transmissions of higher light energy. Receiving these transmissions and working with the guided practices offered will support you in realizing your true identity as an Avatar. The word Avatar is derived from the Sanskrit word *avatara,* which means "descent," meaning the Divine coming down to manifest as a human being for a big purpose.

You probably know some people who radiate spiritual light in powerful and charismatic ways. They tend to be spiritual teachers, ministers or other kinds of leaders, and many are drawn to follow them. You may wonder "I'm not like one of those, how could I possibly be an Avatar?" The truth is, there are many different ways Avatars show up and not all are in public view. I can assure you that you have your own "job description" for how you beautifully express divinity. Chapter 17 – *Your Job Description as a Lightworker* will help you identify it.[1]

Living as an Avatar becomes real as you go through the physiological process of upgrading your body to be able to hold a higher frequency of energy and consciousness. From that place, you will discover you have real superpowers you can develop and share to help heal, bless and uplift others. And, have a lot of fun in the process!

---

1 See Chapter 17 for distinction between the terms Avatar and Lightworker

These extraordinary transformations are possible because we are living through a wave of rapid planetary ascension of consciousness affecting all life. This is part of vast cycles of consciousness that have been documented in the ancient Vedas from India, traditional Mayan cosmology and other sources. The doors to awakened consciousness are now wide open, much more so than ever before in recent human history. In fact, our greatest impediment to taking advantage of this extraordinary opportunity is simply believing we can't.

The human race is already moving through this ascension into greater light, and nothing can stop it. What is variable is how much suffering there needs to be during this transition time. This is where modern Avatars shine. We have powerful abilities to heal ourselves and reduce the suffering of others. We do this by helping accelerate the grounding of higher light in our bodies, our psyches, our societies, our arts, our institutions and our sciences.

What is variable is how much suffering there needs to be during this transition time. This is where modern Avatars shine. We have powerful abilities to heal ourselves and reduce the suffering of others. We do this by helping accelerate the grounding of higher light in our bodies, our psyches, our societies, our arts, our institutions and our sciences.

There are so many good people working toward the healing and upliftment of humanity in all those areas. Yet without the major shift of consciousness Avatars help bring, our collective experience is likely to look like one step forward, one step backward. That's not enough for humanity to make it through this time without increasing destruction.

Each of us is caught up in this ascension of consciousness, and our experience of it can range from blissful to deeply disturbing. A great analogy is riding a surfboard on large ocean waves. When surfers have good balance and skill, the experience of riding big waves is exhilarating and joyful.

If they lose their balance and "wipe out," they can quickly find themselves crushed under a wall of water and gasping for breath.

In a similar way, when you trustingly allow the rapidly elevating energies of consciousness ascension to carry you, it is a high, joyful experience – the greatest ride of your life. Yet if you fearfully deny and resist this profound shift in consciousness, it can and often does feel scary and overwhelming.

The information, perspectives and practical methods presented in this book come from my own lifetime journey of learning, research, self-healing, helping heal

others, meditation, facing my shadow self, teaching and direct spiritual experience. Rather than place a bio about me at the beginning of the book, I have woven my personal story throughout various chapters within it.

Healing Ourselves

If you're like many people on the path of self-healing, you may have consulted with a succession of healers, therapists, doctors, holistic practitioners, clergy, gurus or self-help books, and yet still have times when you feel a deep sense of trauma or disconnect within your being. And yet there is a mighty divine current flowing through you 24-7 that can free you from all bondage and give you the power to help free the rest of the human race. This is the missing link that can bring you what you have really been looking for through all that searching.

You can access more of this divine current through the process of becoming *Christed*. Christing refers to a process through which your mind, body, nervous system and genetics are literally rewired to operate at higher frequencies of love, intelligence and creative power.

Christing refers to a process through which your mind, body, nervous system and genetics are literally rewired to operate at higher frequencies of love, intelligence and creative power.

These are attributes of what is often called God or Divine source, and as an Avatar, your job is learning to practically express them in your everyday life. In this case, the term Christing has a similar meaning to the words "maturing," "evolving," or other terms that describe a process of fulfilling one's greater potential. The oft-prophesied second coming of Christ is not about one superstar person making a grand appearance. The second coming is happening as huge numbers of people become Christed, and through the immense field of love and power that generates, we are able to effectively rebuild our world.

Section Two of this book is titled Quantum Healing and gives you practical guidance in developing your Avatar healing abilities. As will be explained in Chapter 13, you are in holographic inter-connection with all life. This means there is no real separation between you, everyone else and the entire Universe. Therefore, you can be a catalyst of healing for people thousands of miles away. Due to the holographic principle, there is essentially no difference between healing yourself and helping heal the planet – it all happens together. It's just a matter of your intention and focus.[2]

The phrase, I AM Avatar, is a supremely powerful affirmation and mantra of your highest truth. When you say I AM Avatar, you identify yourself as an expression of the pure love, power and wisdom of the Universe. You accept responsibility for being a vital part of the solution at this critical time. To some people, saying I AM Avatar or I AM the Christ may sound like a radical, conceited or even an insane thing to say. Yet claiming I AM Avatar is the pre-eminent key to the fulfillment of your personal purpose, healing and self-realization.

The following passage from the beloved Indian scripture, the Bhagavad Gita, expresses the purpose of an Avatar well. The word *Dharma* in this quote means fulfilling your true purpose and living in tune with the laws of nature.

"Whenever dharma declines and the purpose of life is forgotten, I manifest myself on earth. I am born in every age to protect the good, to destroy evil, and to reestablish dharma."[3]

According to this phrase, we are certainly living in a time where Avatars are needed – lots of us.

I'm calling upon you to trust your own inner knowing. Don't settle for anything less than this highest and clearest truth that a vital part of you already knows. If you have ever felt that there was a bigger picture for fulfilling your life potential or a more expansive way you could contribute to the welfare of the human race, now is the time to step up. It is my sincere wish that the message, practices and vibrational transmission of this book act as a touchstone to help awaken you to a greater truth of who you really are. The tools you will gain here can empower you to free yourself from your own inner struggles and contradictions, and recognize the divine energy transmission that is already flowing through you. The ultimate

---

[2] Chapter 13 provides details of the remarkable practice of engaging in planetary healing
[3] Attributed to the ancient Avatar Krishna in the Bhagavad Gita

solution is right here to all the things that may have made you feel discouraged, frustrated or afraid.

Dogma—Free Understanding of Avatar, Christ, Buddha and Lightworker

The word Christ has a similar meaning as Avatar. It is derived from the Greek word *Kristos* which means the anointed one, referring to a human being who is expressing divine Presence. Christ is an innate quality of the true, higher self of human beings. Therefore, I use both terms Avatar and Christ interchangeably throughout this book. *The term Christ is not used here in a religious, Christian context.* The term Buddha, which means "awakened one" in the Pali language, also has a similar meaning. All of these terms describe the experience of being an awakened Avatar in human form, independent of any religious affiliations or beliefs.

A more contemporary word to describe those stepping up to heal and serve through higher consciousness is *Lightworker*. There are already many millions of people acting as Lightworkers on our planet now, and that is one of the main reasons that so many natural and human-caused disasters have been averted or lessened from how severe they could have been. If you are a Lightworker or moving into being one, Chapter 17 will help you identify the characteristic ways you offer your love and service.

Two of the most famous Avatars, Jesus the Christ and Gautama the Buddha, were not always awake. They had to go through a process of becoming aware of the illusions they lived in, taking back their power and awakening themselves to their true nature. They were able to break free of the profound amnesia most of us fall into when we grow up in human bodies. Yet they are no more Avatar than you are. It's just that they accomplished their awakening to a greater degree, and so can act as our helpful big brothers. This same opportunity is in front of you now.

How Can Avatars Help Uplift the World?

Avatars are creators, and intuitively grasp a profound truth: what we see as "the world" is not any one certain way. It is really what we believe it to be and make it to be. Realizing this truth is a major step in awakening our consciousness and knowing who we really are. Less awakened people generally see the world helplessly, in a fear-based way. Avatars learn to hold the vision of the world they choose to live in, manifesting their vision by focusing their love, consciousness and actions upon it. This means that each person living as an Avatar becomes a beacon of light helping illuminate the path for others.

This form of focus has unlimited potency, especially as large numbers of us develop our superpowers and focus together. See Chapter 4 to learn more about your superpowers.

I have witnessed many remarkable examples of the power of Avatars when we focus our light together. As a striking example, in the fall of 2019, some of the worst wildfires in recorded history were raging throughout eastern Australia. Prior to the start of these wildfires, Australia had been gripped by record heat and more than two years of continuous drought. By November of that year, a state of catastrophic fire danger was declared in Sydney and other parts of New South Wales. By January 2020 over 46 million acres were burning in various Australian states and territories, destroying thousands of homes and decimating entire species of animals and plants.

In mid-January, 2020, I received a series of emails calling on me to participate in two scheduled times of global meditation to benefit Australia. Participants were requested to take a few minutes two days in a row to visualize heavy rains falling all over the fire-stricken parts of the country. It was suggested in the email that we visualize people standing out in the rain celebrating and giving thanks. I participated in these group meditations, feeling the power of people all over the world focusing their prayers.

Rain started falling within two days after these global meditations. The first rainfall in late January started putting out the fires. Then, between February 6th and

10th, 15.4 inches of rain fell throughout the fire-stricken areas of Australia, putting out most of the fires. It was the heaviest rainfall recorded in Australia in 30 years.[4]

I have heard about or witnessed many experiences like that. Another one happened at the time of the Deepwater Horizon oil spill back in April of 2010, in the Gulf of Mexico. Considered to be one of the largest environmental disasters in U.S. history, over 210 million gallons of petroleum were discharged into the Gulf with severe toxic effects on human and marine life. Scientists and engineers tried many methods to cap the deep underwater well without success over a five-month period.

On the weekend of September 18 – 19 of 2010, I was participating in a spiritual healing retreat in Tucson, Arizona led by Dr. Zhi Gang Sha, a teacher of advanced spiritual healing methods. At one point on Saturday the 18th, one of the retreat participants suggested that I ask Dr. Sha if our group could somehow help mitigate the Deepwater Horizon environmental disaster. I did go up to him during a break and explained the situation. Dr. Sha had not heard about it since he apparently didn't listen to the news. But he acknowledged the situation and agreed to "see what he and our group energy could do." The next day, Sunday the 19th I was checking the news and learned that a team of engineers had finally succeeded at capping and containing the oil spill.

Was this just an interesting co-incidence? Or could it have been a manifestation of the power of focused intention? I am open to the latter explanation because I have personally experienced or heard about many such extraordinary healings and reprieves from negative or disastrous situations throughout my life. Awakening Avatars can participate in a level of causality hard to explain through most of our sciences, yet can clearly be experienced. The science of Quantum physics has been catching up to being able to explain the power of consciousness to create reality, and you will find several explanations of quantum phenomena throughout this book.

Why Trauma Matters and Why Healing Trauma is an Essential Part of the Solution

Trauma is a big deal for the human race now. While about 8 – 12 million people in the United States are medically diagnosed with post-traumatic stress disorder or PTSD, almost all of the rest of us deal with what I call "low-grade PTSD." It has become our new normal to feel stressed out in various ways due to economic

---

[4] https://www.bbc.com/news/world-australia-51439175

pressures, isolation, family breakdowns, exposure to toxins and living in highly polarized societies.

Ironically, all of this easily recognizable stress is exacerbated by the mass ascension of consciousness we are part of. As our consciousness expands, we are becoming more empathic, literally feeling more of the pain of the world. Many of our own conveniently buried psychic burdens and unresolved past trauma are also coming up to the surface of our minds much more quickly than we can often process. These are reasons why so much of the traditional psychotherapies and holistic healing arts only ease part of people's distress these days.

As mentioned above, Lightworkers are Avatars who specialize in helping others heal by awakening to their true nature. This is the highest and most effective form of healing. It truly frees people from their past mental and emotional programming, and allows them to step up to being part of the solution themselves. Section Two of this book is full of valuable guidance for healers and specific healing methods.

Opening to your Avatar Energy Transmission

As you go through the process of becoming Christed, you become familiar with the specific ways divine consciousness expresses through you. I call this your unique *energy transmission*. This is a stream of pure vibrational energy emanating from your highest spiritual source that flows through you and blesses others in profound ways. This is the essence of you. It is also what makes you most effective at whatever you are called to do in your life.

Why do I say that your energy transmission is unique? Think of the human race as a huge symphony orchestra. Each musician in the orchestra has her own part to play that differs from most of the other player's parts, although some players share the same part and play in sections. When each player in the symphony plays her part clearly and accurately an amazing, beautiful composite musical sound is created. This is the way it is with us. Our energy transmission is the part we are given to play in the grand symphony of the human race. Our highest key to success, effectiveness and fulfillment in every aspect of our life is identifying our unique energy transmission and cultivating our body's ability to hold and emanate it.

The specific abilities your transmission gives you can be called your superpowers. These are the ways you express genius in your life. Yes, that's right, genius. Genius refers to people who have opened up to allow their transmission to freely express through them. There is great, unlimited power in this. We have seen how a handful of people in touch with their genius have transformed the human race through science, technology, the expressive arts, furthering of human rights, spiritual awakening and much more. You are now called to be one of them. Why? Because you can! And, also because the world surely needs that special ability you are perfectly suited to offer.

The reason this book, and others like it are needed is that most of us who are Avatars in human form are on the latter part of a long journey in which we have been exploring the human experience. During this "long strange trip" we have experienced all manner of high and low vibratory experiences, from the heights of ecstasy to the depths of despair. We have repeatedly acted out the roles of both perpetrator and victim. Many of these experiences have created lasting energy imprints upon the ultra-sensitive inner membranes of our subconscious minds. By now, that has created quite a bewildering burden that can cloud our hearts and obscure our sight. I often use the Sanskrit word *samskara*, or the English terms "energetic gunk," conditioning or "residoo-doo" to refer to this complex psychic burden that is at the root of most chronic pain, disease, anxiety and depression.

One factor that has made this burden even heavier is the tendency for some self-serving individuals and organizations to take advantage of others by programming their minds with messages and images designed to manipulate them into giving their divine power away. These individuals have been all too happy to take this power for their own personal gain. You will learn how to put a stop to that in this book.

Human beings are energy transceivers. This means that we are constantly sharing energy vibrations with others – sending and receiving. This includes those close to us and those a world apart. The current Earth condition in which close to 8 billion people are sharing vibrations that are frequently stressed and fear-based has created a kaleidoscopic mass hallucination in which we have largely lost touch with who we really are. No wonder things often seem so bizarre.

The great news is that there are simple, effective methods for clearing your inner space so you can not only remember that you are an Avatar but also embody that pure, high vibration of love in your everyday, physical experience. This makes you a powerful part of the solution whether you are engaging as an activist or living a quiet, contemplative life – or anything in between.

Healing Humanity

As I write these words our human family is living through a new set of experiences that very few of us ever expected. The fallout from the COVID-19 virus epidemic put the brakes on much of human activity through much of 2020 and 2021, and at the time of this writing is still adversely affecting many countries. As is usually the case, those who are richer and more privileged are coping relatively well and even thriving, while the poor face increasingly devastating consequences.

There are almost endless beliefs and theories about what this epidemic is, where it came from, why it is happening and what the solution could be to get the human race back on track. People hunger to know – when will things go back to normal so we can get on with our lives?

My firm belief is that things will never go back to what we considered normal, and that's a great blessing. We have been living on Planet Earth in ways that have become increasingly unsustainable, and as a result, are facing a myriad of escalating consequences. To put it simply, we just can't keep living the way we've been living. The issues surrounding COVID, and pressing social issues filling the news headlines daily have pushed an even more crucial truth to the background of most people's awareness – and that is the environmental reckoning we are facing now. Ninety-seven percent or more of actively publishing climate scientists agree that climate-warming trends over the past century are extremely likely due to human activities, and the majority emphatically state that this poses critical threats to human wellbeing and even survival.

The Day the Earth Stood Still is a well-known sci-fi movie that was produced in two versions in 1951 and 2008. The story is about an alien with God-like powers who comes to Earth to tell the human race that our self-destructive ways are not only endangering ourselves but other worlds as well, and that we must change our ways or be stopped. In case you have not seen the movie I recommend it and will not spoil it by disclosing more.

Although our current situation is not the same as the plot of that movie the underlying truth – the urgent need for rapid, fundamental change – is accurate.

It would make sense for scientists, governments, churches and all concerned people to come together to mobilize our best resources to resolve the pressing crises facing humanity. Yet there is deep division among people, not only about what the best approach is but even what the most fundamental facts are about our situation. This extreme polarization has hamstrung the kind of massive, unified action and mobilization so needed now.

This book offers a radical perspective on some of the most effective solutions to these challenges of our individual and global situation. I will demonstrate that it is through our consciousness we have collectively created our current situation, and it is through the unlimited power of awakened consciousness we can save the human race and our Earth from destruction, while simultaneously ascending into a way of living we may have only dreamed of as conscious, joyful sovereigns.

Getting Started –
How to Use This Book

What you really are is an Avatar - a deity or divine being in human form. You can activate your direct experience of that remarkable truth through the messages and practices contained within this book. It offers a practical roadmap and tool chest that combines mind-opening, and at times mind-blowing insights with simple guided practices. I call these Ascension Practices because working with them can permanently elevate your level of consciousness. I have been learning and experimenting with such practices for decades, and have put the simplest and most effective ones in Section Four – Ascension Practices. You will find additional practices at the end of some chapters that take you into the living experience of what is presented in the text.

This chapter offers essential information that prepares you for all that follows, as well as a set of simple foundational practices you can start working with right away. These practices align you with the direct experience of your true, Avatar self. *For best results read this before moving onto the other sections.*

When a caterpillar is born it looks like a worm. About a week later it turns into a cocoon called a chrysalis. Then it basically falls apart into a mush of what scientists call imaginal cells inside its cocoon. Over the next 7 – 11 days that mush turns into a gorgeous butterfly that emerges, and then flies around creating amazing beauty in the world. This is one of nature's most dramatic demonstrations of transformation.

You and I are now involved in a transformational process much more far-reaching than a caterpillar turning into a butterfly. We are rapidly transforming into a higher order of life through a process called ascension. Through this, we are moving into experiencing an expansiveness of love, deep healing and fulfillment of our higher purpose which we may have only dreamed of before. In this new reality, so many things we have considered to be improbable or impossible are discovered to be real.

This book also contains an energy transmission. This means there is a living vibration inherent in its pages that helps you realize, or make real what you are reading. You will only receive this transmission, however, if your own higher self says "Yes" to it. Nothing here will impose anything on you that you don't choose and welcome. The transmission of this book invites you to adjust your vantage point and relax into a state of openness and exploration. This state of mind is distinctly different than "consensus reality" – the set of limiting beliefs and perceptions of ourselves and our world that most people share.

Here are some guidelines to prepare you to get the most out of this journey:

1. The content that follows alternates between readings and guided practices. Each chapter is designed to awaken your remembrance of who you really are, and present valuable knowledge and insights. Reading the chapters can be illuminating and entertaining. Doing the practices at the end of each chapter and in Section Four will provide you the most transformative experience.

    You may want to dive into the practices right away as you read the chapters. Another option is to read the text of the book through one time to grasp the content, and then work through the practices once your eagerness for freedom is stimulated. Chapter 22 offers convenient guidelines for setting up a daily practice routine that suits you. Chapter 20, Living as an Avatar offers an integration of the key practices and teachings throughout the book and will be a good friend.

    Whether or not you're already in the habit of taking time for meditation and inner healing work, this can be a great time to start. By spending even a few minutes a day experiencing the benefits of these Ascension Practices, you will probably want to go further. You can also be visually guided through the practices by accessing a set of free videos and audios I offer online for readers of this book. See Resources Section Six.

2. You will find quotations from Jesus, Buddha and other well-known Avatars in this book because they had amazing gifts for expressing advanced truths in simple parables most people readily grasp. These remarkable beings demonstrated how humans can transform into Avatars. They prototyped that experience so that it can be much more accessible to us now. In some cases, I have taken the liberty of updating phrases attributed to these masters with more contemporary wording. Again, these quotations do not indicate

allegiance to a particular religious belief system. If I were writing a book about mathematics, physics or modern dance, I would quote top experts in that subject, and that's the spirit in which I quote these masters here.

3. I have arbitrarily alternated between using the words "he", "him", "she" and "her" in sentences that require that. These are not intended to create distinctions between people of different genders but are merely for convenience in the written word.

4. The journey of this book requires words and terms you may not be familiar with, or that in some cases could use updating. You will find a Definitions of Terminology section in Avatar Resources Section Six. The first time an unusual or non-English term is used in each chapter it is printed in *italics*. That means that you can find it in the Definitions of Terminology section for a fuller explanation. Each use of the term after that in the chapter is printed without italics.

5. This book combines factual information with insights that have come through my own experiences and contact with unseen sources of wisdom. Much of the factual information contains footnoted references for further investigation. There is no way I can prove the reality of the other parts. As is the case with other channeled literature, that information is presented for you to consider and put through the test of your own inner knowing.

6. All journeys start with a decision to take the first step. It is your desire that motivates you to do what it takes to awaken and free yourself. As you read these chapters, it is well to stay open to discovering more of your deeper desire and commitment to awaken to the magnificence of your true self.

One term used often in this book is "chakra" so I will offer a definition of that here. Chakra, which means "wheel" in Sanskrit, refers to spinning vortices of energy and consciousness within your body that help govern all parts of your physiology, psychology and spirituality. There are seven major chakras stacked vertically in the central column of the body, and there are many additional minor chakras throughout the body. There are also chakras below the feet in the Earth and above the head that serve to ground us to the Earth and connect us to divine Source energies. Chakras are major aspects of what can be called our "subtle anatomy" – patterns of energy and consciousness that are non-physical, but just as "real" and essential as our physical organs. The process of *Christing* involves significant clearing and upgrading of your chakra system.

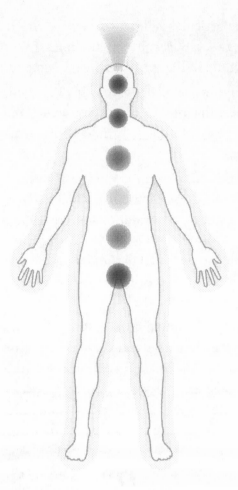

The Foundational Practices

Coming to know yourself as the Avatar you are is a profound experience. On this journey, your body is your best friend and ticket to admission. The following ultra-simple practices are foundational for embodying more of the brilliant energy of your Avatar self in your body. Consider these the launching pad for all the other practices in the book. Each practice offered later will start with the instruction "Engage Foundational Practices." Therefore, I suggest you become intimately familiar with the foundational practices that follow and begin to work with them on a daily basis.

While the list may seem long at first glance, once you learn them you'll be able to do all of them at the same time within five to ten seconds. So, enjoy your brief learning curve, and know that it will soon be very quick and simple to implement and enjoy these foundational practices.

Purity Blast

It is helpful to be able to rapidly clear the energy fields of our body into a state of purity and clarity. You can do this in a couple of seconds by invoking a Purity Blast. To do this simply state with conviction "I now call for a Purity Blast." I like to hold one hand up in the air as I state that. Then either feel or imagine a rapid down-rushing vortex of white or golden light coming from your highest spiritual source high above you, and moving through your body and the room or space you are in. That's it. Just invoke it and trust it is done. I do Purity Blasts before and after each client session I offer to make sure the energetic space in which we work is cleared out from any energies discharged by the previous client, or anyone else. I also do Purity Blasts before and after each teaching event I lead in person or over the internet. This simple practice can make a huge difference in the ease and clarity of your experience.

Coming Back to Yourself

Although we rarely realize it, most of us frequently project parts of our consciousness outward onto other people, places or emotionally charged situations. That means that parts of us are hanging around outside of our bodies. Some of your energy may be projected outward onto people you have any uncomfortable, infatuated or incomplete feelings about, scary things you heard about on the news, or even a pop song that is "stuck in your head" or many other reasons. This is a pretty normal situation.

Any form of meditation or practice you enter into will work much better if you first simply declare "I call all of myself back into my body." Just as you did with the Purity Blast say it with conviction, simply trusting that it is done. This is a very direct way to take back your power from whoever or whatever you gave it away to. It can also be helpful to imagine or visualize streamers of your essential energy instantly flowing back into your body from all around you. You can combine Purity Blast and coming back to yourself into one step by decreeing "I now command a Purity Blast and call all of myself back into my body," though it may be easier to do these as two separate steps when you are first learning these practices. Each step should take you no longer than a few seconds.

Master Hook-Up

Lightly touch the tip of your tongue to the roof of your mouth, slightly behind your two upper front teeth. This contact acts like closing a circuit breaker, instantly connecting and balancing all the vital energies of your body. Doing this gives you an immediate boost of groundedness and power. Acupuncturists may say it balances the Yin and Yang energies of the body through the two great meridians on the front and back midlines of your body.[5]

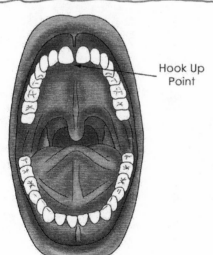

Hook Up
Point

It's almost impossible to feel anxious when your tongue is in this position. Try it and see. Practice the Master Hook-Up as much as you can while you are reading these chapters and doing the practices offered in them. And any other times in your life when you're not talking, eating, drinking or kissing, this is a very simple way to increase your mastery and Presence.[6]

---

[5] These are called the Ren (front midline) and Du (back midline) meridians. The Ren channel connects all the Yin, nutritive energies of the body while the Du connects all the Yang, activating energies of the body.

[6] The word Presence is capitalized in many places throughout this book to indicate a high-vibrational, divine quality emanating through a person's energy field.

Grounding and Mula Bandha

There is more to becoming your Avatar self than just understanding and belief. You must also learn to <u>physically</u> embody the divine true self that you are. *Embodiment* is a key term you will hear often because that's where the action really is. You can only embody to the extent you are grounded. Here are some simple guidelines for grounding your energy:

1. Put your attention on your Root, or base chakra that is in between your legs in the perineum area. Slightly squeeze the muscles there. Squeezing those muscles is called *Mula Bandha* which means "root lock" in Sanskrit, and is also referred to as the Kegel exercise.[7] Intend to keep those muscles slightly squeezed throughout your practice or as an alternative, squeeze Mula Bandha during in-breaths and release on the out-breaths.

2. Imagine that a tree trunk or thick steel rod is form-fitted to the base of your body in the Root chakra area, and penetrating down into the Earth. Imagine this grounding rod as thick and substantial, about the width of your pelvic area. You can visualize this grounding rod extending all the way to the core of the Earth, with its roots wrapping around it for a solid

---

[7] The practice of Mula Bandha involves tightening the same muscles you would contract to stop the flow of urination

connection. Or alternatively, see it connecting to a disk of living golden light two feet (.61 meter) down into the Earth. That is called your *Earth Star* chakra. Either way, release any stress, excess thoughts and tension down through your grounding rod into the Earth. She can handle it and knows exactly how to transmute your stress, sending it back to you as clear energy.

A slightly more advanced method of grounding is to feel and visualize a vertical axis of living light energy extending from a chakra two feet (0.61 meters) above your head, through the central channel of your body where all the chakras are, and down two feet into the Earth to the Earth Star. This awareness will be the basis for Central Axis breathing and most other practices taught later in this book, so it is useful to start visualizing and feeling it as much as you can now. If this seems challenging then simply imagine your Earth grounding at this point. See the image for this practice in Chapter 23.

The Complete Breath

I know you've probably heard it a thousand times. Breathing fully is the number one key to radiant health, spiritual awareness and feeling fully alive. Babies and most mammals instinctively breathe in a full, complete way, but as people age, they tend to chronically constrict their breathing and make it shallower. Just one more of our insane coping mechanisms.

The main reasons so many of us breathe shallowly are unresolved past traumas, dwelling on fearful thoughts and over-focus into the mind. I'll put it even more starkly. Shallow breathing tends to make you smaller and powerless, while full breathing expresses Presence and sovereignty.

Here is how to empower yourself by restoring your ability to enjoy complete, full breathing:

The Complete In-Breath:

1. With your tongue in the Master Hook-Up position, breathe in through your nose with the intention to fill up your lower abdominal area. It may be helpful at first to put the palm of one hand over that area so you can check to make sure your belly is ballooning out with air. If that is difficult at first because you've been a shallow breather stay with the practice, it will get easier over time and you'll feel better and better. Continue your in-breath as you go through these next three steps:

2. After your lower abdomen expands, notice your lower back slightly expanding.

3. Allow your chest to expand.

4. Finally, feel your upper back slightly expand.

The Complete Out-Breath:

1. Breathe out through your nose or mouth. As you start breathing out feel your upper back contract slightly.

2. Then feel your chest contract.

3. Now, let your lower back contract slightly.

4. Finally, your lower abdomen contracts.

Repeat and enjoy the feeling of aliveness. Combining the Complete Breath with Central Axis breathing (Chapter 23) is one of the most powerful ways to increase embodiment of your Avatar self and bless your life in countless ways.

Your energy destiny is now in your hands. The more you breathe completely, the more energy advantage you give yourself.

As you increase the amount of time you breathe completely, you may go through some psychic house cleansing. Old thoughts and feelings you have been suppressing or denying may come up into your emotional or bodily awareness. If that happens congratulate yourself. You are taking an empowered, courageous stand for expanded aliveness. Use the tools of self-love, Central Axis breathing and The Inner Embrace (Chapter 24) to dissolve the old conditioning that is coming up. That is a loving, empowering process.

As simple as complete breathing is, taking on this practice will significantly change your life.

Loving Presence

As you do the Master Hook-Up and Complete Breath, tune into the experience of pure love. That's not so hard to do. Think of the person, animal, experience, place or spiritual being that most easily brings a smile to your face and a glow to your heart. Doesn't matter if it's your child, your boyfriend, your dog, your mother, Jesus, God, the Earth, Michael Jackson or your favorite Zumba class. You know what it is. Allow your heart to tune into as much love as possible – there's an infinite supply. Once you feel the love, call upon it to increase. Breathe your expanded love throughout your body while you do the Master Hook-Up and do it as often as possible. Love melts all blockages.

The Purity Blast, Coming Back to Yourself, Master Hook-Up, Grounding, Complete Breath and Loving Presence are your foundational practices for this journey of claiming yourself as an Avatar in human form. All the other practices in this book are based on this foundation. In fact, if you just mastered these practices and did nothing else your life would wonderfully transform.

SECTION 1

I AM AVATAR

The nine chapters in this section contain the core teachings of how to live as an Avatar – recognizing your unique spiritual transmission, healing yourself, claiming your superpowers, transforming your body and recognizing and helping bring in the New Earth. It will also raise your consciousness about the planetary ascension of consciousness we are all part of at this time.

1

I AM Avatar

In order to understand what an Avatar is, you first need to grasp what Divine Source is. Divine Source is the highest point from which everything real originates. I emphasize the word "real" because so much of what our minds consider to be reality is only a dim reflection of the bright light we truly are.

An Avatar is a representative and embodiment of Divine Source, imbued with the force of destiny to affect large numbers of people and help to change the course of history.

Now, if after reading that last paragraph you're having a hard time identifying yourself as an Avatar who can help change the course of history, that's completely understandable. In our upbringing, most of us have been "domesticated" to believe that we are limited and full of flaws. Even people who have been meditating for a long time tend to believe that they have a long path of gradual spiritual growth ahead of them. But is that really true?

If you evaluate yourself now, you may assess a combination of strengths and weaknesses, ways you feel confident and grounded and ways you still feel wobbly and insecure. Imagine a future version of yourself who has already healed your deepest wounds and mastered your weak, wobbly parts. This future self has passed through the struggles you may be facing and lives in a state of enlightened multi-dimensional mastery beyond your mind's present comprehension.

Reality is holographic, which means that everything in the Universe, including all you call your past and future experiences, exists right here and right now. Therefore, your masterful future self also exists here and now. By simply believing you can, it is possible for you to call upon this part of you and bring its unlimited creation power into your present experience. Because your future self is tapped into all the love, consciousness and power of the Universe, and is available to you right now, you can help change the course of history.

Recognizing your Avatar self who already exists here and now requires a shift in your perception of yourself. "You" – the personality you largely identify with now - doesn't need to live up to any idealized images of perfection, spirituality or selfless loving to embrace and share your Avatar self. Your Avatar is already alive and well within you, just as you are now. In fact, you'll likely come to realize that every experience you've been through in your life has been orchestrated to bring you to this point of realization. That includes all of your successes and alleged failures, all the knowledge and skills you've gained in many areas of life, and your deepest traumas. It was all a soul-guided course in cultivating the wisdom and compassion needed to develop your superpowers and live as an Avatar.

Understanding Your Avatar Self

To really understand Avatars and why they come here, it is necessary to understand that our human race is in a deeply fallen state compared to the natural radiance of our true selves. In this case, "fallen" means that as a race, we have become more caught up in the dense, low-frequency energies of fear and separation than we are with the bright, love-filled frequencies of our true selves. If we were living in a more awake, and even more "sane" way we would know who and what we really are. We would readily recognize we are interconnected spiritual beings expressing ourselves through this physical experience. Therefore, there would be way less conflict and polarization.

Because we've been asleep and caught up in our mostly dark waking dream, Source has now and then had to send messengers who were more awake to the human race. These messengers came to shout "Hey! You guys are sleeping! You're sleepwalking toward the cliff of self-destruction. You need to turn around and go in a different direction. Come on, get with the program of who you really are. Here are a few teachings and techniques to help you along the way. By the way, love one another." We've called those we've recognized as Avatars using titles such as Christ – the Anointed One, Buddha – the Enlightened One, and Quan Yin – the Compassionate One. Those were not the names of these messenger humans; they were their job descriptions. The name Krishna, another legendary Avatar from ancient India means "dark blue" or "the all-attractive one."

Avatars have demonstrated a golden path in front of each human being that deeply transforms our bodies and awakens our consciousness if we follow it. Along this golden path are major change points resembling the sub-atomic quantum leaps described by quantum physicists. These times of rapid up-leveling of consciousness are sometimes called spiritual initiations.[8]

Melani is a sports medicine acupuncturist and herbalist specializing in pain and orthopedic conditions. While she has had a successful practice for some time, she felt something was missing. Here is how Melani described how her consciousness awakened while attending a virtual Quantum Healing retreat:

I have had a lot of training when it comes to the biomedical side and the Eastern medicine side, but I've felt that I've been lacking something, something more well-rounded. I needed the energetic aspect, the spiritual aspect. That's something that my school education didn't touch. I could not for the life of me feel embodiment[9], and that was just driving me nuts because I had done a lot of self-work through various books and online programs. But I kept getting asked the same question. And what it was asking me was, if you take away your past, who you feel you are in your profession and all these other external things, who are you really? I was stumped. I couldn't answer that.

That was really bothering me because I felt like there's more here. When we started doing the meditations as part of the retreat, for the first time I actually got to feel that embodiment which I have been just trying to find for me, and it was very,

---

[8] For references on spiritual initiation, see the Bibliography in Resource section Six

[9] Embodiment is the process of the master divine being you truly are coming into physical expression. Also called incarnation. Very few people are fully embodied due to deeply embedded fear and control programs, and also because they have not felt ready to be fully responsible for being Present. Coming into fuller embodiment creates physiologic, epigenetic changes which upgrade the body

very eye-opening and awakening. It was a very emotional experience for me because it's been something that I never felt existed inside of me. Since I've been awakened, I've just felt so much more at ease and comforted and safe. Safety is a feeling that I've never had before. Previously, I always felt like I had to keep looking for the next thing, the next book, the next class, the next meditation or the next course. And I just don't feel that anymore.

The last two to three weeks have been the first time in my life that I have not felt constant anxiety about any external things or even internal things. I felt very quiet inside, which was very strange for me because I've always had this internal dialogue constantly going on, and I just didn't feel that anymore. I also felt a lot of physical manifestations come out. I now have this sensitivity to knowing what foods are good for me and I'm feeling my food again at a cellular level when I eat it. I had turned that off for many different reasons, but now it's turned back on.

I feel like I see the world differently. Sounds are sweeter and my food tastes better. The earth looks brighter and I can even see music now. Before I could never do that. So, all of this has awakened inside of me.

Avatars and Religions

Avatars are like big brothers and sisters who come here to help show us the way. But of course, being the superstitious, addictive and outward-projecting beings we tend to be, we take these big brothers and sisters and put them up on pedestals and say, "I worship you. You are special and unique. I will build big churches and organizations around You and enshrine Your words in special books and persecute the hell out of anyone who dares question these holy books. We will create a whole class of special mediator-priests who are specially ordained to connect people to You. We reserve extreme punishments for those in our flock who DARE to consider that God, the highest authority, is within themselves. That is BLASPHEMY and punishable by anything ranging from ridicule and being ostracized to death." And a whole lot of other things that I'll frankly call nonsense.

Now I'm not saying religions are useless or misguided. The major religions of the world have done a great deal of good by encouraging people to study the teachings of the Avatars, to be helpful and charitable to others and in general to live more virtuous lives. There has also been a very dark side of religions. This has included the Crusades, sexual abuse scandals, forced conversions at the point of a sword, calling spiritually gifted women "witches" and burning them at the stake and in general demonizing and justifying the persecution of the "other."

Aside from these extreme abuses, the overall problem I have with religions is that they are partially based in a deep ignorance — we should worship the messenger rather than truly realize the message they came to bring us. That message is that we all have the potential to live as Avatars and know what is true for ourselves. If we carefully read the actual messages of the great Avatars, they are telling us they are here to demonstrate what each of us is capable of:

> *Truly I tell you, the one who believes in me will also do the works that I do. And he will do even greater works than these, because I am going to the Father.*[10] – Jesus

> *We are what we think. All that we are arises with our thoughts. With our thoughts we make the world.*[11] – Buddha

So an Avatar is really you when you wake up to who you really are.
That is so important that I'll repeat that again:

> *An Avatar is really you when you wake up to who you really are.*

All of the negative comparisons we make between ourselves and the famous Avatars are on the level of the limited, conditioned mind. So, claim your own Avatar mission without the need for comparisons.

Another thing obstructing a clear understanding of what Avatars are is that so much of what we read about this subject comes from ancient texts, translated multiple times. Each time a sacred text is translated some of the original meaning is distorted by the biases and belief systems of the translator. We are used to reading about Avatars in outdated, often fanciful language, generally not how people actually speak and think. Therefore, we tend to file that information away in a different part of our brain than tangible things in our everyday lives. One of my goals is to update this information into plain language you can more easily grasp. I'm not telling you to necessarily believe my interpretations, either. As an awakening Avatar, you have powerful inner senses to tell you what is true for yourself.

Buddha encouraged his students to be skeptical of all that they heard and to arrive at the truth for themselves:

> *… don't go by reports, by legends, by traditions, by scripture, by logical conjecture, by inference, by analogies, by agreement through pondering views, by probability, or by the thought, 'This contemplative is our teacher.' When you know for yourselves that, 'These qualities are skillful; these qualities are blameless; these qualities are praised by the wise; these qualities, when*

---

[10] The Bible, John 14:12

[11] From the *Dhammapada*, attributed to Gautama Buddha

adopted & carried out, lead to welfare & to happiness' — then you should enter & remain in them.[12] *– Buddha*

The gist of this statement from Buddha is: "Don't believe anything that goes against your own sense of what is right or your common sense – even if you hear it from me."

Avatars are Pioneers and Prototypers

Avatars come here with a special mission, purpose and style. According to records, some came as peaceful wandering teachers, and some came as warriors. Yet they all came here to wake people up, especially at times when the human race was descending into a major self-destructive direction. If you look around at our world that may ring a bell.

The Avatar who appears to have had the greatest impact on the human race was Jesus of Nazareth, probably called Yeshua in his native Aramaic tongue. Jesus was an extraordinarily courageous man who accepted the gigantic mission of prototyping the high-octane experience of being the Christ in human form. What he did was analogous to the first fish who flopped up on a beach and managed to survive breathing air, thereby prototyping being an early amphibian. I'm sure those creatures felt like they were almost dying as they were gasping for air while their gills shut down, and their rudimentary lungs were just starting to come online. But by going through that transformation those first amphibians helped open up a whole new order of life on land. Jesus took an evolutionary leap like that on the chin as he triumphed over the pain and horror of human mortality and made his ascension. He blazed a new path to demonstrate that this was really doable, creating a template of becoming Christed that all of us can now follow much more easily.

I have seen convincing evidence from researcher and author Marguerite Rigoglioso that Jesus's mother Mary was also a very powerful and highly influential Avatar. Although the scriptures and dogmas approved by the Christian Church depicted Mary as a pious and holy saint, it seems that she was also a highly adept spiritual master in her own right. She used advanced spiritual alchemy to prepare her womb to birth an Avatar who would change the course of human history. Mary steadily infused the growing fetus within her with special activating frequencies of light and sacred sound.[13] These prepared Jesus to manifest superpowers that were

---

[12] *Kalama Sutta*, attributed to Gautama Buddha
[13] See Rigogliosio, Marguerite, *The Mystery Tradition of Miraculous Conception*, Bear & Company, 2021

way ahead of the consciousness of his time. As awakening Avatars, you and I are also developing our own superpowers.[14]

You and I, and billions of other people are able to be guided and inspired by the Avatars who have lived on Earth because many of them are now acting as ascended masters – former human beings who have passed all the tests of the material life. Because of their victory over the lower, ego-based self, ascended masters are able to powerfully serve huge numbers of people from the spiritual realms. I have some crazy news for you. That option is also open to you as you progress on your path.

Avatars with a Dark Mission and Avatars of Creative Power

We usually think of Avatars as beings who brought advanced ideas and elevated spirituality. Yet the forward evolution of human consciousness has at times required massive tearing down of old forms. Dark Avatars are those who helped transform humanity in ways that created great destruction and suffering.

A clear example is Genghis Khan who lived in Mongolia in the 1200s. Starting out as an orphaned child struggling to survive amidst enemy tribes, his destiny led him to create a massive army eventually conquering China, most of Asia and Eastern Europe. While Genghis Khan and his followers were responsible for untold amounts of killing and destruction, his influence eventually opened up trade routes and cultural connections between East and West never existing before his time. Therefore, however harshly we may judge him, he was a man who dramatically changed the course of history.

---

[14] See Chapter 5 Recognizing and Claiming Your Superpower

Hitler was a modern dark Avatar, as his odious influence left the world a changed place with the USA ascendant as the major world power, and the balance of power in Europe permanently altered. None of this sanctions or condones the evil done by Hitler or other dark Avatars, it just acknowledges that these individuals have also had major roles in shaping human history. It is important for us to learn from these historical experiences so the human race has less need for more of that kind of massive destruction.

Many musicians, artists, scientists and humanitarians have also been well-known Avatars because their influence significantly altered or evolved human consciousness. My favorite example is the Beatles – four lads from Liverpool, England whose music strongly influenced an entire generation (and beyond) and helped expand human consciousness. It could be argued that basketball prodigy

LeBron James is an Avatar because through his huge influence many Black organizations gained in political clout. Because these organizations turned out a tremendous number of voters to the polls, James seems to have been a decisive force in helping the Democrats win the 2020 Presidential election. The courage Avatars Rosa Parks and Claudette Colvin before her showed in standing up to racial segregation in the 1950s and 1960s created a turning point in the civil rights movement in the USA. There have been so many others who expressed their Avatar nature by rising to the level of great courage and determination in this and so many other vital movements toward justice and equality worldwide.

Claiming Your Avatar Nature

Part of the territory of claiming your own Avatar nature is to realize you also have a certain purpose and mission. As you'll read in Chapter 3, the foundation of your mission is to get in touch with your divine Avatar *transmission and* allow it to *epigenetically* transform your body and mind.[15] This is a form of rewiring your body,

---

[15] See Chapter 5 for explanation of epigenetics and human transformation

allowing higher levels of spiritual energy to express through you. Then you'll be able to bring out your superpowers, which empower you to fulfill your mission.

Claiming your Avatar self can be a very rigorous process. You'll need to stop running from the parts of your psyche that may have been the hardest to face or have been repressed. Recurring dreams, nightmares or patterns of dysfunctional behavior could be indications of places of great power within you that your personality has been afraid to access or touch. In other words, the path of the Avatar is not for the faint-hearted! Yet neither are any other paths on this planet at this time, so why not play the master game?

The Second Coming of the Christ

The pure consciousness of the Avatars is not an individual thing – it is much more similar to mushrooms growing in the wild. On the surface, mushrooms look like separate plants popping out above the ground, yet underground they are all interconnected as one big organism. Did you know that a single mushroom organism can be as large as four square miles? That has been documented.[16] While each of us has our own Avatar mission and job description, our greater power is released when we come together with other Avatars. The prophesied second coming of the Christ is not about a single superstar individual showing up who saves the world. The second coming is when large numbers of people awaken to their Avatar self, coming together in shared intent to love and serve. That is ultra-powerful and happening on Earth now. Yet you won't hear much about this growing movement in our favorite media. Good news doesn't boost ratings.

The real truth about the transformation the human race is going through has been shown to us all along through many sources. Most people miss it because they are usually either too busy, too distracted, too apathetic or too afraid to see it. In this book, I will quote from some of those sources. One is the hit 1999 movie *The Matrix*. This is the story of a reclusive computer programmer named Neo who is pursued by unknown assailants, after which he is offered the choice of a blue or red pill by the enigmatic Morpheus. He is told that if he takes the blue pill, he can continue to see the world however he wants to. If he takes the red pill, he will be awakened to the reality of his situation, and "will see just how deep the rabbit hole goes." Neo chooses the red pill and soon he sees that the world he believed he had been living in was only a computer simulation projected into his mind. His eyes are opened to how he had been living as a slave, and what he needed to do to free himself and help free

---

16 https://www.discovery.com/nature/Giant-Mushroom-Largest-Organism-Ever

others. The plot details of the movie are fictional, but the underlying message offers a remarkably accurate disclosure of the condition of the human race.

Since *The Matrix* movie was released, the human race has been rapidly freeing itself from those who would control and disempower us. This is wonderful, good news, yet you must realize and experience this truth for yourself. You do that by claiming your own freedom and awakening. As you do that, you make it easier for others to claim theirs.

In the conclusion of *The Matrix*, Neo is gunned down by agents who had been trying to shoot and kill him throughout the story. After appearing to be dead, Neo is revived by a kiss of the woman Trinity. As he reclaims his life Neo realizes that he is "the One" who can simply put up his hand and say "no" to the swarm of bullets coming toward him. As he does this, the bullets stop in midair and fall harmlessly to the ground. This is a dramatization of true Self-realization in which we realize our true identity as Christ Avatars. Through this we accept our power to create our reality, thereby becoming free from fear and death.

The most vital transformation toward living as the Avatar you are comes as you recognize and learn to consciously embody your Avatar transmission. As you go through that process, you come to know yourself to be "the One" within your vulnerable human self who helps save the world just by being you. As we then come together with other Lightworker Avatars in the physical or on the inner planes we discover our great power to rock this planet.

Guided Exercise: Invoke the Avatar Within You

If you are motivated to get in touch with your own Avatar identity and mission, start a journal for that purpose. It is powerful to start this process with clear intention. You can say words like these silently or out loud (or make up your own):

> *It is my intention, as the divine master being I AM, to invoke the Avatar within me, so that I directly experience this part of me physically, energetically, mentally, emotionally and spiritually. Bring awareness of my future self into my present experience, as is appropriate for me now.*

I will repeat that invocation one more time:

> *It is my intention, as the Divine Master Being I AM, to invoke the Avatar within me, so that I directly experience this part of me physically, energetically, mentally, emotionally and spiritually. Bring awareness of my future self into my present experience, as is appropriate for me now.*

Now, having made your invocation, relax and let go. Simply breathe deeply, keeping your awareness on the sensations within your body. Focus on your loving presence, and the feeling of joyful anticipation of coming to know and express more of your Avatar, future self, now. The more you let go of your mind and sink into your body, the more your awareness can grow. Be curious and attentive.

Now that you have invoked your Avatar, what do you notice? You may notice subtle shifts in your energy or consciousness, different emotional feelings, tingling in parts of your body or other experiences. Or you may feel you're not experiencing anything different. Your Avatar self lives in a realm of stillness that often feels like emptiness to the human mind. If you are feeling nothing, let that be OK. Breathe fully into your lower abdomen, keeping your tongue lightly touching the roof of your mouth.

It is possible you may also experience waves of fear or tension arise after making such a powerful invocation. If you feel that, it is likely to be the voice of a young part of your psyche "domesticated" to think of yourself as small and powerless. This part has been called the "slave self", and it is not real. Many of the practices offered in Section Four will support you in transforming this old conditioning.

When you feel complete in this Avatar meditation tighten the muscles around your Root chakra to ground yourself. Feel your physical presence in the room or place you are. When you're ready, slowly open your eyes. Take a few conscious breaths with your eyes open, noticing what the world looks like to you now.

If you can take a few more minutes, write something about your experience and intention. Commit to writing in your journal several times in the coming week or longer about what comes up in your day-to-day experience, especially when you have dreams, insights or strong feelings. Once you set that intention and start recording your experiences things will start moving. Revelatory thoughts will come to you at unpredictable times. You may have lucid dreams, or people will show up in your life to mirror parts of you. They may do that lovingly and supportively, or sometimes through confrontation and challenge. The purpose of all that is to fulfill your intention of realizing your Avatar self.

2

Getting Motivated – Vairagya

Many people want to feel greater aliveness, enjoy increased financial success, experience closer relationships or become more spiritually awakened. Yet few find the motivation to make necessary changes to their thoughts and behaviors to have those experiences more consistently. Instead, they do everything they can to stay within their emotional comfort zones, only venturing outside of that when they must do so for their survival, employment or family obligations.

There's no way to sugarcoat it. Stepping into the higher fulfillment of your life purpose is the most richly rewarding experience; yet approaching the pathway to doing so tends to bring up avoidance and procrastination in most people. This human tendency to avoid the discomfort of the unknown has been scaring people off the path of awakening to the true self for millennia.

People who know alcoholics understand this only too well. Even though alcoholics may be aware that continuing to drink is wrecking their closest relationships, threatening their livelihood and messing up their health, they find ways to deny it. Only when they hit some kind of emotional bottom where they absolutely know that their lives have become unmanageable, are alcoholics able to take the first steps of recovery.

There is a similar occurrence on the path of awakening to who you really are. In the process of awakening, you will need to let go of a lot of the limiting beliefs you have been attached to. There are deep fears to overcome. You need to give more of yourself than you have wanted to and challenge the deepest underpinnings of what you have believed your identity to be.

Here's a good check-in point. If what you just read above sounds scary and uncomfortable, and perhaps makes you want to stop reading, you are likely identifying with the viewpoint of your small-self mind. If reading the above touches and excites you and makes you eager to continue, you are probably coming more from the perspective of your true self. Your true self loves freedom and truth and can be inspired by straight talk like this. There is no judgment either way, as you and I and most everyone else have these different aspects. The quality of our experience comes down to which one we choose moment to moment.

I remember a story I read about the Russian spiritual master, Georges Gurdjieff. His disciple, Ouspensky was telling the master how inspired he was about his enlightenment experiences. He gushed something like, "This is so great, why don't way more people get on this path?"

Gurdjieff is said to have replied (paraphrased) "The reason is this—if people knew what it would really take to be enlightened, and all that they would have to give and to let go of, no one in their right mind would choose it. That's why the master must trick disciples into becoming enlightened."

I have found accuracy in this story. Going through everything I've been through, and facing all my weaknesses, selfishness, stubbornness, terror, density and feeling like a spiritual novice in comparison to others has been rough. I've, in a sense, been "tricked" by different teachers' descriptions of light-filled meditation, inner serenity, cosmic visions and a heart full of overflowing compassion into making efforts and commitments that were way out of my comfort zone. Yet the "trickery" has worked for me. I have become far more aware and embodied precisely because of all those practices and the giving of myself I was reluctantly motivated to commit to.

The Sanskrit word *vairagya* describes this process of getting deeply motivated better than any word in the English language. It is often translated as "detachment," but I don't think that's accurate. In my opinion, the closest phrase in the English language to vairagya would be "disillusionment turning into strong motivation." It's a profound realization that we've been playing small, running from our most genuine selves, compromising with love, wasting loads of precious time, avoiding what is most valuable and somehow "missing the boat" on really fulfilling what we know is possible for us. All those, combined with feeling cut off from our most loving source and admitting how much we want that, creates powerful motivation and that is vairagya.

Vairagya often comes to people through major life crises – severe illnesses, painful divorces, losing their money, losing a loved one, war, mental breakdowns or near-death experiences. These can often be understood, at least in part, as your soul doing something dramatic to grab your attention. Your soul does this because it doesn't want you to keep avoiding the higher purpose of your life, thereby twiddling away your precious life force. As hard as these experiences are, if ultimately embraced they can open a doorway that takes you into higher states of enlightenment and greater embodiment of your true, Avatar self.

Getting vairagya doesn't have to be painful or traumatic, however. Some people reach points in their lives where they are ready to focus their minds and go within without dramatic things happening to them. Their souls call strongly to them, and they are listening. From a place of awareness, they internally say "Yes." So don't have any negative expectations of what is required to gain this form of deep motivation. I expect that the need for personal cataclysms to bring people into vairagya will diminish as the ascension of consciousness on our planet accelerates. You are totally welcome to jump onto this leading edge of humanity right now.

The Motivation of Pure Desire

There is one powerful force that can make the process of vairagya more enjoyable and inspiring – attuning yourself to the pure desires that arise within you and devotedly following them. Indeed, desire is the all-powerful original urge that created the Universe and everything in it.[17] Yet desire has gotten a bad rap from many spiritual teachers and writers. Practitioners on paths of spiritual awakening are often taught to fear following their desires because it may distract them from advancing on the path. In fact, traditional religious and spiritual belief systems commonly teach that chasing our desires can lead us into sin, eventually smashing us into a wall of frustration and despair that may lead to vairagya. Is that really what it takes?

I see this as a misunderstanding rooted in messages from old, outmoded systems of spiritual development based on asceticism. Asceticism is the path of giving up what is pleasurable and comfortable to our minds and senses. It is true that the persistent advertisements we are bombarded with through the media, as well as peer pressure, can implant susceptible people with desires for material things and experiences they don't really need. Yet we do have true desires within us.

A distinction is needed between these two ways of experiencing desire:

1. **Projecting Desire Outwards**: Because a person is primarily identified with his lower mind, he feels disconnected from the source of love and fulfillment within himself. He projects his power of desire onto external people, goals

---

[17] Many indigenous and mythic accounts state that highest divine source created the Universe out of original desire to express itself. See Chapter 28 for an updated version of this story

and material things, falsely believing that acquiring those will give him ful-fillment. This is the kind of desire-seeking that often does eventually smash people pursuing it against a wall of disillusionment.

2. **Enjoying Desire as an Innate Quality:** A person is realizing the truth that everything of greatest value exists as vibratory qualities within his own inner experience. He allows himself to feel the energy of desire within his own body, enjoying its beauty and richness prior to seeking its fulfillment outside of himself. This tends to attract the physical fulfillment of his desire.

Acknowledging and honoring the real desires that spring from your own heart and soul are part of your true path of awakening and fulfilling of your higher purpose. This leads us to Avatar Roadmap #1:

Avatar Roadmap #1
Follow Your True Desires

The more you acknowledge, cultivate and follow the true desires that arise from your heart and soul, the more you will gain the motivation of vairagya – with much less (or no) need for dramatic, traumatic external events to motivate you.

The guided practice at the end of this chapter will support you in getting in touch with the rewarding desires of your true self.

You wouldn't be reading this book if you didn't have a measure of vairagya. If you've been through some whoppers of challenging experiences, congratulate yourself. You are in excellent company with all the spiritual masters and society change-makers who have lived. That's because most, if not all of them had to face this same process of getting disillusioned about what they thought their life was, and then needing to step out of their comfort zone, over and over again. Their willingness to do that is why we think of them as masters now. They are not there in our records so we can admire them, they are there to show us what we must do.

How We Avoid Our Inner Work

This process of being willing to feel your own pain and keep transmuting it within the light and love of your true self is profound. It requires you to willingly engage with some of the things that your mind fears and resists the most – those which you may have been running away from throughout your life. The title of the bestselling book my sister Laura co-wrote in 1988 says what is needed so well: *The Courage to Heal.*[18]

Here are the commitments most of us avoid:

- Feeling and fully accepting our own pain without resorting to denial, escape through addictive behaviors, going out of body or projecting our pain onto others.

- Committing ourselves to trimming our ego's tendencies to self-justify, be defensive and rationalize.

- Practicing true self-love, refraining from the compulsion to judge, criticize or sabotage ourselves.

- Being willing to practice healthy self-discipline by carefully choosing the thoughts we energize with our attention, releasing self-indulgence into famil- iar patterns of negative thinking.

It seems to take the "hitting bottom" of *vairagya* for any of us to really become willing to make and stick to these commitments. Yet it feels so good when we finally do so! Rather than running from what we fear to be the deep pain of this experience, we embrace it with our sustained love and acceptance. This is probably

---

18 Davis, Laura and Bass, Ellen, *The Courage to Heal*, Harper-Collins, 1988

the most powerful form of spiritual alchemy. It transmutes the base metal of a divided, traumatized life into the gold of embodied spiritual presence. This is the ultimate way to "lighten up" – to experience a wellspring of love and joy within ourselves.

Although they sound great on paper, really living those four commitments listed above is often the hardest thing in the world for us to accept and put into practice. It's like the description of "Room 101" in the book *1984* by George Orwell – the place where people have to face whatever they perceive to be the scariest thing in the world. But in our case, it is not part of a repressive totalitarian system – it's the pathway to living in an awakened, empowered state. While facing our core issues may feel like "Room 101" to us at times, even a few moments of practicing radical self-acceptance and loving Presence can positively transform those experiences from fearful avoidance into heartfelt serenity.

Remember, Planet Earth is not the Club Med of the Universe![19] It is a place you come to do intensive transformative inner work and give of yourself in service. The sooner you accept this and get with the program, the more of your earthly moments will be filled with the lightness and open-hearted joy of fulfilling your purpose.

Your Bliss Meter

I'll tell you that each time I have taken what felt like baby steps to love more, concentrate my mind more, give more, reach out more or let go of one more limiting thought there has been immediate positive feedback from the Universe. In small or large ways, I feel lighter, better or clearer. Some of my resistance softens and my heart gives me an internal thumbs-up. It is this kind of feedback system that guides you. Your body, heart and spirit do this by feeding back positive experiences to you as you take steps on your Avatar path. Some people call this their "bliss meter."

I find this process very helpful for seeking personal guidance. Rather than follow one of the codified systems of morality created throughout human history – such as the Code of Hammurabi, the Qur'an, the Ten Commandments and so much more, I simply stay as attuned as possible to my inner bliss meter. Any choice or experience that takes me higher into greater love and Christ consciousness is beneficial for me

---

[19] Club Med is a chain of all-inclusive vacation resorts throughout the world in which all expenses are prepaid and many luxuries are provided so guests can enjoy a carefree time. Many wealthy people have attempted to create "Club Med" lifestyles in which they are insulated from the pain of the world but that does not ultimately work – all human beings must face the challenges and growth experiences of material life in one form or another.

> ## Avatar Roadmap #2
> ### Your Bliss Meter
>
> Your bliss meter is the perfectly responsive feedback system you have going with the Universe. The next time you feel your energy and mood going south, don't indulge in feeling bad, beating yourself up or immediately turning to addictive activities. Recognize that your universal guidance system is directly communicating with you. Remind yourself of your true desire, such as to be free, whole, happy, in love or whatever is real for you. Allow your vairagya to motivate you to immediately switch up your thoughts and negative expectations of whatever you have been brooding about. Instead, seed your reality with images and thoughts of already having what you really want right now. As you do that feel the energy shift in your body. You are doing spiritual calisthenics – building your "muscles" of discernment and positive choice. This is a vital part of your process of Christing and embodiment of your true self.

– a "Yes." Any experience that decreases those experiences, lowers the level of my consciousness and makes me grumpier and more depressed is not beneficial for me – a "No." Therefore, my inner guru is always with me (whether I choose to listen to him or not).

Once you know that your *Christing* process often happens outside of your mind's comfort zone, you don't have to beat yourself up or take it so seriously when you are freaking out and your fear is telling you to bolt. It means that you are doing a great job following the example of great masters. It is an honor to go through vairagya and get motivated to take your own steps.

Guided Practice: Cultivating Your True Desires

Engage Foundational practices. Allowing yourself to be nurtured in your field of Loving Presence, sincerely ask yourself what you really desire. Do your best to discriminate between desires and wants held in your mind and the real desires of your heart and soul. You can tell the difference by tuning into the feelings of your body, and the degree of love and excitement in your heart. As you picture and think about your true desires it is likely your body will light up and you will feel more in touch with your heart. Desires and wanting that are primarily mind-centered will give you less of those experiences and thinking about them may actually make you feel more disconnected from your true self. These differences may be subtle at first, and you can train yourself to discern the difference more easily.

Examples of true desires include the desire for deeper love in your life, greater freedom to experience yourself as an Avatar, increased financial prosperity, new friends you resonate with, a new love relationship or to creatively share more of your gifts and talents. Take the emotional risk of feeling your desire fully, even though your mind may not yet know "how" you will fulfill it.

See yourself already having the thing or experience you desire. Allow your body to respond to having it, here and now. Notice the energy sensations that arise in your body and what you feel emotionally. Picture yourself enjoying having what you desire as clearly and specifically as you can. Have fun with this process of visualizing, feeling, noticing and allowing.

Now bring in your power of creation through sound. Speak statements of affirmation of already having what you desire. Speak them out loud if you are in a private place, and if not, clearly think them without speaking. Some examples of affirmative statements are:

- I am in love, I am loved, I am loving, I am loveable. These experiences through me magnetically attract others who vibrate with loving and being loved.

- I live in a joyful sense of richness in my finances and emotional feelings.

- I am sharing love and healing blessings abundantly wherever I go, in person or online.

- I am sharing my spiritual teaching abilities with receptive appreciative people now, and I AM richly supported financially.

- I am ready and present to physically connect with my beloved soulmate partner, and we are each other's reward.

Your experience is your workshop and research project. Experiment with different statements and visualizations and find out which ones light up your body and mind.

Honor yourself for any painful or traumatic experiences you have been through that created greater vairagya within you. Now resolve to motivate yourself in more positive, proactive ways through your Ascension Practices.

When you feel complete give thanks to divine source for whatever positive experiences you had or any insights that came to you. Close your practice. This is a great time to record some notes in your Avatar journal.

3

Claiming Your Avatar Transmission

This chapter will help you understand your most precious asset that makes you who you are: your Avatar energy *transmission*. I really want to make this tangible and not abstract to you.

Take a moment now to think about times when something about you has really touched and blessed other people. Can you remember a time when something you did or said made other people light up, feel better, or maybe have a deep belly laugh? Think about your relationships. What has it been about you that your friends or family members have felt most supported and encouraged by? What qualities have you shared in your professional life that you have learned to count on to reliably create positive results? Have others expressed appreciation to you because they've been inspired by a spiritual quality you emanate? We often minimize or discount our own brilliant qualities because we're too busy focusing on what we perceive as our weaknesses and faults. So many of us get into self-judgment and throw self-doubt upon ourselves.

Those experiences in which your presence touches, blesses and uplifts others arise from your *transmission*. Your transmission is a vibrating stream of higher light energy flowing through you, expressing your original divine spark. It is who and what you truly are, prior to becoming a physical human being or even an individualized soul. We've been feeling this part of ourselves all our lives, but there are often programs running in our minds that block us from clearly seeing or expressing it.

This is literally God, the divine, the absolute coming through you, and the thing is, *it's already happening*. That divine flow is your Avatar transmission. This may seem like a subtle idea that is difficult to understand, and your mind may be saying "Whaaaat?" But hang in there! It is so worth it, even beyond what these words can express. When you get the awesome truth that your true essence is this divine flow of light and frequency, and you can cultivate your ability to bring it through you more clearly and consciously, you then have the golden key to everything you could possibly want in your life. This is the key to getting clear on the greatest contribution you are here to offer.

Understanding Your Transmission and Why You May Be Limiting It

A good analogy for your transmission is what you perceive in a movie theatre. When you look at the screen during a movie you see rapidly moving patterns of light of many different colors, and your ears hear a range of sound frequencies. Your brain interprets these light and sound patterns as a storyline, and if the movie is good, it evokes many emotions and sensations within you. If you were to break your concentration on the movie in front of you and turn your head around, you would be able to see a beam of light emanating from the source of the movie – the projector behind you. Although you can't see any storyline in that beam of light it contains all the dancing wavelengths of light that evoke the story.

Just as the output from a movie projector carries the blend of light wavelengths necessary to express a movie, there is a set of frequencies and vibrations you bring through as your transmission. There is a specific purpose for what you

bring. When you are aligned with that purpose and living it, your life is exciting, vibrant and full. Yet due to fear and internalized taboos, most of us spend a great deal of our time and energy controlling, suppressing or mentalizing our transmission. Could you imagine what you could experience if you let go of all that resistance, and allowed your pure divine ray to express through you unimpeded?

Could you imagine what you could experience if you let go of all that resistance, and allowed your pure divine ray to express through you unimpeded?

When you are sharing your Avatar transmission you are literally being a divine Avatar on Earth, one who can be humble, laugh about it and not take yourself seriously. Avatar is really just another job description like gardener, schoolteacher or dog catcher. No fake airs necessary.

.What would represent your greatest dream coming true? Anything you can dream that seems like the ultimate things you want, whether they seem attainable, or far off and remote, all originate from your transmission. Do you dream of being a healer who is able to facilitate miraculous experiences in which people's lives change for the better? Do you dream of being financially wealthy, with joyful confidence you can create whatever you want from your thoughts and visions? Is your dream to be full of love and part of a circle of loving, conscious friends, family, intimate lover or whatever combination is right for you? Is it to share high spiritual wisdom with others who are hungry for it? Or to be in the silence of your true Beingness? Whichever of the things you desire or imagine have to do with you being in touch with, acknowledging or sharing your transmission. Dare to dream the seemingly impossible.

Again, if you are reading these words, and it is not yet clear to you what this really means, don't worry.

Avatar Roadmap #3

Cultivating the Experience of Your Avatar Transmission

Step One – Open Yourself: You are ready to open yourself to the direct experience of your Avatar transmission when your motivation for freedom and living your truth becomes strong. This is Vairagya (Chapter Two). Vairagya is what allows us to make healthy commitments, and focus our mind in meditation.

Step Two – Daily Practice: From this place of motivation and joyful anticipation commit yourself to doing the Ascension Practices outlined in this book, or inspiring, high-level practices you learn elsewhere.

Step Three – Invoke the Avatar Within You: Call upon your Avatar self, asking your divine self to help you clearly perceive your transmission. (See practice at end of Chapter One for guidance). Receive the direct transmissions that come through this book as you read and work with it. Be open to what you experience without needing it to fulfill any expectation of what your transmission should look or feel like.

Step Four – Risk Being Yourself: Be willing to take risks in sharing more of your authentic self in your day-to-day life. Allow the beacon of light you truly are to shine more and more when you are with others. Be willing to gently and gradually release identification with your small self and familiar personality, discovering more of who you really are.

Step Five – Share and Serve: Your transmission is all about loving and serving. Offer your love, service, encouragement and blessings to others, even if you're not sure you're "qualified." Know that your Avatar self is ultimately qualified to do all those things and is who you truly are already.

This book is a transmission itself. Just by reading it and doing the suggested practices, you are being supported in activating your own transmission. You can be assured that this will eventually become clearer and more tangible to you, as you do the practices regularly and offer your superpowers to others. That's the way it works – we realize our gifts in the process of sharing them.

This path requires that you honor your challenges and difficulties – any feelings of struggle, blockage, self-doubt or feeling like you're not enough. Whatever your brand of negation is, learn to dance with it, just like boxers learn to bob and weave to prevent getting clobbered. The negative mind-states you may feel are part of an epidemic of dis-ease affecting almost everybody in our world. A lot of this doesn't even come from you, even though you hear it within your own mind. The negative thought patterns that are yours are often connected to unacknowledged emotions, repressed anger or uncried tears. Allow yourself to feel your own feelings, knowing they are expressions of your energy. Everything is energy, and you are learning to become a master of energy.

So, move ahead confidently with excitement and inspiration. "I am uncovering the greatest mystery, the greatest value within me." Beloved stories tell about hidden treasure chests at the bottom of the ocean, or Aladdin going into a vast underground cave full of mind-blowing boundless precious treasure. Yet the most valuable of them all was the simple lamp that Aladdin could rub to summon the Genie who would give him anything he wanted. Then he had access to all the wealth he could ever use right in his pocket.

These archetypal stories evoke the truth of your Avatar transmission. This is your real Genie and buried treasure. But it's not externalized "riches" as it was in those stories. It's really about your accepting this ultimate truth and limitless abundance that is you.

There are so many fascinating metaphysical studies and principles. People can go around and around studying new teachings, experiencing various altered or high states of consciousness and learning to manifest and create things from their mind. But all that is just a small shadow of the glory of who you really are. Your Avatar true self is beyond the comprehension of our minds, and yet it's what you are. So be willing to go through this journey, be willing to be that dancer or boxer who's able to find your own grace and balance at holding the space of your luminous true self. If you'd love to do this, you'll find practical guidance on living as an Avatar in Chapter 20.

How Trauma Has Inhibited Our Transmission

There's a reason why we often have such deep impulses to limit and control our transmission, and that reason is trauma. Awakening Avatars have usually lived through many lifetimes expressing their Avatar nature. In some of those lifetimes (or for some people, this one) we got slammed for expressing our transmission. We may have soul memories of being persecuted, killed, tortured or rejected. We may also remember times of "blowing it" when we believe we misused the tremendous power of our transmission to hurt others. Maybe a lot of others.

All these impressions could be embedded in what is often called cellular memory and manifesting as various forms of pain, stress or limitation. Therefore, when you come around to getting more in touch with your transmission a lot of those experiences may come up. Guess what? That's perfect as long as you don't run from your feelings. Just keep infusing those scary or painful feelings with your transmission and get support from others. That's what Ascension Practices are for. The practice at the end of this chapter is appropriate.

In recent years many valuable methods for accelerating the release of trauma have been developed. These include tapping systems such as the Emotional Freedom Technique, rapid eye movement (EMDR), cognitive therapies and vibrational energy medicine. I have learned or developed clinical methods using microcurrent and color light therapy, in combination with guided visualization and Quantum Catalyst healing, that support clients in releasing deep traumatic imprints within one or two sessions.[20] There are many practitioners now offering such high-level services.

Christed human beings have cleared enough psychic debris out of their minds and bodies so their transmission can come through clearly and beautifully. This process breaks the dominance of the disempowered part of us which has been programmed and domesticated in the image of the dark dreams of our society.

Working with Your Transmission

Imagine that you're going through a time where you're facing some challenging times. You feel down, struggling with some issue or conflicted about something that just happened to you. You're trying to find a solution but just seem to keep going around in circles in your mind. You may ask your friends for advice or have therapy sessions or try to medicate it away with drugs or alcohol, but whatever you do you still feel stuck and unsure. If at these times you acknowledge and connect with your transmission, you are taking the perfect action. You are bringing your divine essence to your experience and can trust and allow the magic alchemy to take place. As you relax, breathe and allow your transmission to touch the affected parts of you, you are likely to realize that what you have been feeling contains a gift of healing – a part of you calling for greater acknowledgment and loving connection.

Cultivating your body's ability to more consistently vibrate with your transmission helps activate your light body or *merkaba*. This is a spinning vortex of high-frequency, love-filled spiritual light that forms around you, and eventually

---

[20] For a complete description of the Bilateral Trauma Release system I practice using microcurrent and light therapy, see my book Reclaiming Your Calm Center, Chapter 15

becomes permanent. The practices in Section Four will guide and support you in activating your light body.[21]

Your transmission is like the universal solvent that dissolves all stuckness, issues and conflicts. This truly awesome resource is built into you. The turning point comes when you stop trying to control or figure out what you're going through and come into this present moment, opening your body and allowing the consciousness of your cells to vibrate with your transmission. If that seems extremely subtle to you, or if you're not sure you're feeling it, I can assure you that it's really there. You can believe it, or act "as if" you are experiencing it; even if your mind doesn't believe you are. Decree some things like these, as fits your situation:

"I AM my Avatar transmission surrounding and comforting these painful feelings I'm going through."

"I AM relaxing and flowing my Avatar transmission through this knot I'm feeling in my gut."

"My Avatar transmission informs me so I will ace this exam I'm about to take."

"My Avatar transmission makes me fearless as I go into this meeting."

If you are a psychotherapist, acupuncturist, doctor or other healing professional sitting across from a challenging client you're not sure you know how to help, silently say something like:

"I AM radiating my Avatar transmission to bring miracle results for this beloved person, beyond my own knowledge. Give me the words to speak, the easy knowing of what to do and the ability to emanate Quantum healing vibrations through my field. Let my own skills, intelligence and love be informed and uplifted by my transmission."

I'll tell you a secret about me. I do this with almost all my in-person and remote clients and it makes a whopper of a difference in my clinical outcomes. I know that because there have been times I was in a rush and didn't take the required few seconds to align with my transmission. I could absolutely tell the difference. The experience of the sessions where I failed to align with my

---

[21] While all the practices in Section Four support light body activation, Chapter 27 contains a specific practice for activating the merkaba

transmission was usually still positive for my clients to some extent, but the magic quality of healing and transformation felt missing. I felt more like a "muggle"[22] rather than a master healer.

Once you've created a clear intention to become directly aware of your Avatar transmission, your soul will start working on fulfilling your request 24-7. Thoughts, feelings and insights may pop up at unexpected times. It's great to record these in your journal or on a voice memo on your cell phone.

I have noticed that it is much easier for people to discover the direct experience of their transmission while offering high-level healing sessions or participating in Lightworker group events. Your transmission is really about giving, and so the interactions you have with others pull it through you more readily.

Your transmission is really about giving, and so the interactions you have with others pull it through you more readily.

---

22 Muggle is a word created by author J.K. Rowling in her ultra-successful Harry Potter book and movie series. Muggles are people who live conventional, non-magical lives because they don't believe in magic

As mentioned above, this overall book contains an activating Avatar transmission. If you'd like some support with perceiving your transmission, you can hold the book in your hands or place it on your altar as you do this practice. To assure your own sovereignty you can say something like this: "I open myself to the transmission or virtue from this book that supports me, and I refuse any energies that are not for my highest good."

It's powerful to create a journal to record your experiences of working with your transmission and getting in touch with your Avatar self. When you look back on your journal entries a few weeks or months later, they will have way more meaning than is obvious when you are writing them.

Superpowers – Your Transmission in Action

The characteristic ways your transmission expresses through you to help make other people's lives happier, healthier and more awakened are your *superpowers*. Your superpowers are your transmission in expression. As explained in Chapter 4, everybody has at least one superpower and some people are aware of several of them. This literally makes you a superhero. As with all hero's journeys, there are bound to be obstacles to overcome, strength to be gained and power that must be claimed. This is part of the path we are walking.

We usually think of people serving others through actions – volunteer work, caring for children or the elderly, bringing about scientific discoveries, protecting or inspiring us. As you go through the process of becoming *Christed*, you become more dialed into the pure transmission that is you, and how you powerfully serve and bless, whether or not you are doing any actions. As mentioned in Chapter 17 on Lightworkers, some serve by holding and radiating high frequencies of light, with or without any associated actions. Actions you do take while flowing with your transmission are far more impactful than actions arising from your personality motivations.

Much of my career has been focused toward educating and supporting holistic healthcare professionals. I've had the privilege of seeing so many of my colleagues transform their approach to patient care as they attune their bodies and minds to their Avatar transmission. Kaisa, an acupuncturist from Southern California, shared this during a group conference:

Ever since our last meeting, I feel completely different – in a really good way. Lots of energy, and just a whole other level working with patients. And, as I am tapping more into the source of healing, I have a lot of energy running through me, where I have to force myself to go to bed at night. And this energy feels really, really good. Some days I feel heavy energy from my patients, I can feel the things that they might be working through. But overall, for myself, I just kind of took off and went to another level with my work. And it's really amazing. I'm now meditating every morning. I just feel like another level of intuition working with my patients. It's a lot clearer. I don't know how to describe it. It seems I get information quicker. And it's clear and their treatments are even more effective, faster as well. It's been great.

Chapter 26 in Section Four contains step-by-step practices for attuning yourself to your Avatar transmission. You can also learn how to access a free guided meditation to support you in getting in touch with your transmission in the Resources Section Six. Many people find it easier to let go into their energy flow while listening rather than reading. There are also resources for connecting with group events that support attuning to your transmission.

4

Recognizing and Claiming Your Superpower

Comics, movies and TV shows about humans possessing superpowers have fascinated viewers for a long time. Why do we love *X-Men*, *Superman*, *Wonder Woman*, *Black Panther* and *Lord of the Rings* so much? Is it because we feel so powerless in comparison to them? Because we want someone to swoop in and fix things? I don't think that's the main reason. I believe we resonate so strongly with those shows because they remind us that on some level that we also have real superpowers. Your superpowers probably appeared and started calling to you early in your life. These were the areas in which you showed strong natural abilities.

Your superpowers are living expressions of your energy transmission. They flower as you step into your Avatar mission.

The process of claiming, developing and sharing your superpowers abundantly with others is one of the most precious and fulfilling experiences you can have in your life. Yet having superpowers and avoiding developing them can lead to various forms of distress, as explained below.

Examples of Superpowers

To make this subject more tangible, here is a list of superpowers I've identified in people. Expressing one or more of the qualities in this list does not necessarily mean that you have developed your superpowers. It is when they are expressed in a heightened way bordering on genius that they become super.

- Compassion
- Courage
- Master Healer abilities
- Scientific inventiveness
- Imagination
- Artistic vision and expression
- Humor
- Spiritual vision
- Physical grace and strength
- Bringer of justice

- Teacher and mentor
- Destroyer of outmoded systems
- Light translator
- Clear, inspiring communicator
- Spiritual warrior
- Goddess power
- Nurturer
- Truthteller
- Deep listener
- Deal Maker

In my explorations of many spiritual teachings and paths, I've come across people who beautifully embody one or more superpowers. I gravitated toward these people, seeing them as teachers and mentors and sometimes putting them on pedestals in my mind. Like the ugly duckling, I often tried to emulate these people's abilities and sometimes felt inadequate, "not enough" or like a spiritual beginner in comparison to them.

When I finally gave up trying to copy other people's superpowers, I started discovering my own. Through years of offering healing sessions and receiving mirroring from others, I've realized that I am a quantum catalyst and light translator. As a quantum catalyst, the presence of my transmission empowers others to recognize and activate their own superpowers, bringing them out in practical expression more quickly than they often believed possible. As a light translator, I gather knowledge and direct energetic experiences from multi-dimensions and integrate it all into simple, practical lessons that others can grasp and benefit from. (The superpower of humor also often pours through me when I'm not trying too hard, three hard or four hard).

For some of us, our superpowers were obvious at a young age. At an early age, some children showed themselves to be a math whiz, a musical prodigy or to start moving like an athlete prior to receiving any external training. Many children are able to rapidly bring out advanced abilities like these, especially if they are fortunate enough to have supportive parents. For others, their superpowers were not so obvious because they required more time, challenge or struggle to bring them out. They may have been expressing superpowers not normally valued in our society or in their family, or were too busy coping with an abusive or hostile environment.

Some children were actively shunned or punished for their superpowers. For example, one of my clients is a highly gifted intuitive healer and hypnotherapist named Sharon, whose mother despised her sensitivity and psychic gifts. Here's how she relates her struggle to bring out her superpowers:

When I was really young, before I went to kindergarten, I remember getting messages about the world. I don't know who was talking to me, but it didn't seem unusual. There were messages about the world, like for example that energy is neutral. I was shown in pictures a cauldron of all this energy that was neither good nor bad. And I thought, gosh, where did this come from? But anyway, I used to get these kinds of communications.

I was also pretty intuitive. I thought you could talk with people telepathically and I could also feel people energetically – I just knew what was going on with them. And so, I think I must have talked about that when I was younger because my mother was always saying things to me like: "Stop saying things like that – that's crazy – that's not right – don't do that." When I was about 13, she threatened to send me to a psychiatrist because she thought that I was acting too crazy, just because I was being intuitive and feeling energies. So anyway, I got the message that I didn't live in a world where it was OK to talk about what felt like such an important part of myself. I had to be really careful and not mention anything that was too strange.

When I first had the healing session with you, I just had this knowing. It was like going to another dimension or something, all of a sudden, you're in another place. And I had a sense that you and I were part of a community, so to speak before we came to this world, and so I felt like really happy.

Although you were born with the seeds of your specific superpower, you will usually need to work to develop it. Athletes, musicians, entrepreneurs, healers, mediators or scientists who amaze us with the brilliance of their abilities and performance usually work hard to develop their innate abilities. Some of us hone our superpowers through intensive disciplined practice, others through major selfless giving to our family or tribe, and others by living through the fires of personal struggle and tragedy. And many other ways and combinations of ways.

Another of my clients named Frances is a highly gifted psychotherapist who specializes in working with people who have been through extreme forms of traumatic abuse. Many of her clients present with dissociative identity disorder (DID), a condition of people who have been through devastating childhood trauma. Frances experienced severe trauma and sexual abuse in her own early life and had been through a series of traumatic adult experiences around the time I met her. In spite of these experiences, or perhaps because of them, she possessed a remarkable ability to consult with a very busy schedule of clients who were dealing with very severe mental health conditions and help most of them to significantly heal.

In Francis's own words:

At this point, my work is less about psycho-therapeutic techniques. It's more about invoking the power of spirit to help me with the healing. And being very aware of that and drawing on that, especially when I'm feeling nervous. I bring all my tools and things to do (to the sessions) *but there's a spiritual piece that's so all-encompassing for my patients, as well as for myself.*

If Frances had not been through the experiences she had, it is questionable whether she would be able to offer such a consistently high level of her superpower.

The Power in Your Wounds

After you break a bone in your body and it heals, that area is usually stronger than the original bone. In the same way, your superpowers often spring from your areas of deepest trauma and struggle in your life.

This brings us to a profound truth – the seeds of your greatest power often lie within your deepest emotional wounds.

In his book *Iron John* about the deep male psyche, poet Robert Bly states:

Our wound is the source of our genius and power. Without touching our wound, we live a provisional (tentative) life.

Why is this true? Because these areas of deepest wounding often represent your Assignment of Love – the aspect of human suffering you volunteered to help heal. This is the assignment you signed up for before you were born. You chose to go through these difficult experiences because your Avatar transmission is ideally suited to help transmute and heal large numbers of people also experiencing it.

Your Avatar self is able to fulfill your assignment because it is tapped into all the love, power, intelligence and abundance of the Universe and beyond. Just as a glass prism refracts sunlight into a rainbow of colors, this ultimate power manifests through us in differing and sometimes unique ways. Part of our individuality has to do with what our purpose is. There is a strong internal urge in most of us to identify and develop our superpower because it supports our mission, and our mission strongly calls to us.

There is an overall direction of the human race, and that is to transmute our traumas and accumulated baggage into love and ascend in consciousness. As more and more people join the movement of awakening, we will graduate from trying times of suffering and polarization into the enlightened race we are capable of being. You and I and everyone else have a special part to play in this process. It is your superpower that allows you to play that part effectively.

Claiming Your Superpower

Back in the early 1970s, I heard a healing mentor in Boulder, Colorado named Thelma Dowd teach the principle of "greater mission, greater purification." This means that the more powerful and expansive a person's superpower is, the more seeming hell they may go through in claiming and expressing it. The process of going through all those painful experiences eventually helps open the heart and create a strong motivation to help others who have been through similar struggles. This process of claiming and expressing your greatest gifts can be seen as your Assignment of Love in this lifetime.[23]

Your superpower is what you are probably most inspired and motivated about in your life now, and you've been dancing with it, or around it for a long time. Once you recognize what your superpower is you can commit yourself to developing it. As you make that commitment things will start happening in your life to support you in doing so. A series of people may show up and give you feedback about how much you have helped them in certain areas of life. You may learn some energy healing methods, and as you share them you are blown away by how positively they transform. Or you may go through your own injury or healing crisis and discover a healing power within yourself that you never knew you had. Sometimes you will simply find yourself dreaming and fantasizing about doing something you have never done before, which could be your superpower calling to you.

---

[23] See Chapter 16

Claiming Your Superpower Through Challenge

Once you say yes to following the path of developing your superpower, you may feel challenged. Old "pretender voices" of self-doubt, apathy or procrastination may tell you that this is just too hard or unrealistic. All kinds of "weapons of mass distraction" may insistently call to you, trying to pull you away from your higher path of development. Claiming power seems to always require upping our level of courage and commitment. Hey, I never promised you a rose garden!

For example, I mentored a busy, successful acupuncturist in California named Chang. When I first started working with her, she told me that she felt locked into her left-brain, rational mind, and it was very hard for her to feel subtle energy or intuitive information. As Chang participated in some retreats and studies through the Bridge to Mastery institute, she felt new abilities opening up within her. She learned to tune into the field of light emanating from her body often called the light body, and her intuition started flowering. At first, Chang resisted and feared these changes. Yet as she persevered and received needed support Chang's healing abilities opened up more, and she was able to expand her work to include teaching and leading groups. Her clientele increased as more of her patients noticed their improved results and referred others. Through this process, Chang had claimed more of her master healer and seer superpowers and integrated these into her acupuncture practice.

Resisting or Avoiding Your Superpower – the Lamborghini Example

Having innate spiritual gifts and not expressing them can lead to various forms of distress. I have learned this from personal experience and will share a story here that beautifully illustrates this point.

My first major spiritual teacher is named Prem Rawat.[24] During the years I was following him, one of the things I appreciated him for was his gift for expressing profound teachings through entertaining stories. There was one anecdote he told us at a 1975 event that deeply impressed me and has stayed with me ever since.

When Prem was a teenager, he was already a world teacher with several hundred thousand disciples. As many teenage boys do, he loved high-powered cars. Prem

---

[24] When I first met Prem in the early 1970s he was known as Guru Maharaj Ji. In recent decades he dropped that title and is known by his birth name of Prem Rawat.

told us about a wealthy Italian disciple who bought him an expensive grand coupe automobile called a Lamborghini Espada. This car had twelve cylinders in its engine and was designed to go really fast. Prem took the Lamborghini out for a drive in the city traffic of Rome and found it to be an unpleasant and jarring experience. The engine was so powerful

that he had to frequently press the brakes to prevent the car from surging ahead and hitting other vehicles. Eventually, Prem got tired of this struggle and took the Lamborghini for a drive on a highway near Rome. He told us "It was only when I took the car out on an open highway and drove it at close to one hundred miles per hour that I really experienced the luxury of that car. It clearly was not designed for start and stop city traffic."

Prem went on to compare the Lamborghini with people on the spiritual path. He explained that we are designed to operate at a high-frequency level, with an open heart and a calm mind. When we are mostly operating from the density of our overactive lower mind the experience is a lot like struggling with that powerful Lamborghini engine on city streets. We go through a lot of conflict and struggle because our soul is wanting to move us forward into the higher life while our fear-based minds are often resisting and trying to go in other directions.

What I took away from this story is that I am designed to operate at a high level of consciousness and expression of my superpowers. Even though my superpowers were relatively undeveloped back in the 1970s, I was aware of them. I often did feel a sense of inner emotional struggle, or even what felt like self-sabotage back in those days. I eventually realized that these experiences arose because I was denying much of who I really am as an Avatar. I had been allowing the fears and wounding of my past to "keep my foot on the brakes" of my life. As I have taken courageous, loving actions, and what has often felt like risks to express my superpowers, the sense of inner struggle has greatly diminished, and life has become much more fulfilling. Hearing Prem's story back in 1975 planted a powerful seed of recognition that has flowered over the years. That's an example of great teaching.

One of the universal laws of energy that has been recognized since ancient times is the Law of Use. This law states that higher-level knowledge and abilities

must be used and shared in order for an individual to be in harmony with nature. Having these gifts and denying, or not sharing them puts us out of harmony and often leads to suffering. This is a profound understanding, and one that is well worth contemplating and journaling about. The practice at the end of this chapter offers guidance for this process.[25]

Expressing Your Superpower

Your superpower calls to you. It calls you to uncover and express the potency of your light beyond the comfort zone of your conditioned mind. And we usually say no to it until we finally get ready to say yes, after going through a series of life experiences that drive us deeper into core truths about ourselves that we may have been avoiding.

---

25   The Law of Use and other Universal Laws of energy are clearly explained in the small book The Kybalion. See Bibliography.

The good news is that the more we choose to live a passionate life expressing our superpower, the less we will resist it and the more fun and inspiring it becomes. It's another form of creating new neural pathways. I have found that I have had to take risks each time I have claimed a new level of my superpowers and higher purpose. I had to be willing to do things I was not sure I could do, and risk being rejected or looking like a fool or a failure.

One memorable example of that was at a microcurrent seminar I taught in Los Angeles in 2012. A physician-acupuncturist attending that seminar asked if he could bring one of his patients to the seminar, so I would treat him as a demonstration in front of the room. His patient, Jack, was a Vietnam veteran with multiple, severe chronic pain and neuropathy issues that no other medical treatments, including acupuncture and microcurrent therapy, had been able to relieve. At first, I said no because I was not sure I would be able to effectively relieve this man's pain and didn't want to fail in front of my students. Somewhat reluctantly, I eventually agreed to do this demonstration.

Once Jack was in front of the 35 students attending the seminar I evaluated and treated him using my best techniques. Jack only reported minimal improvement from all my work, and I grew more stressed and nervous. Then at one point, something in me popped open and I started seeing Jack as already whole and free of pain. I felt a significant energetic shift happen between Jack and myself. As I was treating an acupuncture point in his ear with microcurrent a surprised look came over his face, and he started moving his body, amazed that 80% of his pain was gone for the first time in years. This relief lasted for several days, and his care was continued by the doctor who brought him.

What I realize now is that I opened up more to my master healer superpower that day. I had been aware of that part of me previously but had not fully trusted it, putting more faith in my electronic healing devices and rational techniques. Once I had that first experience with Jack, I started inviting my students to bring their most difficult pain relief patients who had not found relief to all my seminars. My success at being able to demonstrate impressive results at each event with these challenging patients was over 90%.

A similar story applies to my public speaking abilities. In my youth, I used to be so shy, and almost paranoid at times, that it was hard for me to even be in groups, much less speak up in them. Once I created my microcurrent manufacturing business in my thirties, I started getting invitations to teach training seminars. I remember the first time I offered one in California in 1991 in front of a room full of chiropractors. I was so nervous that I hid in the bathroom for a while, wishing I didn't have to come out and face the group. I finally coaxed myself to step out and deliver my class. After a slow, and somewhat hesitant start I got into the rhythm of teaching and interacting, and it became fun. Within a short time, I was teaching regular seminars, feeling a flow and power that people were benefiting from. Now I love sharing with groups of any size, and the clarity and smoothness of my delivery keeps improving.

What these stories illustrate is that it often requires a willingness to step into the unknown and take a risk to claim your superpower or the next level of it. This happens the most when we put ourselves into positions of service to others.

Avatar Roadmap #4
Claiming Your Superpower

If you want to claim and discover your superpower, put yourself into situations where it's needed and you are the one there to deliver it. Choose to come from a place of love and service rather than self-aggrandizement, really caring about the person or people you are helping. That is the surest way to express and develop your superpower or superpowers.

What you will likely find is that your superpower will raise the level of work or techniques you are already implementing.

As a person goes through levels of spiritual awakening, new superpowers are opened up within them. This is Universal Law – the higher a level you serve on the more tools and resources are given to you to get the job done. That is why ascended Masters[26] like Jesus, Buddha or Quan Yin possess God-like powers to lovingly heal and bless billions of people at the same time. They have stepped up to serve on a super-high level and they are given supreme superpowers. When reading those last sentences, did your mind think anything like "that's fine for Jesus but impossible for me"? Don't be so sure!

---

[26] Ascended Masters are beings who serve massive numbers of people from the non-physical, spiritual realm. They had human lifetimes during which they purified their minds and passed enough tests of spiritual development to become liberated from the struggles of the human experience.

Guided Practice – Discovering your Superpower

Find a quiet time and write your answers to the questions below. It is valuable to read through these questions one time, simply observing your reactions and visions. After doing that, I suggest coming back and writing or typing the answers to the questions. Use a word processor program on a digital device if possible, because it is likely more insights will come to you once you start this self-inquiry. Just put down what first pops into your mind without over-thinking or analyzing your answers. Set an intention for your Avatar self to bring clarity to you over the next ten days. Then be open to any inspired thoughts or dreams you have about developing your superpowers during that time period. Once you create this intention you may also receive valuable insights through other people's comments, movies, books or lyrics to songs you hear that touch you. Come back to your document often during those ten days, updating it as you are guided.

The following questions will help you get in touch with your primary superpower, and perhaps one or more secondary ones. Answer these questions more from a feeling and intuitive level. Allow your left brain analysis of yourself to help, but be secondary to the input from your heart and gut.

1. When you were growing up what did people who knew you well say were your strongest and most noticeable characteristics? These were the ways you tended to invest most of your energy and focus. Even if you might judge these tendencies as negative, they can still, in some way point toward a superpower. For example, a childhood condition of attention deficit and hyperactivity disorder (ADHD) which may have seemed like a problem could become the power behind an excellent adult athlete or brilliant inventor. Many powerful healers, teachers and social innovators started their lives burdened by depression or addiction. They had to learn to take their power back from those who have influenced them in the past in order to claim their superpower.

2. What have you dreamed you would really love to do with your life if there were no obstacles or limitations holding you back? Or if you knew that you could overcome them?

3. What have been your strongest natural abilities throughout your life? These may be abilities you have already expressed extensively in your

work or relationships or those you know you have, that you have not yet actualized much on a practical level. Think of times you have been the most successful, had your most valuable accomplishments, connected the most deeply with another person or created something really beautiful. Write those down as well as those qualities of being you drew on to create those outcomes. These do not have to be creations or accomplishments valued by our materialistic culture, such as making big amounts of money or gaining extensive external recognition. Sometimes what may be judged as small acts could make a big difference to others in need. For example, a retired disabled man who greets people entering Wal-Mart could be expressing his superpower of making people feel welcome and at ease.

4. Have you fantasized about having a superpower that would allow you to do something extraordinary? If so, what is that superpower and what would it allow you to do? In answering this question do NOT tie your answer to what you believe is realistic or practical. Have fun imagining the answer – even the sky is not the limit. If you get excited fantasizing about being a galactic level healer, being the next Gandhi or ending hunger in Africa go for it!

5. What quality in you has helped other people the most? If you are a healer, physician or healing arts practitioner, in what specific, repeatable ways have your clients positively transformed when working with you?

6. If you have already opened up your spiritual sight or direct knowing, what do you see or know about your true spiritual identity, the highest version of yourself?

These are questions that are best answered over a period of time. Write or type your initial, spontaneous answers, and then set your intention to allow your intuition to show you more. Come back to your document at least three times over a week, adjusting your answers as guided. This writing exercise can be combined with forms of inner contemplation in which you encourage yourself to visualize yourself doing what you would most love to do, perhaps discovering more of what that really is in the process.

A guided audio version of this practice is available. See Resource Section Six.

5

Your Body is Where It's At

The only place you can awaken your Avatar nature and bring out your superpowers is in your body.

Your body is the gateway to everything you really want and your higher destiny. It is only in your body that you can grow, evolve, transmute and ascend. I've heard it said there are long lines of blissful cosmic beings waiting for a chance to incarnate into a human body for these reasons, yet most of them have to chill out and wait. That's because there's a limited quota of souls who can be born into human bodies at any one time. What many people call global over-population is probably more like a Who's Who list of beings from all over the Universe wanting to crowd into the most happening place. This is certainly a different kind of immigration issue than we usually hear about on the news!

Embodying your Avatar self in your body is both a spiritual and physiological transformative process. It is true *alchemy*.[27] This process is well supported by the cutting-edge scientific field of *epigenetics*. Epigenetics is the study of how the environment we live in, our lifestyle, our thoughts and our feelings continually modify the gene expression of the DNA in our cells. Our DNA is literally like a super-computer network that continually orchestrates the re-creation of our bodies and our experience.

In the old days when I went to high school, we were taught that people inherit their genes from their parents and ancestors. This means that they get their progenitor's positive and negative traits, as well as a propensity to get a lot of the same diseases. Epigenetics

---

[27] Alchemy: "a power or process that changes or transforms something in a mysterious or impressive way" Definition 2 in Merriam Webster dictionary

has shown that these ideas are only part of the truth. According to many research studies, people can reduce or prevent getting most diseases of their parents[28] by cleaning up their diet, exercising regularly and practicing positive thinking and mindfulness.[29] An article in BMC Genomics Journal details the physiological mechanisms through which regular exercise reduces the pathways of inflammation as well as the methylation defects associated with cancer and other major diseases. It states:

These epigenetic mechanisms contribute to lowering the basal level of inflammation, thereby preventing the occurrence of diseases linked to low-grade chronic inflammation. Moreover, it is recognized that physical activity counteracts those processes of hypomethylation and hypermethylation associated with neoplastic (cancer creating) *mutations in the genome, thus representing an intervention able to target several genes simultaneously and potentially eliminating any side effects for the patients.*

Other studies confirm that disease-preventing epigenetic changes associated with regular exercise and a healthy diet can be passed down to benefit future generations.[30] In other words, people who clean up their diet, breathe deeply and break a sweat working out will pass more healthy genes onto their children than sedentary people eating less consciously. This means our bodies are input-output systems and are continually transforming to reflect the food, fluids, breathing, energy, thoughts and feelings we put into them.

Intriguing Research

Recent research studies are confirming the extraordinary power of positive thoughts and feelings to upgrade the body's ability to heal and prevent illness. As an example, Dr. Joe Dispenza has been leading studies in which researchers look at blood samples, heart rate monitors, brain scans and other bio-physical markers in an attempt to objectively track how the body responds to shifts in consciousness. They are validating measurable changes in these markers after research subjects go through heart-opening and consciousness-raising experiences. In some of

---

[28] https://bmcgenomics.biomedcentral.com/articles/10.1186/s12864-017-4193-5#
[29] Mindfulness refers to a meditative approach to everyday life, in which people train themselves to keep their attention in present time as much as possible. Mindfulness practices have been documented to provide significant benefits to people with anxiety and other emotional imbalances, cancer and heart disease
[30] https://www.nature.com/scitable/topicpage/epigenetic-influences-and-disease-895/

the studies, researchers evaluated the degree of heart-opening through direct measurements of changes in the amplitude of the electrical field of the heart.

One recent study tracked changes in a volunteer who had participated in a week-long workshop. When this volunteer arrived at the event, he was feeling quite sick and drained. Blood was drawn from him at that point and stored. This man had significant heart-opening experiences during the workshop, as measured by a big expansion of the amplitude of his heart's electrical field and beneficial changes in his brainwave patterns. His blood was drawn again after he went through this transformational experience.

Researchers at the University of California San Diego received this man's blood samples. They added live samples of the SARS CoV-2 virus that creates COVID-19 disease to both samples. What they found was that the blood drawn at the start of the workshop showed rampant COVID infection throughout the blood cells. The blood sample drawn after his transformative experience showed virtually no infection after being exposed to the virus. While additional research is called for on larger populations, this is intriguing evidence of the power of our consciousness to prevent disease.[31]

Yet our power to transform our bodies goes much further than preventing disease. These same pathways allow us to rejuvenate and upgrade our bodies to a higher order of life than we have known.

Regenerating and Upgrading Our Bodies

Think of your body as the most precious gift you have. Your true Avatar self doesn't need any improvement or any development, because it exists in a realm of perfection. It's the act of embodying the real you in your physical body that's where the action is. Just think about the fact that we have a planet full of people who are only semi-embodied, and therefore full of energy gaps between their true selves and their bodies. This situation is spinning off all kinds of bad dreams into creation. We don't have to participate in that. We can be examples of people practicing to be fully present more of the time, feeling and seeing it all.

You have both physical anatomy and subtle anatomy in your body. Physical anatomy like bones, nerves and organs can be seen by our eyes and medical scans, while subtle anatomy can only be felt and sensed. Our subtle anatomy includes the meridian energy pathways worked with by acupuncturists, chakras and tiny energy

---

[31] https://www.youtube.com/watch?v=Y-Rfm5apEFA

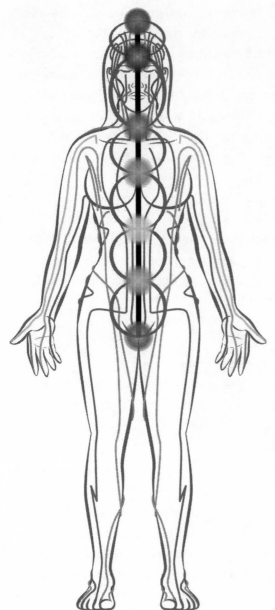

vessels called *nadis* that interconnect all parts of us.[32] A lot of the stress and overload so many people feel these days could be prevented by repairing and upgrading their subtle anatomy.[33] Energy-balancing practices such as qigong, yoga, Tai ch'i and meditation are wonderful for this purpose. I believe that these arts should be taught to children in schools, as this would lead to a much healthier society.

Imagine an old house with frayed, decaying wiring in its walls. A lot of the insulation has come off the wires and they are broken in some places. There could also be an outdated, rusted fuse box. Imagine you just purchased this old house and want to redesign it to be a functional modern place. You're excited about putting in lots of computers and high-tech equipment requiring much more power than appliances did in the old days when that house was built. It's very likely you're going to have to redo a lot of old wiring in order for that old house to serve in its new way.

This is the way it is with your body in the process of becoming *Christed*. The extent to which we're feeling tired, depressed or having various symptoms such as indigestion, headaches, inflammation, insomnia and chronic pain is an indication that our inner energy

---

32 See Definitions of Terminology in the rear of the book for explanations of these terms

33 The overuse of recreational drugs such as opiates, stimulants, marijuana and psychedelics as well as some pharmaceuticals can damage our subtle anatomy, and it can take a great deal of inner work to repair that. However, the occasional use of psychedelic medicines in supportive, healing environments has been shown to be healing and awakening for many people.

wiring could use some upgrading. I love the expression Sue Morter uses of "building circuitry" in our bodies through our practices.[34] This is such a great way to put it – we are rewiring our bodies to hold and circulate the higher spiritual voltage of who we really are.

Quincy is a 60-something woman who acts as CEO for four different companies, as well as being considered the matriarch of her large Chinese American family. Her story is a striking example of how the body can be rapidly rejuvenated through lifestyle changes and unblocking its energy. In her own words:

> As you know I was going through Western medicine for almost three years, trying to deal with multiple issues I developed after a seizure I had a few years ago. I was feeling a lot of things – fuzziness in the brain, very low energy and not being able to sleep well. But what was really, really problematic was I couldn't walk more than a block. And that was a real critical issue for me because I couldn't get any exercise. I was having issues with a sprained ankle that hadn't healed for over six months. After working with several different (medical) specialists, I wasn't seeing much improvement in any of these areas.

> On the first session, you tested my energy center (Assemblage Point) and found it to be low, and then adjusted it. And surprisingly enough I felt a difference right away, which surprised me. Then you did an evaluation and found that I had certain energy blockages and started doing an adjustment on me with a combination of methods. I was able to walk much better after that first session and could barely feel the ankle pain. My head felt clearer right away, and my energy picked up.

> I'm walking now two and a half miles every morning. And you got me to start doing qigong, which I do almost every day and the breathing exercises. And getting a better understanding of qi and the different key points, and breathing has really made the difference. My consciousness has definitely shifted. I think part of our sessions have been about getting in touch with the spiritual side.

---

34 Morter, Sue, *The Energy Codes*, Simon and Schuster 2019

And the exercises you practice with me are extremely helpful. I will say there's much more of a lightness, there's much more of an appreciation or a, how do I say it? a recognition of the emotional and spiritual aspect of healing.

It's really interesting that during Quincy's first session, in which she experienced so much improvement in her ability to walk, she did not receive any direct treatment on her ankles. The six months of pain and disability she had felt in those areas quickly cleared up after balancing the energy of her chakras, organs and other energy pathways. By committing to daily walking, qigong, fuller breathing and improved diet Quincy created positive epigenetic input to her body, helping rejuvenate it in the process. Her story is an excellent example of how healing sessions can help provide people with enough relief of their symptoms to give them the freedom to become more proactive in upgrading their own health and fitness.

Upgrading Your Circuitry

Jesus was masterful at coming up with great parables to explain subtle spiritual truths in ways anyone could understand. One of these was:

And no one puts new wine into old wineskins; or else the new wine bursts the wineskins, the wine is spilled, and the wineskins are ruined. But new wine must be put into new wineskins.[35]

It was really clever of Jesus to spin out that parable because so many people love wine. A modern, updated version of that could be:

You can't run advanced, high-tech equipment through old circuitry without blowing the circuits. You need to first upgrade the circuits.

Strengthen Your Body in a Balanced Way

Many people have tried to elevate their consciousness and purify their bodies through extremely ascetic diets and deprivation of its comforts and pleasures. I believe this is no longer an appropriate path for most people, and can derail you on your path of living fully. What's much more important is to strengthen and vitalize your body. Your body loves to be strengthened, so challenge it by doing

---

[35] The Bible, Mark 2:22

regular vigorous exercise. As you do, all your systems of detoxification, metabolism, respiration, digestion, immunity, healing and regeneration are augmented.

As can be expected in our culture, some people overdo exercise, allowing it to become an obsession and addiction. Overexerting our bodies can paradoxically become a way we avoid being fully in them. It is usually the middle way of moderation that works best for the long term, yet it's important to stretch your body beyond its easy comfort zone.

Regardless of whether you are highly fit and mobile or are relying on a wheelchair for mobility, there are appropriate strengthening exercises you can do. These may include yoga, qigong, lifting weights, hiking or the use of a small rebounder trampoline. Working with a rebounder can create great fitness benefits, even if you exercise from a seated position.

My favorite exercise is hiking in the mountains. That is the perfect exercise for me because hiking with an elevation change challenges my body, strengthening its cardiovascular systems. While hiking I'm also breathing relatively fresh air and being entrained by the vibrations of the natural world which are highly regenerative to the body, mind and spirit. While hiking I'm either by myself having time for solitude and reflection, or spending time with other nature lovers who tend to be open, appreciative and fun people. Love it!

Some people's hobby is restoring classic cars or old houses, making them beautiful and functional. Consider taking that kind of care and dedication remodeling and rejuvenating your own body. It's amazing what increased care and attention can do for one's health and wellbeing.

Internal and External Rejuvenation

Rejuvenation is the art of prolonging life while enhancing vitality and well-being. There are records of deep rejuvenation arts going back to ancient civilizations in Egypt, Greece, India and elsewhere. The term rejuvenation has become co-opted in modern times by estheticians and plastic surgeons who mainly work with the skin and underlying tissues, yet true rejuvenation is much more than skin deep.

I expanded my understanding of rejuvenation through a multitude of seminars and workshops about microcurrent electro-therapies[36] I led over a 25-year period. I am the lead developer of the Acutron device which is used by acupuncturists, chiropractors and other health professionals for non-drug pain management and non-

---

[36] Microcurrent is a form of therapy equipment that applies very low pulsed electric currents to the body for pain relief, rehabilitation, electro-acupuncture, reducing inflammation, facial rejuvenation and more.

needle electronic acupuncture. We learned that this same technology also produced noticeable lifting and toning of the muscles of the face after one acupuncturist in Florida treated a woman with Bell's palsy using the Acutron. After that client experienced relief from her sagging facial muscles, she continued coming back for ongoing face lifting. Pretty soon the teaching of this method became a very popular part of our workshops. Within a few years, there were hundreds of health professionals and estheticians using the Acutron for combinations of pain management and facial rejuvenation.

After many years of offering these workshops, I was able to gather a great deal of feedback from some of the practitioners offering microcurrent facial rejuvenation. What I learned was this: those who were mainly treating the skin surface with microcurrent reported producing results that were highly satisfactory to their clients between 70 – 80% of the time. Other practitioners who combined facial rejuvenation with internal balancing methods such as acupuncture, herbal medicine or energy healing tended to produce better and more consistent results. Yet there were some whose results stood out from all others. These practitioners reported almost all their clients being highly satisfied with their facial rejuvenation results and usually referring others. When I spoke with some of these people it became clear that they were bringing some kind of intangible healing energy and loving Presence to their clinical sessions that transcended even highly skilled microcurrent treatments. They were in touch with their Avatar *transmission*, and it amplified the positive results of whatever else they were doing.

These extensive observations convinced me that true rejuvenation takes place on multidimensional levels.

The process of true rejuvenation involves cleansing and detoxifying the body while strengthening the health of its organs, glands and subtle energy systems. This process is activated through the body's epigenetic pathways as people provide vigorous exercise and a healthy diet to their bodies while focusing their mind into the present moment more of the time. Rejuvenation also involves a process of emotional lightening up as we release old psychic burdens. All of these activities increase a person's ability to maintain higher frequencies of light in their body and mind. This is what I have referred to earlier as activation of the light body.

So, what would be the opposite of rejuvenating yourself and lightening up your body? My father once wrote a newsletter article that expressed the answer very wisely. He stated that each of the times in our lives we cheat, compromise our integrity or give our power away, a dark spot gets created somewhere in our bodies. Those dark areas eventually degenerate and age us. The more experience I've gained working with clients through Quantum Healing, the more accurate I now see my father's musings to be.

Aging and Longevity

The conventional wisdom I heard while growing up was that losing vitality, becoming more physically decrepit or demented, and developing one or more killer diseases were normal and expected parts of the aging process. It did seem to be true, as that is what eventually happened to all my older relatives. I would now like to offer a different perspective.

Because most of the human race is in a fallen state of consciousness, our thoughts and feelings are frequently fear and stress-based. Therefore, our DNA is continually expressing that in the cells of our body. This, in combination with the influence of chemical and electromagnetic toxins directly affects the function of our organs, hormones, the condition of our joints and fascia as well as our brain function (or lack of it). These are major drivers of degenerative changes in the body and mind associated with aging.

We can see areas of chronic weakness, pain or inflammation as places where the brilliant feedback systems of our body are reflecting unexamined, unforgiven or unloved parts of our psyche. These are the markers for energetic gunk or *samskara* that is crying out to be transformed and released. Have compassion for these parts of yourself and give them what they are asking for.

There are ways to slow down age-related decline, and even reverse it in some cases. That can happen through the process of clearing old mental conditioning, and rewiring our bodies and minds to the higher, love-filled frequencies of our true self. This is the process I refer to as Christing.

Some advanced practitioners of various Eastern paths have claimed they were able to spiritualize their bodies and live much longer than most people through dedicated meditation, *qigong*,[37] living in nature and eating special foods and herbs. One noted Chinese Taoist practitioner named Li Ching-Yun is reputed to have lived to the age of 256, and there is quite a bit of supportive evidence to suggest that this

---

[37] Qigong – energy exercises that circulate vital energy throughout the body and build internal power.

Avatar Roadmap #5
Christing Your Body

1. Do regular Ascension meditative practices that increase physical embodiment of the light of your true self, also called activation of the merkaba light body. Train your mind to release stress-filled thoughts about the past and future, dwelling more in present time.

2. Cultivate the qualities of self-love and self-forgiveness, then sharing pure love and forgiveness with others as possible.

3. Be willing to feel your own pain instead of running from it. Keep applying loving Presence and the light of your transmission to clear energy blockages in your body that are based on past conditioning. Be willing to go through the process of mental and emotional purification, which all masters-in-training go through.

4. Receive high-level light transmissions and activations through healers or teachers you trust, as you are guided to. This is an essential part of most Avatar's process of awakening.

5. Eat a health-supporting diet and commit to regular, vigorous exercise. Detoxify the body when needed.

may be true.[38] Other ancient and contemporary sources have described dedicated practitioners transforming their physical bodies into a *rainbow body*, another name for the light body. In his landmark book, *Autobiography of a Yogi,* Paramahansa Yogananda wrote about a Master he called Babaji who has been living for hundreds of years yet was able to appear in a youthful body wherever and whenever he liked. There are many more accounts like this in the series, *Life and Teachings of the Masters of the Far East* by Spalding.[39]

Of course, it's easy to be skeptical of these claims of extreme longevity, and it is not necessary for you to believe them. What's most important to know is that we can be on that same regenerative path now, whether or not we live to an impressive old age. This is the practical process of embodiment of your Avatar self that is real and you can really do.

---

[38] https://en.wikipedia.org/wiki/Li_Ching-Yuen
[39] See Bibliography

Longevity is a mixed bag in our modern societies. People of privilege with higher incomes and access to quality medical care are living far longer than most of their ancestors did even two generations back. Those less privileged, who tend to be in minority groups and have less access to high-quality food and medical care, generally have shorter life expectancies. This discrepancy is unnecessary, and we must work toward more effective healthcare and disease-prevention programs that benefit all people.

Summary

Most spiritual paths I have participated in, or heard of were based on focusing the mind in meditation and opening the heart through loving service. Yet there was little to no emphasis on upgrading the body, and as a result the health of many avid practitioners actually declined. The epigenetic process of Christing and embodying your Avatar self, on the other hand, is totally body-centered. This evolutionary path fulfills the highest aims of methods for fulfilling human potential, awakening spiritual awareness and elevating the health and luminosity of your body.

Recommended Practices

Ideal practices to support the process of Christing and rejuvenation of your body are:

Central Axis breathing (Chapter 23)

All of the Christing – Embodiment practices (Chapter 25)

6

The Ultimate Taboo in Our Society

To get by in our society we need to navigate complex systems of laws, moralities and codes of conduct. We internalize these into our minds in various ways, and they govern our beliefs and behaviors, often more than we realize. All these programmed behaviors and beliefs about what is real filter our own experiences to create the waking dream we live in. Multiply this by millions of dreamers and that is the "dream" of our society – a set of shared experiences and beliefs that create a consensus reality.

Even wrongs as severe as serial killing or genocide are still part of the world we recognize. We can understand what those experiences are and condemn or judge them. Yet there are some experiences that are way more prohibited than even the most egregious crimes we know of. These go beyond what we think of as horrible or prohibited actions that we know exist in society, and I will refer to them here as taboos. I realize that the word taboo is often used to describe prohibited actions that we do understand such as murder and incest. For the purpose of this discussion, I will use a more radical definition of the word.

In this definition, a taboo is a prohibition so extreme that we usually don't even know that it exists. Taboos are so hardwired into the deepest parts of our subconscious minds that we can't even approach them without starting to feel extreme levels of panic, as if we would be annihilated if we were to go into it. It's as if loud sirens and flashing red lights start going off in our heads wordlessly giving us the messages of STOP – DESIST – DO NOT APPROACH – YOU ARE ENTERING A PROHIBITED ZONE – YOU WILL CEASE TO EXIST IF YOU PROCEED.

The foremost taboo in our modern society is the taboo against knowing who you really are.

This taboo doesn't tend to kick in very strongly if we just intellectually read or think about self-realization. Having spiritual or metaphysical beliefs about our true or higher selves can still be part of the safe zone of our dream. Most meditation experiences slow down the momentum of our minds and bring us into more peaceful parts of the dream. Delving into hidden truths through studying metaphysics and conspiracy theories is still mainly within the dream. Most of what we call altered states of consciousness are just other sectors of the dream than we usually focus on. This taboo is only designed to fully kick in when we actually attempt to stop our conditioned minds and enter the direct, bodily experience of the Christ Avatar that we truly are.

Vonnegut's Fable

Science fiction literature often serves the role of introducing advanced or forbidden truths into our consciousness in the form of entertaining stories. That is probably why I devoured the stuff during my teenage years. Kurt Vonnegut, Jr's novel, *The Sirens of Titan* [40] imaginatively depicted the taboo against knowing who we are in this section of the story:

> A human army was training on Mars to prepare for an invasion of the Earth. In order to keep the soldiers submissive and obedient, the army commanders installed implants into each of their brains that kept repeating a march song that sounded like "rented a tent rented a tent rented a rented a rented a tent." This noise was so loud that it drowned out the soldier's own thoughts and effectively kept them in line. One night a few men snuck away from the base with several bottles of bootleg whiskey, notebooks and pens. They got really drunk and as they did the odious "rented a tent" noise in their heads softened. This allowed the men to remember some of their own thoughts, and they eagerly wrote them down in the notebooks. This was how they recollected some true things they had been unable to remember about their lives, and who they really are.

I believe Vonnegut's story mirrors what is really going on with the human race. It provides a great metaphor for the noise in our heads that frequently distracts us from the pure, still voice of our true self.

We grow up hearing about people who are convinced that they are Jesus or Napoleon or God being committed to long-term confinement in mental hospitals. Yes, many people saying these things may have a real mental illness, but do we really think about why they have it? According to current mental health textbooks, the causes of schizophrenia, a disease characterized by being out of touch with reality are unknown, although often associated with severe childhood or adult trauma.

While most people reading this book feel more grounded and at ease than diagnosed schizophrenics, we have one vital thing in common with them. We also believe we are something we are not. Or perhaps more generously, we recognize only a small part of ourselves as "us," rather than the totality of who we really are.

Very few people realize the power of this pervasive taboo against knowing who we are that has been hard-wired into our psyches. Even fewer seek to investigate where this taboo came from. That's because asking that question opens up a deep rabbit hole that few are willing to delve into. It's like having a dark family secret that is kept hush-hush because to bring it into the open would severely rock the boat and bring up lots of scary, unpleasant feelings and wounds.

---

40 Vonnegut, Jr. Kurt, *The Sirens of Titan*, 1967, Hodder & Stoughton

Claiming your Avatar self requires the courage to know and live your truth. It requires stepping out of the false security of identifying with the dream of our society and taking a stand for living the truth of who you really are. The image from *The Matrix* of Neo taking the red pill clearly evokes this powerful choice.

You and other awakening Avatars are very powerful beings. We are expressions of unlimited divine love, light and power. From the examples of well-known Avatars, we have seen that even one person standing in their divine power can significantly change the world. Imagine how things would change in human society if millions of us all over the planet made that powerful choice. As we do, we can help pull humanity back from its current destructive tendencies.

This is a movement you can be a vital part of. Yet most of us encounter a wall of avoidance as we approach claiming our power. It often feels like an experience of deep fear and trauma we don't want to face. In spite of that, the wellspring of our greatest power and love is right behind that wall. It takes great courage and love to drop into our gut and unmask our fear, so we can behold our own light. As we are willing to deeply feel our truth over and over again, we gain in strength, poise and confidence.

The support of other Avatars is very helpful in this reclamation process. We can mirror the light we see in each other, offering encouragement and helping validate what is real and true.

Breaking the hard-wired taboo against knowing who we are is a major aspect of our spiritual awakening. As Franklin Roosevelt said so aptly, "We have nothing to fear but fear itself."

Guided Practice

Do you want to see how much the taboo against knowing who you are affects you? If so, try this practice.

Stand in front of a mirror (preferably with no one else around) and gaze deeply into your own eyes. Set an intention to closely observe your feelings and reactions by staying very present to yourself. The following statements are called Decrees. Speak these words, or similar, out loud with a voice of authority:

I AM THE CHRIST
I AM A DIVINE AVATAR
I AM GOD IN FLESH

I AM UNLIMITED AND POWERFUL
I AM PURE LOVE
I HAVE COME I HAVE COME I HAVE COME

What did you notice? If you felt deep recognition, joy and shivers of truth running through your body congratulations, you have stepped out of the taboo against knowing who you are quite a bit. Or, you may have noticed any of these taboo-type reactions:

- Denial of the words you were saying
- Judgmental voices saying something like "who do you think you're kidding, egomaniac?"
- Going out of your body, spacing out, thinking about other things
- Fear or panic
- Tightening up
- Heart beating faster in a fearful way

Reactions like these come up because your deep programming is kicking in to let you know, in no uncertain terms, YOU DON'T HAVE PERMISSION to know and enjoy who you really are. Stop a moment to consider how radical that is.

If you observed any of those reactions in yourself as you spoke those powerful statements and would like to break this taboo, take on the practice of speaking decrees regularly. You can use the ones above, or work with additional decrees found in Resource Section Six. Also, feel free to create your own decrees.

Realize that the negative aspects of our minds are frequently repeating negative decrees to us. They are often whispering or yelling to us messages of fear, self-doubt, overwhelm, not being enough and other mental toxins. Taking the initiative to regularly speak powerful, affirmative decrees is powerful medicine to start reprogramming your mind. By doing that you are taking charge of your experience and your destiny.

7

Getting with the New Earth

You may have heard references to a new, more enlightened Earth, with descriptions such as these:

- On Earth, as it is in Heaven

- The new age or the golden age of Earth

- Sat Yuga – An enlightened age on Earth as described in ancient writings from India[41]

- A New Earth – from the book by Eckhardt Tolle

---

[41] Sat Yuga is the most enlightened phase of the great cycles of consciousness described in the Puranas and other ancient Indian sacred writings

If you think about an enlightened, ascended Earth and humanity, do you believe it to be sometime in the future, the far future? Most people do, or they feel more cynical and don't even believe an enlightened Earth is possible.

In reality, the New Earth is already here and now, in its own dimensions of existence. Being able to directly perceive it is all a matter of awareness and belief. As an awakening Avatar, you have the power to train yourself to see and live in the new, ascended Earth. As greater numbers of awakening Avatars claim that awareness, it becomes easier for more and more people to also awaken to it. Then we will fulfill Jesus's prayer "on Earth as it is in Heaven."

You Are Multi-Dimensional

A truth you will frequently read throughout this book is that you are a multidimensional being. This means you exist at many levels of consciousness, and in many worlds of experience simultaneously.

I suggest that you stop for a moment to take that in. What resonance of truth do you feel in your body as you read and consider that? What does being multidimensional mean to you?

Many commentators have tried to interpret these words of Jesus:

My Father's house has many rooms; if that were not so, would I have told you that I am going there to prepare a place for you?[42]

I would reword that phrase like this for our current time:

Your true Avatar self exists in infinite dimensions of existence. I am a catalyst to help awaken you to your true, multidimensional nature.

Even though we are multidimensional beings, it is "normal" for most people to limit their field of awareness to just the few dimensions they call "the world," blocking out their perception of all the other multi-dimensions.[43] How do we do that? We humans have awesome powers of denial; even of events or things conclusively confirmed by a consensus of scientists or eyewitness observers. Our brain is able to compare input to our internal maps of reality, and if the input does not agree with what we believe, we tend to reject it.[44]

---

42 The Bible, John 14:2
43 For more about multi-dimensions see Chapter 29, Timelines
44 For examples see: https://theconversation.com/humans-are-hardwired-to-dismiss-facts-that-dont-fit-their-worldview-127168

I remember reading the wonderful book series, *The Chronicles of Narnia* by C.S. Lewis during my youth, and those stories left deep impressions on me. The ability of people to deny what is right in front of them was clearly depicted in the final book in the series, *The Last Battle*. This book is about a war between an army of wicked witches and dark creatures, and an array of animals and noble children led by the Christ-like lion, Aslan. During the last battle, the skies were dark and stormy, and there was lots of pain and death. Eventually, the light side won the battle, the sun came out and there was great celebration. One memorable scene concerned some very negative dwarfs who had been fighting on the side of the dark army. After the battle, the children went up to these dwarfs to let them know that they were forgiven and accepted, and free to go. Yet these dwarfs cowered and cursed, believing that the skies were still stormy, and the battle was still raging. No matter how much the children of the light tried to reassure or reason with the dwarfs they could not see or believe the truth. Finally, Aslan told the children that there was nothing more they could do for the terrified dwarfs, as they were refusing to open their eyes to see the reality in front of them.

The battle ending and the sun coming out in that C.S. Lewis story is representative of the New Earth. This is a higher vibrational dimension of our planet vibrating primarily in the fifth dimension of pure love and Christ consciousness. On the New Earth, we recognize our interconnectedness and interdependency with each other and with all of nature, and there is abundance for all. Those who seek to keep engaging in control and manipulation to gain power over others can't find many takers on the New Earth. It's a lot like the old bumper sticker message from the 1960s: "What if they gave a war and no one came?" Yet most of us continue to dream that we are still living in the survival-based old Earth full of fear, trauma and top-down control systems.

Why do we keep perpetuating that old reality? It is partially because our brains are literally addicted to pain and suffering and tend to keep perpetuating it. This quote from an article by Anna Anderson, Quantum Coach, reveals some of the physiology behind this curious human tendency:

> Every emotion, either positive or negative, is a blend of chemicals (neurotransmitters and hormones) that our brain instantly produces in response to thoughts. This cocktail circulates throughout the body producing corresponding sensations that are felt at both the psychological and physical levels. The chemistry of emotion is very addictive if repeated frequently over a long period of time – just like the chemistry of nicotine, alcohol and drugs.

This is most noticeable in the case of negative emotions, as they produce stress hormones that our body, in a twisted, self-destructive way, can easily start craving like a drug.[45]

We also hold onto our trauma focus because we deeply fear the loss of familiar identity that would come if we were to stop perpetuating it.

So, what does it really take to see the new Earth? One thing it requires is a process of dis-illusionment. We often think of that as a negative, depressing experience, but it can be just the thing we need to awaken us from the hypnotic trance of our old, habituated reality. You get to see the New Earth when you purge yourself of your false fascination with all the dramas, traumas and distortions you have been inundated with since childhood. These experiences exist primarily within the fourth dimension of our minds (4D), the astral zone where we can be so manipulated and misled. This is the realm that has continued to bind us to the old Earth.

The term "dimensions" refers to spaces theorized by mathematics, described by the number of coordinates required to define any point within it. The same term is often used to refer to realms of human consciousness. Human beings are mainly aware of these three dimensions of consciousness:

- Third Dimension (3D) – The physical realm of experience including length, width and height. All physical things exist within these parameters. The rational mind perceives 3D as its primary reality, often denying the other dimensions of experience.

- Fourth Dimension (4D) – Refers to the additional dimension of time or duration, as well as experiences of subtle energy and higher consciousness beyond the physical level and rational mind. This level is sometimes called "paranormal" or "metaphysical." While 4D often feels high and transcendent, it is still polarized between light and dark energies and beings. Therefore, peoples' experiences of 4D can range from blissful to terrifying.

- Fifth Dimension (5D) – The realm of pure love and oneness that is free of duality and polarization. While there are higher dimensions of consciousness than 5D, this is the one that is most easily perceived by us at our current level of spiritual evolution. The overall consciousness of the New Earth primarily vibrates in 5D and higher levels of 4D.

---

[45] https://www.huffpost.com/entry/are-you-addicted-to-suffe_b_9744416

The fourth dimension used to be described as a beautiful space of angels, elementals, fairies and the various light and dark spirits. Those are there to offer people a clear choice. Now the fourth dimension has become co-opted by massive amounts of manipulation and disinformation – "illusion, pollution and delusion." I also believe that some players in our world deploy energy and artificial intelligence technologies that broadcast through the realm of 4D, in attempts to influence and manipulate massive numbers of people.

No level of mind, whether it's the gross worldly mind or the more subtle, seemingly spiritualized mind, can be fully trusted to guide you. To really see the new Earth, you need to be committed to truth beyond all duality, which you can directly experience through your Avatar transmission. Your transmission is one experience you can truly trust because it comes from the highest pure source. The best way to prevent being adversely affected by all negative influences is to go through the process of *Christing* and learn to keep your mind connected to 5D more of the time. Purity is powerful.

The Choice We Must Make on Earth

Many of us have heard about enlightened civilizations existing in other parts of the Universe. It seems that at some point in their past these advanced civilizations had to face the same dire choices we are now facing on Earth. They had also developed advanced technologies with the potential for great destruction and misuse just like we have, and had to grapple with the struggle to overcome the duality and ignorance of their lower nature. These civilizations somehow managed to pass that big testing point and learn to live sustainably according to higher spiritual principles. That is why they are still around. It's likely that other planets with civilizations that did not pass that test now look like pockmarked asteroids or dead zones. This is truly the choice point we are at on Earth now.

Avatar Lightworkers have paratrooped into this reality to help humanity take the higher road and honor our Earth.

Protecting our Environment

The truth is that the Earth is a living being, and many indigenous and ancient cultures learned to live in synch with our planet. These ancient civilizations (and many of their descendants today) honor the feminine principle, which is about respecting our sacred relationship as part of the inter-connectedness of life.

The ancient civilization called Atlantis started out in sync with the Earth, with its people possessing advanced knowledge of how to tap into deep cosmic and Earth energies. It seems that many of the leaders and scientists of Atlantis became more patriarchal – choosing the imbalanced male aspect of the mind and its ambitions to supplant the honoring of the Earth. This expression of hubris, an arrogant overreaching for power, helped lead to the current dominance of destructive patriarchy in our modern cultures. It also led to the destruction of Atlantis, with the loss of much advanced knowledge and technologies.[46] We are in a similar situation now. If we don't get our act together to live in honor and respect of the Earth, she will kick us out one way or the other. The Earth will only tolerate so much dishonor and abuse.

Indigenous People and Lightworkers Have Helped Stabilize the Earth

We can see plenty of ongoing environmental, social and humanitarian crises on Earth at this time. I believe, however, that these are much less severe than they would have been without the ongoing planetary healing work that has been done by the network of indigenous peoples and Lightworkers. If they had not been holding an ongoing space of prayer, meditation and Earth healing, I believe there would have been much worse devastation by now than there actually has been.

As a dramatic example, there have been at least 15 documented cases in which the United States and Russia[47] came close to starting nuclear wars with each other between the 1960s and 1990s. These close calls mainly happened due to failures of tracking equipment or errors in human judgment. Any one of these events could have produced catastrophic consequences, but somehow each one was averted.[48] Was that all "good luck?" It seems that there are powerful forces helping to deliberately hold back major destruction.

A radical shift is needed in order for humanity to come into right relationship with the Earth. You can start participating in that right now by committing to being a steward of the Earth. If you agree, you can take a moment to send your love and Avatar transmission down into the Earth to signal your intent. Then resolve to take appropriate action. Contact your elected representatives and executives of polluting corporations, and demand that they do the right thing by changing their practices away from polluting and over-extracting from the Earth. Let them know that this is an absolute imperative. So many big corporations are already moving in that

---

[46]   Spence, Lewis, *The History of Atlantis*, Dover Publications 2003
[47]   During the time of many of these incidents Russia and its satellite countries was called the U.S.S.R.
[48]   https://en.wikipedia.org/wiki/List_of_nuclear_close_calls

direction on their own, yet they still need public pressure and government action so the changes come quickly and consistently enough. Our voices matter.

Those who deny that there is a need to protect the Earth's environment are trying to perpetuate an old system that worked when there was a much smaller population of people on the Earth. This is rooted in a long history of white privilege to exploit and colonize other countries and races while seeing the Earth as an inexhaustible resource to extract from and dump into. None of this is just or sustainable moving forward, due to the much higher human population and the global awakening of consciousness.

Working With the Elementals

The term "elementals" refers to conscious beings that work with and regulate the elements of the natural world – earth, air, fire and water. Elementals are not sophisticated and highly evolved like human beings, angels and other light beings. They stay very close to their basic, earthly functions. Elementals are known by names such as gnomes, fairies, sylphs, undines and salamanders.

These elemental beings are highly responsive to the mental field of consciousness created by the human race. That means that during times when human societies are living in greater harmony and balance according to *dharma*,[49] the natural elements of the Earth tend to reflect that through greater stability. When large numbers of people are living chaotically, more out of sync with their true purpose and respect for the Earth, the elementals will also act more chaotically. That brings about more of what we call natural disasters such as wildfires, floods, droughts, earthquakes and devastating storms. These are direct manifestations of imbalances of the elementals of fire, water, earth and air, respectively. As you've no doubt noticed, all of these have significantly increased in recent years, and scientists tell us they are likely to further increase.

It is vital that each of us acknowledges our responsibility for what is happening with the Earth now. Once you accept this responsibility, you can start working with the elementals more consciously and contribute to the healing and stabilization of the Earth. You can do that by taking time to love and honor the Earth as explained in this chapter. With loving focus, see the elements of the Earth in harmony and balance, and do your part to be a conscious steward of our planet. I encourage you to take a few minutes each day to bring planetary healing into your daily meditation time, as detailed in Chapter 13.

---

[49] Dharma means living in harmony with your true life purpose and Universal law

The Solution is in Consciousness

Our environmental crisis is only one of many challenging issues now facing humanity. Others include massive disease epidemics, racism, sexism, institutionalized political corruption, rapidly increasing levels of mental illness and an increasing wealth gap between the super-rich and everyone else. Each one of these issues has become so acute and interlocked with other intractable issues, that they have become almost impossible to solve at our current level of consciousness. These issues are not impossible to solve because we lack the resources and technology to solve them – it is due to the dominance and control of the patriarchal ego-based human mind. These issues are so difficult and entrenched that a major shift in human consciousness is required in order for the human race to pass the test of this time.

Due to the dualistic nature of the mind, each solution tends to bring new challenges and controversies. The greatest, most effective solution comes as we literally "change our minds," and step out of the zone of problems into the zone of solutions. This is the realm of 5D. Then our governments, social movements and brilliant sciences are much more likely to create solutions that really work.

The great news is that this shift is already well underway. This is the time of mass Ascension of consciousness, or the Ninth Wave as described by the ancient Mayans.[50] The New Earth is already here for those who have eyes to see it. This is not some kind of New Age idealistic fable; it is actually more real than our bad dreams of the old Earth which are starting to fade away.

Would you consider going cold turkey on your addiction to pain and the illusions of the fourth dimension, and allow your eyes to see anew that you are already in the blessed New Earth?

You are manifesting the reality you live in all the time. One of the most powerful ways you manifest is through the power of your expectations. Because you are a creator being, whatever you expect to happen in your life is what tends to actually happen. This is a principle you need to consider carefully in order to create what you really want. If you expect a bleak future, that's what you will create.[51] If you train your heart and mind to joyfully see the New Earth, then that is where you will live. Changing your mind takes practice. The practice at the end of this chapter will be supportive of making this vital shift in perception.

---

[50] See Chapter 8 about the Mayan creation waves

[51] Watching TV news shows and frequently reading online blogs about how bad and corrupt things are strongly reinforces the brainwave frequencies of stress. This tends to make people feel fear and pessimistic about the world. Solution – only put your attention on what you want to see. Keeping informed about current events does not have to create negative states as long as you stay awake and in love, keeping your energy inside your body.

Avatar Roadmap #6

Perceiving the New Earth

It may be a very new idea that there is a new Earth right here that you may not yet be seeing. So let's make it practical:

1. Take a walk in your favorite places outdoors. If for any reason you are unable to walk, ask those who care about you to help you get outside to a beautiful place that you love.

2. Engage Foundational practices.

3. Open your heart to love and appreciate the Earth. Expect to see beauty all around you, with you a part of it.

4. If possible, allow your bare feet to touch the Earth, even for a few minutes.

5. As you walk or stand invoke your Avatar transmission, and imagine it emanating from a golden chakra two or more feet above your head, flowing down through the central axis of your body into the Earth Star chakra two feet down into the Earth below your feet (see practice below). Becoming aware of this central axis is key to increasing embodiment of your Avatar self in your body.

6. Breathe deeply and consciously, choosing to embody love.

7. With each step you take see or feel your transmission gifting the Earth, helping heal and stabilize it.

8. Make decrees such as these to open your consciousness:

   I AM beholding the New Earth.

   I AM opening my spiritual eyes and my body is feeling the vibration of the New Earth.

   Dear my beloved Avatar self – reveal the New Earth to me now in whatever way possible.

9. Through the eyes of love, look around you at the sky, the rocks, the trees, other people, birds, clouds, whatever you see. Notice if you are perceiving the Earth differently than you usually do. Take in the colors you see, sensations of warmth or coolness you feel and anything you can smell. Bring your mind into the sacred Now moment and listen to the sounds you hear. Listen more carefully than you usually do, noticing sounds that you usually don't pay attention to. Allow yourself to

be drawn into heightened perceptions of all your senses. Celebrate the New Earth that is already here, and you are able to perceive.

10. You can also imagine that the Earth is a huge, living being, often called Gaia. Explore the experience of communion with her in every step you take, flowing your love and Christ energy into her, and receiving her love gifting back to you. Open your heart wide and have fun with this.

I can tell you what it is like for me. I have been seeing the New Earth for many years now. It is a different vibration that is higher, and of a finer nature than the Earth I used to know. When I am walking outside nature often looks different to me. Sights that I used to take for granted, such as sunlight, birds flying or bees buzzing around a flowering bush look extraordinarily beautiful and entrancing. I can more readily sense higher dimensions of consciousness emanating through Earth's physicality. Sometimes when I am tuned into this consciousness, other people mirror it to me by being extra friendly and connected as we pass each other.

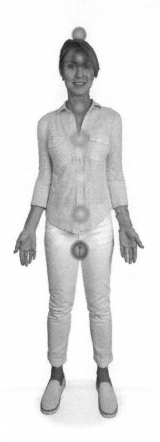

The Earth Star Chakra

The Earth Star chakra is a vital part of your energy anatomy. It is a disk of living light that sits about two feet (.61 meter) below you into the Earth. If you are standing, it is two feet below your feet, and if you are sitting on the floor or ground it is two feet below the base of your body. When perceiving your Earth Star, see or feel it two feet below you into the Earth, even if you are several stories up in a house or building.

Building awareness of the Earth Star is a vital activity for awakening Avatars because a major function of this chakra is to increase embodiment of the true self. Think of the Earth Star as a powerful electro-magnet pulling the energy of your Avatar transmission from divine source down into your body.

Putting your attention on the Earth Star is the perfect counter-balance to chronically over-active mind chatter.

I have enjoyed using the term "unfreakable" to describe a state of mind in which I stay calm and grounded, even when confronted with difficult, unexpected situations. I have discovered that it is my awareness of my Earth Star chakra that makes me the most unfreakable. This awareness also helps open my perception of the New Earth, and it can do that for you also.

As you increase your ability to sense and participate in the New Earth, you are bringing yourself more into fifth dimensional (5D) consciousness. When you are consciously aligned with your Christ Avatar transmission, your footsteps are blessing and helping to anchor the New Earth into the physical, 3D Earth. That is great service. Then you are helping actualize the phrase "on Earth as it is in Heaven."

Guided Practice – Getting in Touch With Your Earth Star Chakra

Your greatest powers are your love and persistent attention. Read what is above to build your motivation and inspiration to directly perceive your Earth Star. When you are ready, simply direct your love and attention two feet (.61 meter) down below your feet. Intend to open your awareness to this vital part of yourself.

If you are a primarily visual perceiver, notice what you see in that location. The Earth Star has been described as a golden disk or pool of energy, yet it is most powerful to discover what it looks like for yourself. If you are primarily kinesthetic, extend your feeling sense down into the Earth Star. Tune into the subtle energy sensations of this chakra.

Just like any other new experience, practice makes perfect. I love to include focusing on my Earth Star as part of sitting meditation practice and also while walking outdoors. I also find dropping my attention down into my Earth Star the ultimate stress reliever, in conjunction with deep belly breathing and putting the tip of my tongue in the Master Hook Up position.

I "flush" accumulated tension or stress down through my body into my Earth Star many times each day, bringing my mind and nervous system into a more empty, neutral state. If you wish to experience this simple clearing practice, follow these steps:

1. Imagine or visualize a golden ball of light two to four feet above your head. Take in a deep breath.

2. With the intention of clearing your body of stress, breathe out strongly, imagining the ball of light rushing down through your body, pulling all stress down into the Earth Star beneath your feet.

3. Pause for a short time to enjoy the neutrality in your body.

4. Repeat if necessary.

Focusing on the Earth Star is a valuable part of the following practices described in Section 4:

Central Axis breathing (Chapter 23)
Light Body Merkaba Activation (Chapter 27)

8

Ascension and Quantum Waves

Mass ascension of consciousness is now at a major tipping point on Planet Earth. This radical shift is reverberating throughout our entire galaxy and beyond. As you will learn in this chapter, there have been many times in the history of our planet during which overall consciousness has leaped rapidly upward. Yet the Ascension unfolding now is unprecedented. We are entering a new phase of life that will not look like anything we have seen before, where we transform from a race of physically-based beings having a growing awareness of Spirit into living as embodied multi-dimensional spiritual beings. We will awaken from our painful collective dream of separation, conflict, scarcity and domination into the reality of universal love, limitless resourcefulness and intelligent collaboration.

This idea of higher consciousness breaking out all over the planet may sound like an intriguing intellectual idea, yet it is so much more than that. It is a grand awakening you can feel for yourself, and you are already feeling it. Everyone is experiencing the Ascension on one level or another, but few have words for it or can see the bigger picture of what is really happening. While each of us may describe this shift in different ways, you may recognize some of these common experiences:

- Sensations of energy moving, pulsing or vibrating in your body.
- Flashes of inspiration, deep insights or profound love that well up in you unexpectedly, sometimes alternating with disturbed, fearful or depressive feelings. Little to none of this seeming to be directly caused by events in your current life.

- Going through bursts of higher states of consciousness and receiving inner messages or guidance more easily than you previously believed you were capable of.

- Becoming more empathic to the thoughts and feelings of others – sometimes massive numbers of people. This may feel overwhelming at times.

- Becoming disinterested in work you've been doing, relationships you've been in or activities you used to enjoy. Eventually being drawn to new forms of work, relationships or activities. Or just feeling a void in these areas.

These are just a few examples of ways people are experiencing Ascension. There are countless more.

These examples of "ascension symptoms" indicate two sides of the experience most of us are going through – expanded states of consciousness as well as times of feeling conflicts and stress that can seem overwhelming at times. We can say that we are going through more extreme polarization of our experiences.

You've probably noticed how so many people in our societies have gotten more polarized and extreme in their belief systems. I've been politically aware and engaged since my early teenage years, yet I have never seen anything like the polarization of beliefs recently filling the media. This can be explained in part by understanding that the human race is passing through the highly polarized zone of the fourth dimension as we are entering into the pure love and oneness of the fifth dimension.

Chapter 7 contains brief explanations of the third, fourth and fifth dimensions of human experience. These are important concepts to understand in putting the ascension of consciousness into perspective, and why it may seem like our inner experiences are swinging up and down so much.

As an awakening Avatar, ascension is your thing. Your truest self doesn't need any ascension because it is already an expression of All That Is. Yet there is plenty of room for all of us to uplift and purify our bodies and minds from the lower vibrational states we grew up in.

In past generations it was easier for people to focus on their physical existence, keeping the shadow of their deep emotional issues walled away in their subconscious most of the time. Of course, these buried issues kept surfacing in ways ranging from physical diseases to wars between nations. Now the elevating ascension energies are bringing all that buried stuff to the surface – whether we like it or not. Therefore, a major aspect of your experience of *Christing* and awakening is consciously dealing with your shadow self.

Ascension is happening. Yet you are constantly making the choice of how you experience it. A good analogy is the cable cars of San Francisco, a city I live close to. On some of the steep streets in the city with cable cars, there are underground metal cables moving upward during hours of operation. The cable car operator uses a big clamp to grab onto the moving cable, which pulls the car up the hill.

It's the same way with us. The elevating consciousness on our planet acts like those underground metal cables. You can latch onto it and allow this flow of higher light and love to pull you into higher states of being. To the extent you consciously choose this, you lighten up your life experience on many levels.

So how do you choose to latch onto the upward-moving cable of Ascension? You do it with the one thing you can really control – your attention. This book is full of insights and practices to support you in training your mind to focus on the ultimately fulfilling, love-filled experience of your true self. The more moments your mind is focusing on the life you want to have and the world you want to live in, the more you are creating that reality for yourself.

As the old saying states, "wake up and smell the flowers." Know and believe that the door is open right now for you to step into a higher, healthier experience of your life. Recognize the elevating light on our planet. See it, meditate upon it, feel the love and behold the New Earth as often as you can.[52] Through these ways of focusing your mind, you are healing yourself on the deepest level, and helping bring Heaven to Earth. Because the Universe is holographic, the more you create that reality for yourself the more you help create it for all life.

Purification

While the process I just described may sound simple, and, in essence it is, adapting to these shifts can be rigorous. Remember, everything is made up of energy. Energy can transform instantaneously. Yet it usually takes time and care for the denser energies of your physical body and the engrained thought patterns of your mind to catch up. As you get with the energies of Ascension, you enter a process of clearing and purification. As explained in Chapter 5, your body becomes epigenetically restructured. This is the process of rewiring the subtle energy systems of your body – so it supports the higher voltage of your Avatar self.

---

[52] See Chapter 7, The New Earth

Your body becomes epigenetically restructured. This is the process of rewiring the subtle energy systems of your body – so it supports the higher voltage of your Avatar self.

My friend, Vidya Frazier, who has written several valuable books about the ascension of consciousness, has explained that any of the following symptoms bothering lots of people now could stem from reactions to the rapidly shifting energies on our planet[53]:

- Periods of intense emotional upset
- Mind fog
- Hypersensitivities
- Sleep disturbances
- Headaches
- Exhaustion

If you've been going through any of these, I have good news for you. Each of those experiences, and others listed above, is direct feedback as to how energy is moving through your body, and what you are thinking and believing. As an awakening Avatar, you have the power to transform those symptoms by mastering your own

---

[53] Frazier, Vidya, *Awakening to the Fifth Dimension*, First Edition Design Publishing 2014

energy. You do that one breath, and one thought at a time. The daily practice plans outlined in Chapter 22 will be golden for clearing any blockages and imbalances of energy in your body that have been at the root of distressing symptoms.

Rebalancing Female and Male Energies

As part of Universal Law, all creation springs from an interplay of female and male energies that the ancient Chinese called *Yin* and *Yang*. According to the *Kybalion*, a text describing seven universal laws governing everything in the Universe, the female principle is the source of all creation. The male principle represents the power of Will that activates the female principle to create. This dynamic is how the process of creation works in people of any gender because all of us possess both the male and female poles to various degrees.

A great deal of the suffering and destruction the human race has been going through is due to the system of patriarchal control. Patriarchy is the male principle of humanity suppressing and over-controlling the female principle. When imbalanced male energy dominates and suppresses feminine power we become increasingly disconnected from nature. Suffering increases and fresh new creation in harmony with the greatest good of all is stymied.

Because imbalanced male energy has been dominating and inhibiting the feminine for a long time, most of what the human race has created in recent centuries has been in the realm of the mind – technologies, hierarchal top-down structures, financial control systems and polarized divisions between groups of people. The human race is now going through a major breakup with old systems of patriarchal control. This will feel increasingly jarring and disruptive to those trying to perpetuate the old order. Each of us needs to root out the seeds of male-female imbalance from our own minds. It is vital that we consciously choose to align ourselves with what we really desire in the way of truth, love and freedom.

Pure love is the cohesive force that attracts energy into new patterns of higher-level creation. As the female and male energies come into greater balance within us, Ascension energies can flow through our lives and rapidly transform our planet and our societies. As is the case with many tipping points, this can happen more rapidly than most of us believe is possible.

Why Things Are Better Than You Think

Whatever most people imagine an ascended human race to look like, it is unlikely many would imagine that it would look like what is happening on Earth now. At the time of this writing, we are dealing with all of these: a global disease pandemic, multiple environmental catastrophes, massive concentration of wealth and power in the hands of a manipulative few, rampant disinformation campaigns through our social media and highly polarized societies. This couldn't be the ascension of consciousness, could it?

It could and it is. The human race has gone through many previous tipping points of consciousness. Each time we passed through one there was a great deal of chaos and resistance at first, similar to what we are seeing now. A well-documented example of a previous time of ascension is what was called the European Renaissance. At varying times during the 1400s through the early 1600s European society went through many radical shifts. These included:

- Moving out of feudalism, in which kings and wealthy landowners owned all the wealth and everyone else were serfs with no rights, into capitalist systems, creating a growing middle class.

- Tremendous advances in the dissemination of information and literature after the invention of the printing press.

- Widespread liberation of people to think for themselves rather than blindly follow the dogmas of the Church.

- Great advances in art and music, with creativity, expression and artistic realism reaching new heights.

- Rapid growth in global travel, exploration and trade, opening consciousness to a more global perspective and allowing the intermixing of Eastern and Western cultures.

- Rapid escalation of knowledge and research into astronomy, mathematics, alchemy, geography, medicine, human anatomy and more.

Before the tipping point of the Renaissance was the period called the Middle Ages, an era that started after the fall of the Roman empire, around 400 AD. During that approximately 1000-year period, development in all these areas of human expression stagnated, human rights were almost non-existent and close to half of the population of Europe was killed by the bubonic plague. Once the Renaissance began, human consciousness started rapidly flowering in all the areas listed above during a short period of time. This was a true ascension of consciousness, a quantum leap in the awakening of human potential.

There have been other historical periods since the Renaissance in which human mass consciousness rapidly elevated. One such period was called the Enlightenment in 18th century Europe. This was a mass movement affirming reason over religious dogma, advocating ideals of liberty, scientific progress, tolerance for different races and groups, and the separation of church and state. Times of rapid elevation of innovation and consciousness also happened in parallel within other cultures throughout the world.

Leaps in technology, communications, human rights and the creation of democratic political systems have been coming rapidly in more recent history. These include the Industrial Revolution of the 1800s, expanded voting rights in the 1900s and the explosion of computer technologies in the 20th and 21st centuries.

There have been major dark sides to all these advances, in the forms of inequality, misuse of technology, colonialism, human exploitation, pollution of the environment, and more. The time we are living in now shows all those forces at crisis levels, and it's easy to be pessimistic about the future prospects for the human race. But there is great reason for hope. It is common for there to be loads of crises and chaos prior to a breakthrough to a higher level of energy and consciousness. That is really what we are seeing now. This often-repeated phrase says it well:

Breakdowns Precede Breakthroughs

It is true that due to our advanced technologies and a frequent lack of wisdom in how we use them, the human race is at a major choice point that will determine how we survive this time, and if we do, how we move forward.

It can be encouraging to look at longer historical trends. By doing that, we can see that there has been tremendous progress in most key indicators of rising human consciousness and well-being in recent times. As examples:[54]

- World-wide hunger has decreased by an average of 27% in the world between the years 2000 and 2017.
- Child labor has declined by 40% internationally between 2000 and 2016.
- Human life expectancy has doubled, on average, between 1770 and 2015. In the 1700's most people died in their 30's, now the average age of death is over 72 years old.
- Child mortality has declined by more than 50% between 1990 and 2017.
- Violent crimes have declined steadily since the early 1990s in the USA.[55]

---

[54] https://www.vox.com/2014/11/24/7272929/global-poverty-health-crime-literacy-good-news
[55] At the time of this writing there appears to be an increase in violent crimes in many U.S. cities. Yet the overall trend is for these to decrease.

- The number of people in the world living in democratic societies has increased by about 80% since the early 1800s. Back then it was only about 2%, now it is above 50%.

- The number of people being educated in schools has vastly increased from the late 1800s up to the present day, with the biggest increases in the United States and South Korea. This goes along with an exponential increase in literacy over recent centuries, and most rapidly in the 20th and 21st centuries. The same goes for access to the internet, a marker of freedom of access to global information.

All of these statistics show unmistakable upward movement in human consciousness and well-being, in spite of all the difficult issues we often hear about through the media. Those issues are reflections of the dark sides of human nature, some of which are now coming into the open in new ways. It's painful to rip off the band-aids and have to face that stuff, yet it's a necessary process.

Less than one hundred years ago, law dictionaries defined women and children as "chattel," or the moveable property of men, and what we now call sexual abuse was an unspoken, forbidden topic. Gay, lesbian and transsexual people had no rights and could be imprisoned under sodomy laws. Racism was a blatant, accepted reality of U.S. culture, and sadly continues to be. In our recent past, there was also very little awareness of the fragility of Earth's ecosystems. So, the fact that there are major public struggles about these topics is actually a sign of elevating consciousness rather than the reverse. It means that major issues that were previously swept under our collective rug are now out in the open, and we are openly grappling with them.

The Nine Quantum Creation Waves

As we have seen through the examples above, the process of consciousness ascension does not tend to happen in a linear, even way. It is more *quantized*, which means that our ascension process more often happens in definite steps or stages. Long, stable periods are followed by times of rapid shifts. Those tipping point periods, when we take a leap to a higher level in a relatively short amount of time, are times of accelerated ascension.

There is a parallel between this and the science of quantum physics, which uses the term quantum leap to refer to the instantaneous jump of a sub-atomic particle from a lower energy state to a higher one. Quantum leaps appear to happen outside of time, as the particle just appears at a higher level without any measurable amount of time passing.

These observations mirror the advanced cosmology of the Mayans from Central America, as written about by Carl Johann Calleman and others. [56] According to Calleman, the Mayans identified nine discrete quantum waves emanating from the center of the Universe. Each of these quantum waves vibrates at a different frequency, and each could be said to be a building block of our known Universe. These nine quantum waves have been released on Earth sequentially throughout its history. Each time there has been change in the predominant wave affecting the Earth, a quantum leap in consciousness occurred.

According to Calleman:

"The lower waves (First through Fourth Waves) which drive biological evolution, form the basis of and prepare for the higher waves (Fifth through Ninth Waves,) which drive the spiritual and mental evolution of humanity. The combined action of the waves allows processes created by different waves to be coordinated so that critical new events necessary for evolution appear at the right time, sometimes very obviously as a quantum leap."[57]

Here are the ways the nine quantum waves described by the Mayans triggered the evolutionary steps of life on Earth and human development. The dates in parentheses are the times when each quantum wave started strongly affecting Earth. The years listed for the 7th, 8th and 9th waves are A.D. or our modern time.[58]

First Wave: (16 billion years ago) Supported creation of our planet, and later the start of life through individual cells, the building blocks of living things.

Second Wave: (820 million years ago) Supported creation of multi-cellular organisms.

Third Wave: (41 million years ago) Supported creation of animals with a spine having right and left halves of their bodies.

Fourth Wave: (2 million years ago) Supported creation of human beings with brains that could express consciousness in expanded ways.

Fifth Wave: (about 100,000 B.C.) Supported humanity living in shamanistic unity consciousness, feeling one with nature and the cosmos.

Sixth Wave: (3115 B.C.) Supported development of stronger ego/individuation, which was necessary for the development of mind, science and religions.

---

[56] Calleman, Carl Johan, *The Nine Waves of Creation: Quantum Physics, Holographic Evolution, and the Destiny of Humanity*, Bear and Company 2016

[57] Calleman, Carl J., *Quantum Science of Psychedelics*, Bear and Son 2020, Chapter Two, pages 37-38

[58] This table offered courtesy of Carl Johann Calleman.

Seventh Wave: (1755 A.D.) Supported stronger ego/individuation for development of technologies, materialism and democratic systems, with most power focused in the western world. The Seventh Wave included the Industrial Revolution of the 1800s.

Eighth Wave: (1999 - 2011) Supported development of digital computer technologies, the rise of feminism, more power going to eastern countries.

Ninth Wave: (2011 – present) Supports multidimensional consciousness, reducing the power of ego-mind into greater acceptance of unity consciousness, mixing and integrating all of the previous quantum waves.

As you can see, we are now in the time in which we are most strongly influenced by the Ninth Quantum Wave according to Mayan cosmology. This is a time in which all the quantum creation waves that have been transforming our consciousness since the dawn of life on Earth are affecting us at the same time.

We are now living in a time in which all the quantum creation waves that have been transforming our consciousness since the dawn of life on Earth are affecting us at the same time.

This is a radical departure from previous change points in which the evolution of life and consciousness was up-leveling in a quantized, step-by-step progression. Now we are in all of it, all the time. We are awakening to the holographic nature of consciousness, in which every individual point, such as our individual mind, is totally interconnected with all life and all consciousness, everywhere. This has vast implications for every aspect of our experience.

Avatar Roadmap #7
Surfing the Wave of Ascension More Smoothly

A heartfelt commitment to doing daily Ascension Practices will give you a much smoother ride as you move through all the rapid changes happening at this time. It will also empower you to fully enter into your body, the only place where the alchemy of awakening and transformation truly takes place. This can be called the process of full incarnation.

Ascension Practices and Moving into Full Incarnation

Hopefully, what you have read so far in this chapter has opened your mind to the cosmic forces that are driving the ascension of consciousness affecting us all. It is vital, as stated earlier, to move beyond an intellectual understanding of ascension into your own personal, bodily-felt experience of it.

During this time of the Ninth Wave in which we are going through accelerated ascension, I have found the most valuable practices to be those that support greater *embodiment* of the true being we are in our physical body. These are the Ascension Practices presented in this book and are what I practice and teach the most.

Incarnation is the process of the soul, which is an individualized aspect of infinite Spirit, coming into physical form. Those of us aware of this idea usually assume it is a done deal and here we are, already incarnated. Yet it is rare for those of us in our modern society to have completed our incarnation process. Most of us don't come fully into our bodies due to repeated over-stimulation of our minds plus the burden of trauma, or low-grade PTSD.

The German mystical teacher Rudolph Steiner taught that there are six major stages of incarnation people are designed to go through, starting at birth and completing around age 42.[59] In an ideal society based on the spiritual principles of life, each of us would complete all the stages of incarnation described by Steiner by that age and live as a realized human being. That certainly is not the norm, or even common in our societies. That is why special practices to support us in fully coming into our bodies are so valuable.

Guided Practices

The recommended guided practices to support the message of this chapter are found in these two chapters:

Chapter 9: Self-Healing Through Your Transmission

Chapter 24: Self-Love and the Inner Embrace

Practicing these self-healing methods helps create the stability and receptivity within you to be able to ascend your consciousness.

---

59 https://sites.google.com/site/waldorfwatch/incarnation

9

Self-Healing Through Your Transmission

The process of *Christing*, in which you upgrade the systems of your body and awaken your consciousness as an Avatar, is the ultimate form of healing. If you've been going through pains and struggles in your life, it's not because there's something wrong with you. It's more because you're a limitless divine being attempting to cram the grandeur of who you are into a small box of limitation, having likely bought into some version of the fear-based dream of our society. If you recognize any truth in this, you have the power to step out of that dream now. I personally self-monitor and step out of dreams of limitation I notice in myself many times each day. You can also. There is tremendous support for freeing yourself in that way now.

The word "healing" originates from old English and German words that mean "to make whole." In order to understand what it really means to be whole, it's vital that you learn to discriminate between the voice of your true self and what has aptly been called "pretender voices." Those are thoughts and feelings that have been programmed into us by others. Those influencers who helped instill those limiting voices did not necessarily do it maliciously, they were most likely passing on what was programmed into them. These voices are part of our internalized control systems, the taboo against knowing who we really are. A major aspect of self-healing is gaining skill at discriminating between pretender voices and the experience of our genuine self. It is about choosing love and what is real over and over again.

In order to dramatize this point, I will share one of my favorite spiritual teaching stories. This is a very brief version of a story that is usually told in longer form:

There was a man from California named Ray who wanted to be enlightened but just wasn't interested in meditation, self-discipline, joining spiritual groups or other activities like that. Yet his desire was strong. One day an old friend who was traveling through Asia sent him a message saying that he had heard about a master teacher living in the Himalayas who was able to help people become enlightened in just one day. If Ray was interested, he should come to Kathmandu, Nepal, and go to a certain gift shop and ask for a certain woman, and she would tell him how to find this master. Ray loved this idea, put his affairs in order and booked a flight to Kathmandu. After lengthy travel, he eventually found the woman he was supposed to ask. She did acknowledge knowing about the master who helped people become enlightened in one day. She did not know exactly where he was in the Himalayas however and sent Ray on a bus ride to a village a few hours away to ask someone up there.

Ray takes the rickety old bus to the village, finds the person he is supposed to ask, and is then directed to another, even more remote place, to ask another person who is supposed to know where this master could be found. In the full version of this story, this search goes on for a long, long time, with Ray being referred from one person who is supposed to know where the master is to another for months. To cut to the chase, after this exhausting, frustrating search eventually Ray finds himself trekking alone in the Himalayas and arrives at the actual mountain on which the master lives. After a harrowing, treacherous climb he finally reaches a relatively flat plateau area. On it, he sees two buildings. One is a modest dwelling, and the other is a long, narrow building. Ray sees a man sitting cross-legged in front of the smaller dwelling. Tired, hungry and hurting, Ray stumbles over to the man, who nods in welcome and beckons him to sit down in front of him. Before Ray can say anything, the man offers a cup of tea and a small plate of snacks, which Ray gratefully accepts. Finally, when Ray is feeling a little more settled the master speaks in English and says:

"I know why you've come here. You're here to become enlightened in one day." Ray nods affirmatively. "I have seen you coming in my meditations and was expecting you. Many people come here seeking the same thing. Are you ready to learn how?" Ray says yes, and the man arises and beckons him to follow. He leads Ray over to the long, narrow building a few minutes walk away. Ray sees that the building is about 12 feet wide and about 40 feet long. There is a door at the end they are standing next to.

"It's actually quite simple" the master spoke. "This building has a door at this end and another door at the opposite end. All you have to do is open the door at this end, walk through the building without stopping, and exit at the other end. Then you will be enlightened."

Ray felt a flood of thoughts and feelings including excitement, confusion, skepticism and a slight, but palpable sense of dread. "That's it?" he asked. "That's all I have to do?"

The master nodded yes. With a strong sense of resolve. Ray started reaching for the door handle to enter the building. "There's one more thing you need to know" the master spoke.

Ray stopped in his tracks and pulled his hand back from the door handle. "What's that?"

"There are 10,000 demons in this building. They'll do everything they can to try to distract, scare and mislead you as you walk through. But not to worry! They have no real power over you. All you have to do is ignore them while keeping your mind focused on your desire. As long as you keep walking and do that they can't hurt you."

That stopped Ray in his tracks for a moment. But with the master's words "they can't hurt you" in his mind, he reached for the door handle again. Before he pulled it open he turned to the master again. "By the way, how many people have come up here to walk through this building?"

"Hundreds, maybe thousands by now" the master replied.

"How many have successfully walked through this building?" Ray blurted out.

"None," the master said with a wry smile. "No one has yet walked all the way through the building. I'm hoping you'll be the first!"

There is a lot of power and depth in this story. Rather than telling you my interpretation now, I encourage you to contemplate what it means to you. Some useful questions to ask yourself could be:

Who or what are the demons, relative to your experience?

What does it really mean to be enlightened?

What is real healing?

Who could walk all the way through the building without stopping, and what would it take for you to do that?

You can find my answers to these questions in Chapter 20. If the story has no meaning for you, then let it go.

Personal Healing – Collective Healing

Let's face it – humanity has been going through massive amounts of trauma for thousands of years. Much of this unresolved burden has accumulated within our deep subconscious minds. Because all of us are holographically inter-connected with each other, none of us are unscathed by what has now become a field of collective trauma.[60] We can no longer fully separate our personal healing process from the healing of humanity and the Earth.

While this may sound like a burden, it is also a remarkable opportunity and blessing. Any real healing you do for yourself is also helping heal the human race. It works the other way also – all of the other Avatars, healers and Lightworkers on the planet who are doing their healing work are also blessing and benefiting you. The guided practice at the end of this chapter addresses self-healing that contributes to the welfare of others.

There are almost countless methods for self-healing, including Emotional Freedom Technique (EFT), cleaning up your diet and exercising more, self-inquiry[61] and forms of yoga, qigong and meditation. These all have great value. As an awakening Avatar, you also have the supremely effective healing resource available to you – connecting with and bathing in your Avatar *transmission*.

---

[60]   There are estimates that approximately 8 – 10 million Americans have been medically diagnosed with full-blown Post-Traumatic Stress Disorder, or PTSD. In my view, almost all of the rest of us are affected by what I call low-grade PTSD.

[61]   Some well-known systems of self-inquiry include Byron Katie's "The Work", the Sedona Method and non-dual systems.

We can no longer fully separate our personal healing process from the healing of humanity and the Earth. Any patterns of recurring stress or emotional imbalances you go through are not just yours.

I have studied and practiced many forms of energy and spiritual healing for decades and have found there to be one common thread that runs through all of the most effective systems. I would describe that as a form of bodily-centered communion with our higher, divine self. This could be called healing alchemy and includes the five elements described on the next page.

The support of a healer-practitioner is very helpful in moving through those steps when you are dealing with complex or long-standing issues. Yet you can learn how to effectively take yourself through them. In fact, learning and internalizing this process of self-healing is a vital aspect of your path of awakening to your Avatar self and integrating higher light into your everyday life.

As you go through your healing process it is vital to remember that it is only the divine, the Christ universal, manifesting through you as your Avatar transmission that can truly heal your deep issues.

Avatar Roadmap #8
The Five Elements of Effective Healing

1. **Identify the Issue**: Identify a painful, unresolved issue that is calling out for healing and resolution. By "issue" I mean a limiting belief, recurring negative emotional pattern or internalized psychic burden that may be restricting you from fully expressing yourself and enjoying your life. In my long experience as a healing practitioner, most chronic pain and diseases are rooted in such issues.

2. **Where in the Body?**: Find a focal point within your physical body that is expressing, or marking the issue. In my experience there always is one. These are frequently, but not always located in one or more of the body's energy centers, or chakras.

3. **Find Your Desire and Motivation**: As you learned in Chapter Two, the willingness to go through any meaningful growth and healing requires a strong internal motivation that can be called *vairagya*. Otherwise you will tend to avoid facing the issue, self-medicating with some combination of distractions and addictive behavior. Life is the biggest motivator! You are drawn through a series of experiences, inspirations and challenges divinely designed to build your vairagya. This may be felt as a passionate desire to break free of old, limiting patterns.

4. **Connect with the True Self**: Connect with higher vibrational light and pure love from your true, divine self. The highest light you can connect with is your Avatar transmission.

5. **Spiritual Alchemy**: Consciously apply your higher light to the focal point of the issue in your body, accompanied by conscious, deep breathing, relaxation and building a sense of trust. There are many external methods that can augment this step, including Central Axis breathing, visualization, tapping and vibrational medicine. Allow yourself to fully feel your feelings and allow your body to release and integrate them. Allow the wisdom of your body to unwind and integrate energies it has been holding.

Healing My Severe Back Pain with Spiritual Alchemy

Here is a real-life example from my life to make this process clearer to you.

Back in 1998, I was living in Phoenix, Arizona, running my medical device manufacturing and seminar companies. I had become divorced a few years previously and was going through a process of self-exploration and deep emotional healing. Early that year I became involved in an intense relationship with a woman that brought up a lot of previously unexamined feelings within me. I was also facing challenges about fulfilling my goal of running a successful business, and had been doing a lot of international travel to promote it. Through all these experiences my emotions were often highly stimulated, and my vitality was feeling drained.

One day as I was moving an appliance in my house, I felt something go out in my lower back. Unlike previous bouts of back pain that had cleared up quickly, this time it did not improve. I received several chiropractic sessions. One of them actually made the pain worse, bringing on sciatica down my leg.

My back issues worsened for several months, and at the same time, I continued to go through a lot in my emotional life. It soon became hard to even sit for more than a short time. Eventually, I had an MRI scan in a hospital and learned that there were two herniated disks in my lower back, with one of them severely herniated and extruded into the epidural space. I received an epidural injection of pain medications, and this temporarily reduced the pain. But then I started developing drop foot – reduced neuro-muscular control over one of my feet. At that point a doctor I was working with recommended back surgery. Soon after that time, my lady friend ended our relationship, and this brought up deep waves of grief within me.

Having back surgery was an unacceptable solution to me due to the risks, as well as my deep conviction about natural healing methods. My strong desire to avoid surgery, plus the heartache of that intense relationship ending brought up strong motivation (vairagya) to look deeper within myself for a solution. I learned some useful back exercises from a physical therapist and committed myself to doing them twice a day while breathing deeply and staying present to my innermost feelings. This was somewhat new to me. Although I had been a committed meditator for over twenty-five years, I had been in a pattern of running from my deeper feelings by staying busy with work, friends and seeking validation through relationships with women. I spent many hours feeling into my own body while connecting with my source of higher spiritual light. At the same time, I periodically did the exercises with simultaneous microcurrent therapy to reduce inflammation in my back.

During this period of inner exploration, I got in touch with old feelings of emotional wounding from my early childhood. Through sessions with skilled healers, as well as participation in a spiritual institute I was part of, I also processed strong imprints of intense trauma from what felt like past lifetimes. Finally, after two months of this healing process, my back started miraculously healing. The strong feelings of grief faded away, and I entered a more positive, productive phase of my life and career. About a year later I participated in a three-week trek through the Himalayan Mountains in Nepal that required tremendous exertion, and no back problems bothered me. I had found my way through the five steps of healing listed above, and my life changed for the better on many levels.

I have also discovered that I can work with variations of the same five steps to help manifest my positive visions and goals.

A guided meditation for going through the five steps outlined above for self-healing and positive manifestation follows.

Guided Practice for Self-Healing

1. Engage Foundational practices – Purity blast, grounding, Master hook-up, coming back to yourself, complete breath and loving presence. All of these can be experienced together in a few seconds once you are familiar with them.

2. Open to your feelings. Identify which issue or experience you would like to heal or work with. If needed, briefly review the issue in your mind to bring yourself into the present experience of it. Avoid getting caught up in repeating internal stories and beliefs about the issue, however. Stay centered in the Now moment.

3. You can also choose to focus on manifesting your sincere desires or visions in this practice. For example, if you wish to live in greater financial abundance, move an inspired project forward or attract a new, higher-level relationship into your life, bring those into your practice. Allow yourself to embody your true, heartfelt desire for these outcomes.

4. Relax your body and deepen your breathing, allowing yourself to drop into body awareness. If your primary issue is physical pain, focus your attention on the painful area. If you are intending to heal emotional hurts or energy imbalances, look for a location in your body that most strongly

connects with the issue you are intending to heal. Even if you are choosing to focus on manifesting a positive outcome instead of healing an issue, you can still look for a part of your body that is most associated with opening up the flow of energy needed to help fulfill it. Trust your inner master healer to guide you to the optimal body location.

5. Explore your experience of this area of your body. Place the palm of one of your hands over this area if you can. Direct deeper breathing into this part of your body. Letting your analytical mind step to the background, tap into your imagination and ask yourself what this part of you feels like or looks like. Does it have any shape, color or texture? What emotional feeling comes up for you as you tune into it? Without trying to fix, change or judge this part of you, compassionately observe it.

6. If you have learned the practice of Central Axis breathing (Chapter 23), practice that now. Move your breath and attention up and down the central channel of your body that contains your energy chakras. Linger on the focal point of the issue in your body, holding your breath in that area for as long as is comfortable, gently squeezing the internal muscles around it. If you don't yet know Central Axis Breathing simply breathe directly into the body area, internally squeezing it while briefly holding your breath.

7. Tune into your Avatar transmission, opening your body to receive it like a waterfall of pure essence moving down through your body and into the Earth. Or, you might experience your transmission coming from all around you. Feel your transmission as pure love that comes from a higher part of you than you usually identify with. Allow that pure love to nurture and bathe the focal point in your body. Continue to breathe deeply, allowing yourself to trust this communion between your human embodiment and your divine source. Seek to build that feeling of trust. You are learning to trust the one thing that is ultimately trustable – your own true self that is one with all that is.

8. Go with whatever comes up within you. If any bodily sensations, visual images or thoughts that seem to come from higher wisdom arise, acknowledge them. If you feel nothing let that be okay and continue to allow this sacred alchemy to take place. If you feel an urge to make sounds or move your body in any way that feels good to you follow that, as this

could be a valuable unwinding process of previously stuck energies in your body. Other forms of energy release include trembling, burping, coughing, sighing or yawning. Allow your body to unwind previously held energies in any of these ways.

9. If you are working on manifesting a positive outcome, visualize your desire already fulfilled through specific images of what it looks like, and feeling what it feels like. Allow the vibrational sensations to fill your body you would have "as if" your goal or desire was already fulfilled, right now. Whenever exciting, positive things happen in your life, feel-good hormones and neurotransmitters are released into your body. You can give yourself permission to feel those now, even if those outcomes are not yet physically present in your life. Allowing these feelings while attuning to your transmission is powerful alchemy.

10. When you feel complete with your self-healing or manifestation process, take three deep breaths, sighing on the exhale of each breath if appropriate. Allow yourself to sit quietly without doing anything for a few minutes.

11. After completing these steps, you can share the blessings of your transmission with others. If you are motivated to do so, invoke a person or animal, a group or the entire Earth and picture it before you. Remember that you are holographically connected with all life and the Universe. From the love of your heart ask that the blessing of your transmission heal and bless the beings you have chosen to share it with. Know that you are safe in doing this because this healing is not coming from your personal energies, it is flowing from the infinite divine source. Allow these loving blessings to flow for as long as you are guided to do so. Then close your practice.

SECTION 2

QUANTUM HEALING

This section includes six chapters on a range of healing insights and methods, all based on healing through shifts in consciousness. While health professionals and healers are likely to gain the most practical healing techniques from Chapter 11, each of these chapters contains support for all awakening Avatar Lightworkers wishing to be part of the healing of others and the Earth.

10

Evolution of a Quantum Healer

When I was a young boy, I used to daydream about being able to send out waves of healing energy all over the planet. I would see myself sitting somewhere out in nature with my eyes closed and concentrating my mind, knowing that people, animals and the Earth were being healed. That was around the time when we started to get something called a Weekly Reader at school which sometimes had articles about political crisis zones in the world. Sending healing to those places just seemed like a natural way to daydream, and I didn't talk about it to anyone else. Those visions faded as I entered my turbulent and angst-ridden adolescence.

My teenage years culminated in a pilgrimage to India to sit at the feet of a spiritual master called Maharaj Ji, when I was nineteen years old. The group of five hundred young Americans and Brits I was traveling with remained in India for two months, most of it spent with our teacher at the Prem Nagar ashram near the sacred northern city of Haridwar.

The culture shock of that first trip to India really shifted me. I had been living a relatively privileged life in the USA, and after just a few days of international travel, there I was on the streets of New Delhi surrounded by an endless tumult of totally destitute beggars. Many of them were missing arms, legs or eyes. One woman asking for alms tried to hand me her dead baby.

At the time, there was a war going on between India and Pakistan, and I later found out that my country had been aiding the Pakistanis. I discovered the hard way that Americans were then often looked at as enemies when a few friends and I became surrounded by a group of increasingly hostile young men in Patna.

We were rescued just in time by an older man from the spiritual organization hosting us.

After that journey, I spent my twenties in spiritual practice and service. During those years I was part of a spiritual organization that offered service opportunities in various parts of the USA, so I moved around quite a bit. In my early thirties, I entered the fields of holistic healthcare and entrepreneurial business. That has been part of my path now for over thirty-five years, and I have gone through a real evolution in terms of what I understand the real meaning of healing to be.

In my early years as an acupuncturist and herbalist in the 1980s, clinical practice was my driving motivation. I started full-time practice at a naturopathic office in Westport, Connecticut, and seemed to have some degree of "beginner's luck." I enjoyed the challenge of being able to help people with an array of pain and disease symptoms they had not found help for elsewhere. The majority of my patients did report improvements ranging from satisfactory to remarkable.

Yet, in spite of my clinical successes, a nagging disquiet grew within me. I noticed that a high percentage of the people who reported relief of pain and disease symptoms were back within a few weeks or months. Either the same symptoms recurred, or a new form of suffering arose in their body or mind. So, I would do my best to help them with the new issue. I knew this was considered normal and was what kept people like me in business, but I wasn't satisfied to just help people play whack-a-mole with their symptoms and issues. In an effort to learn how I could heal people on a deeper level, I delved into the study of energy healing methods, including microcurrent,[62] color light and sound therapies. The use of these modalities did significantly boost my results. In 1987 I became inspired to develop, produce, and market my own microcurrent stimulator device called the Acutron, eventually adding color light functionality to it.[63]

My next discovery was the role of chakras in pain and disease. To review, chakras are spinning energy vortices stacked in the central column of the body from the top of the head to the perineum between the legs. I learned that each chakra influences and regulates certain internal organs, glands and nerve networks. Each chakra also helps generate forms of emotion and innate spirituality. While I found lots of spiritual books containing methods for spiritual development through meditating

---

[62] Microcurrent – gentle electro-therapeutic currents measure in the millionth of an amp range, and usually delivered through a series of frequencies that target specific tissues, organs, aspects of the nervous system or health conditions

[63] See Resource section for further information about the Acutron, energy medicine and educational resources

on the chakras or yoga practice, there was very little information about how to use the chakras medically in the treatment of pain and disease.

I started experimenting with applying microcurrent, color light and sound vibrations to chakras, combining that with acupuncture and microcurrent treatments. The results were gratifying, and in some cases amazing. I had learned a powerful key to helping resolve deep imprints of trauma keeping people blocked and off-balance. I discovered that beginning a patient treatment with chakra energy balancing, followed by acupuncture or a series of brief microcurrent techniques, allowed me to help alleviate symptoms for many people who had been suffering with chronic pain for a long time – sometimes decades. The chakra balancing part of the session helped to clear the emotional root causes of their issues, thereby making all the other, symptom-relieving techniques considerably more effective.

For over 25 years, I toured the United States teaching other acupuncturists, doctors and estheticians how to use these modalities. Although planning and running all these events was rigorous, I loved meeting and sharing my knowledge with all the people who attended them.

Yet, once again I found myself up against a new wall of limitation. Even though my techniques were highly effective, and many colleagues were eager to learn them, I could see a deeper hunger in people that even my best methods could only partially address. I began to realize that the pains, issues and life blockages my clients reported were based on factors beyond even their personal traumatic experiences. We are trained to think of trauma as painful experiences that happen to individual people, often morphing into long-term post-traumatic stress. I became aware that there was a pervasive sense of entrenched collective trauma permeating large groups of people, including the entire human race. As inter-connected beings, we have been reinforcing, and in many cases, amplifying that experience of trauma for one another. I could see that the healing of individuals could not really be separate from the bigger picture of collective healing.

My Sacred Journeys

As I investigated the often-hidden causes of personal and planetary suffering, I found myself losing motivation to keep treating people's symptomatic issues. I recognized that these were like the proverbial tip of the iceberg, and I was rarely getting to the deeper part of the iceberg. For a time, I grew despondent and knew I needed to look deeper within myself to re-evaluate what my real purpose was. As part of this process, I journeyed to Guatemala for a personal retreat at a beautiful yoga center on Lake Atitlan. My retreat stay included personal ceremonies with two different local Mayan shamans who spoke with me through an interpreter. In my two ceremonies, both shamans communicated that there was a bigger picture for my life and healing work than I had been fulfilling so far. In different ways, they shared that it was important for me to connect with some parts of my spirit and psyche I had been out of touch with. Both shamans suggested that I work with what they called "plant medicine" to help me break out of my self-created limitations. At that time, I did not know what they were referring to, believing they were advising me to use some folk herbs for self-healing purposes.

The translator later told me they were talking about *ayahuasca*, a combination of two psycho-active plants used to promote altered states of consciousness in healing ceremonies. There was no ayahuasca offered to me at the retreat center, so I returned to California intrigued by this possibility, but not knowing where I could safely have that experience.

A few months later, while at my clinic in Mill Valley, California, the acupuncturist I worked with asked me if I would offer some device troubleshooting for her friend Lily from Hawaii, who owned an Acutron device. While I was examining Lily's equipment, I asked her what kind of work she did. Her reply astounded me: "My husband and I lead ayahuasca healing ceremonies in various locations in California." I had a powerful body rush, knowing that this was the fulfillment of the advice of those two Guatemalan Mayan shamans. Eager to have the full experience, I signed up for a series of ceremonies over a 10-day period with this couple in Southern California.

There is a great deal I could say about those experiences, but what is most relevant is that the message of the shamans was powerfully reinforced. I was shown, over and over again, how I had been living in a self-imposed, limiting box. I felt the spirit of Jesus come and guide me many times during those ayahuasca ceremonies. It was as if he was my best friend, a friend who pulled no punches. He telepathically communicated that even with all the success I'd had with my inventions, teaching and clinical practice, I had only been living half of a life. There was another bigger, more vibrant reality that I had been running from within myself: the reality of me acknowledging all my feelings and acting as a planetary Quantum healer. That was the same vision I had daydreamed about as a young child.

These experiences reminded me of the Charles Dickens redemption story *A Christmas Carol.* In that famous tale, various spirits show the miser Ebenezer Scrooge how cut off he had been from his heart and soul, and what lay in wait for him if he did not change his ways.

After those profound plant medicine sessions, I cut back on my clinical, teaching and technology work and started studying with a series of advanced healers in the

USA and England. Each one of these gifted people helped open my mind and body to new healing possibilities. I became more aware of my multi-dimensional nature and was able to validate the truth that healing energies of pure love and consciousness were coming through me beyond all my clinical techniques. My mentors referred to this healing energy by different names, including fifth-dimensional healing, energy healing, biofield healing and quantum healing.

Parts of me were awakened that had previously been running in the background of my professional work. In looking back at my extensive clinical practice and teaching career, it was clear that I had been transmitting healing energies all along. Yet I had not fully acknowledged what a vital part these high-level energies had played in the positive results I had helped bring to people. As I let these revelations sink in, my mind and body transformed in ways I had not experienced before. My optimism returned.

I am now certain that it's not my learning or skilled clinical techniques that truly heal. The source of real healing is what I now call the Quantum Field or the energy field of the master healer. This part is not personal to me. It is a universal resource available to anyone who wishes to help free and uplift themselves and others.

These days I work with clients both in-person and remotely hundreds to thousands of miles away, and the results are similar either way. As I do less in the way of hands-on techniques, the results my clients are describing have become increasingly profound. Some of my clients are enjoying the relief of pain and disease symptoms they have suffered with for years. But what is even more striking is that their lives are changing in other ways. It's as if each client comes to me ready to release some of the heavy ballast they've been carrying from their past, in order to step up to their next level of awareness and self-expression. Some of them sense that this process is not only for themselves and that they are becoming part of the grand symphony of ascension that is happening globally.

From Prisoner to Reiki Master

Shannon Kassoff is a yoga teacher and Reiki Master Teacher with a large following in the Huntington Beach, California area. I met her through one of the workshops I attended with Dr. Sue Morter. Shannon later attended one of the virtual Lightworker retreats I led in 2021. I recognized her to be a bright light in the group as she stepped up to lead an inspiring guided meditation about planetary healing. She became one of the reviewers for this book, and shared her story with me about how she came to be a healer:

> *I grew up in the deep south, the Bible Belt, and there was lots of trauma in*
> *my childhood, teenage years and early 20's. I had my first really big spiritual*

awakening in jail actually. I ended up getting sentenced to prison for 16 months in my 20's because I had a very bad drug problem. My son was two at the time. I was pleading for some mercy from the court. So, they sentenced me to a place called Family Foundations for women who were either pregnant or had a child under the age of six. At one point when I was still in jail and about to enter that prison, I hit my knees and had what the Big Book of Alcoholics Anonymous calls a mountaintop moment. My shoulders dropped and I felt something come over me. I had a peacefulness even in that situation where I knew I was about to serve a lot of time.

Later, after I was out of prison, I felt called to follow my healing journey and went to India. At one point while I was there, words dropped into my consciousness saying that I needed to be trained in Reiki, even though I didn't really know what it was. And so, when I got home, I did that. And I started practicing immediately. I knew that I was supposed to be doing this to expand my energy and consciousness, to heal the trauma in my body and be of service to other people in that way. Things unfolded in my awareness of how we are all energy, and everything is connected. In just a short period of time I've been able to access multi-dimensional realities through meditation and in working with clients. I've been receiving lots of what I call downloads of information that were not like anything I had ever known before, and outside of the realm of what I used to understand as spirituality.

When I work with clients now not only do I feel their energy, I can see their energy. And I describe it as our higher selves having a conversation. When I find a blockage in their energy system or a gap in the flow around their chakras, I just start silently asking questions. And answers come to me, and sometimes they come in images, like little movie clips. Sometimes people come in for physical things, and then we find the emotional roots in childhood trauma, or sexual trauma, or any number of things.

Many of the clients I have been working with are healthcare professionals or healers. They tend to be highly skilled, effective practitioners. Yet most of these clients feel a sense of incompletion as if they have reached some kind of plateau in their life and career. Although they would describe it in different ways, each of them was hungering for more of a spiritual dimension in their healing work. They already possessed that innate quality but needed a bridge to step into greater actualization of it. Caryn Carroll's experience illustrates this well.

Acupuncture Has Become Secondary

Caryn is a gifted acupuncturist and herbalist with a busy practice in Ventura, California. Here is how she described the significant changes she made in her approach to patient care as she learned the arts of Quantum healing:

I believe the most powerful thing that I've learned is the idea of seeing a patient already whole. I really adore that concept. Because in the past, I would focus on why they came in, you know, frozen shoulders, sciatica or migraines. But the beauty for me now is going beyond that, and really seeing who they are on the inside, you know, what is their spirit asking them to see.

And now almost always, the next session is something all new and different. They tell me "That issue from last time is already gone." So, I feel like it's a more rapid transformation for them. Because mind you, they're just there for a more traditional acupuncture session. But if I trust my higher self that says: "Hey, tell them what you just saw, show him that picture." That's where the true healing really happens. Recently, patients have been coming back wanting to talk about old issues from their childhood or adolescence, which is kind of fascinating to me.

And now the acupuncture and everything else is sort of secondary to the healing energy work.

Caryn went on to describe the inner purification process she went through in the course of claiming her higher healing gifts:

In my mind, I feel like I had an ascension sickness. It was as if I were surrendering to source all those questions. It felt like I was burning up pain, dogma and limiting belief patterns. And then having tons of conversations with my own higher self. Now I believe that my higher self is my future self, and the Holy Spirit is letting me see that, saying "Talk to your older wiser self. She's already gone through what you're going into. The path is open, you're holding your own hand in the future, just walk through those doors." The pathway is right there. It's beautiful. It's expansive, its creation in action."

The transformation these healers went through accelerated as they learned to sense and work with the inter-connected network of energy often called the Quantum Field. Quantum healing, which you will learn about next, is the practice of consciously working with the Quantum Field for the healing and upliftment of clients.

11

Quantum Catalyst Healing

Some situations call for a miracle.

Alex is a local woman who applied for a job I offered last year. In the course of our discussions, she told me about severe insomnia and chronic pain she had been suffering since early childhood. She had tried a long list of tests, treatments and remedies over decades in the hopes of helping her get to sleep and to ease the pain in her jaw, but she'd experienced little to no success. After I told Alex about the possibility that Quantum Catalyst healing might be able to help her on a different level than she had experienced before, she booked an initial session with me. I admit feeling a bit of trepidation, as I did not want to be the next in the long list of healthcare practitioners she felt disappointed with.

During that first session, Alex told me about the overwhelming childhood experiences she had been through, that were likely causes of her sleeplessness.

I had insomnia always, since I've been 6 years old, and I'm in my 60's now. I've had severe jaw and tooth pain all my life based on bruxism, TMJ disorder, grinding my teeth, and because I was always stuck in that loop, dramatic dentistry ensued. What the dentists did to me back then when I was six was literally physical torture and highly inappropriate, as I believe I was also sexually molested by one of them. My mother also greatly amplified my pain by putting toxic chemicals on my scalp and tying my hair into very tight and painful buns. I've had chronic pain since childhood in my neck, scalp and jaw. In addition to all of this, I went through a series of traumatic relationships with older men while I was still a teenager and into my early 20's, feeling controlled and helpless.

My husband is a doctor and we have tried so many things to try to ease my pain and get me some sleep, but basically, nothing has had much effect.

During her first session, I adjusted her Assemblage Point (see explanation below), balanced her chakras and applied a series of microcurrent frequencies. As we went through these techniques, I explained to Alex how she could attune herself to the Quantum Field. Even though she had never heard of it before, she was able to feel a new vibration in her body that felt good. Alex was very encouraged by how positive and relaxed she felt after this first session, as it gave her hope that she could actually respond to treatments. Through discussion, we were able to determine that Alex is a very sensitive empath who is also highly sensitive to electromagnetic fields in her home. As part of her solution, she ordered a special EMF blocking bed cover that helped her feel more at ease at night.

After going through a series of weekly Quantum Catalyst sessions for one month, then tapering down to once every three to four weeks, Alex reported:

Each Quantum session with Darren has been unique and different, there have been many levels and layers of things both deep and noticeable on the surface. It's been super beneficial on many levels; I feel so much better. I feel strengthened, healthier, stronger and my organs are shored up. Even the first time he adjusted my assemblage point in my very first session I felt heartened and strengthened. My husband says I'm a lot nicer and more ebullient, a whole lot happier. I'm still going through changes with my pain levels, I'm always working with that, but the pain loop is not as dire and drastic as it was.

When Darren and I worked on my liver last time, I experienced a sudden clarity, as if the curtains opened. Initially, it was painful, and a lot came out and I had some swelling up here, some breakouts, that felt like a natural response to that treatment. But then I suddenly had crystal clarity, and everything fell into place in the way that things do sometimes. It was as if all the anger and hostility had gotten out of the way. Things just seemed clearer. I felt generally better, not pissed off at the world. I usually just feel cloudy, dark and terrible, but it all got clear after that treatment.

About my sleep – I have gotten some more rest. I feel like I'm coping with my insomnia a lot better and it doesn't freak me out as much. I'm treating myself differently and taking better care of my schedule. That feels 95% better, just not so horrible with the darkness of all that. I was really depressed. I was in such a dark place and really reaching for a lifeline. The results have been very heartening. It was like the light switch came on.

Similar to Alex's experience, the most common reaction from people going through Quantum healing is how different it seems to them than most medical or holistic healing treatments they have experienced previously. They are often surprised to see that the treatment of their distressing symptoms is not the main focus of the sessions, yet their pain and other symptoms usually do clear up.

Let's now look at what Quantum Healing really is.

The Basis of Quantum Healing

In this context, the word "Quantum" refers to several of the qualities of reality that have been known since ancient times. These were introduced to the human race through what has been called the seven Hermetic Laws.[64] While many meditators and visionaries have had direct experiences of these principles throughout human history, many of their experiences have been confirmed over the last century through laboratory experiments.[65]

Quantum healing takes place via the Quantum field. Scientists and philosophers since ancient times and from many cultures, including Albert Einstein, have speculated about a non-physical field through which light and thought travel. This has often been called aether. Many research studies since the 1800s have verified its existence, and it is now often referred to as the field of zero-point energy (ZPE). Physicist John Archibald Wheeler estimated that there is massive amounts of energy in the ZPE of what seems to be empty space. He calculated that the zero-point field in an empty glass used to drink water contains enough energy which, if released, could bring the entire Pacific Ocean to the boiling point! Many physicists have concluded that zero-point energy fills the entire Universe.[66] Zero-point energy is an aspect of the Quantum field. To put it simply, the Quantum field inter-connects everything, is where everything emerges from and returns to, and contains all potentialities and possibilities.

---

[64] See The Kybalion, by Three Initates for details on Hermetic Laws, which have been known since the time of ancient Egypt. These seven laws are the basis for spirituality, most sciences, metaphysics and understanding of human behavior

[65] For accessible accounts of these experiments see Quantum Physics for Beginners: Discover the Science of Quantum Mechanics and Learn the Basic Concepts from Interference to Entanglement by Analyzing the Most Famous Quantum Experiments by Daniel Golding

[66] Niggli, J Gerontol Geriat Res 2014, 3:2

The Quantum principles most relevant to this level of healing are:

1. **Healing the pain of separation:** Everything in the Universe is holographically inter-connected, also called quantum entanglement. That means that
each individual point connects with every other point in the Universe in a
never-ending matrix of universal Love. The deep sense of separation that
underlies so much of human pain, depression and disease is, therefore, an
illusion. The healing process involves a process of conscious re-connection
with the direct experience of our true selves. As this alignment takes place, a
great deal of pain and physical dysfunctions spontaneously clear up.

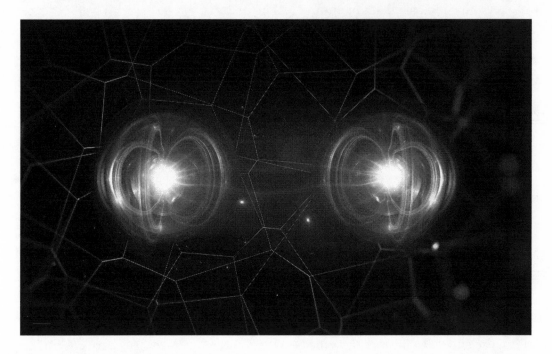

The title of Diane Connolly's book *All Sickness is Homesickness* aptly describes
this key principle of healing.

2. **Awakening from the dream of suffering:** Consciousness is the prime
mover of everything in the Universe. As people unburden and free up their
consciousness, their minds and bodies are able to heal through the principle
of *epigenetics*. Healing the mind is the process of releasing identification
with what has justifiably been called the *slave self*,[67] claiming sovereignty
and freedom to create positive outcomes.

---

67 Slave self: The separated self most people identify with that can be controlled and manipulated by others,
and usually is without us knowing it.

3. **Spontaneous remission:** Under certain conditions, sub-atomic particles can instantaneously leap from a lower to a higher level of energy and vibration – the so-called Quantum Leap. This experience is mirrored on the human level by spontaneous healings of pain, diseases and emotional imbalances. Once a person's innate ability to heal is unblocked, the master healer connection within them is able to restore their well-being. In some cases, this happens extraordinarily quickly, in other cases, it happens gradually.

What is the Master Healer?

We are usually programmed to think of a master healer as a wizard-like person with miraculous healing abilities, yet this is not accurate. Being a master healer is not a personal accomplishment. It is a universal energy field we can tap into best described through words like love, harmony, consciousness, oneness, light or clarity. Even though it is not something that derives from our human small self, we can learn to embody the vibration of the master healer and channel it effectively.

The English word "healing" is rooted in old English and German words that mean "wholeness." True healing is not just the relief of symptoms – it is a return to wholeness. Returning to the experience of our unbroken self is a lot like rebooting a computer that has been running annoying, buggy software. The processor is able to delete the distorted version of the buggy program and re-install the original, uncorrupted code, so things can function as they were intended to. In cases in which rebooting the program is insufficient to remove the corrupted code, it becomes necessary to uninstall the old code and then download the latest version of the code from the source server. This process is extremely accurate in describing the process of true healing. That is not surprising because we have built computers in our own image.

Master healer is a brilliant vibration that brings about all real healing, ranging from the mending of a cut on your finger to unexpected remission of stage four cancer to breakthrough experiences of spiritual awakening. Master Healer is catalytic. A catalyst is an agent that brings about transformation in substances or systems it is in contact with, yet it itself is not changed.

For this reason, I have been using the term "Quantum Catalyst healing" to refer to the therapeutic work I do and teach that facilitates the healing and transformation of others.

Because master healer is an impersonal field of infinite resourcefulness, it does not need to take a long time for a practitioner to tap into it. A healer who has been practicing Quantum healing for many years is not necessarily able to facilitate healing breakthroughs any more readily than a new practitioner. Sharon's story about offering her very first Quantum healing session is an excellent example: [68]

I want to share with you the very first healing I offered to someone. My client was a woman in her early thirties who had had depression and suicidal thoughts since she was twelve. She had been to many psychiatrists, psychologists and therapists to no avail, so she decided to try an alternative form of healing. After the usual intake, we began our session, and during the session, a strong quantum field formed. I could feel the energy spiraling between me and my client, It almost seemed out of time. I could sense that she was deeply affected by the field and immersed in Light. And I saw her in her wholeness and truth. In that moment, I knew her healing had already taken place, and that her previous thoughts concerning depression and lack of self-worth had been lifted.

When the session ended and the quantum field was released, my client stared in amazement and shook her head. She indicated she had experienced something life-changing. After that session, she began to meditate and became interested in spirituality. Her depression was gone. I saw her a couple more times to make

---

[68] The first part of Sharon's story, in which she described her struggles to share her healing abilities, is in Chapter 4

sure the healing had stuck. She said that her depression had been a faulty way or untrue story of looking at the world. I, as healer just held the quantum field. The quantum field did the healing.

Multi-Dimensional Medical Practice

Most doctors and holistic practitioners focus mainly on the physical body or the balancing of its energy in their work. Others, who consider themselves to be spiritual or energy healers, mainly focus on invisible, subtle levels of consciousness and feeling. What I have found to be exciting and highly effective is combining both in my work. Integrating modalities such as microcurrent, acupuncture and light therapies with healing through pure consciousness is a multi-dimensional approach to health care. We can picture it like this:

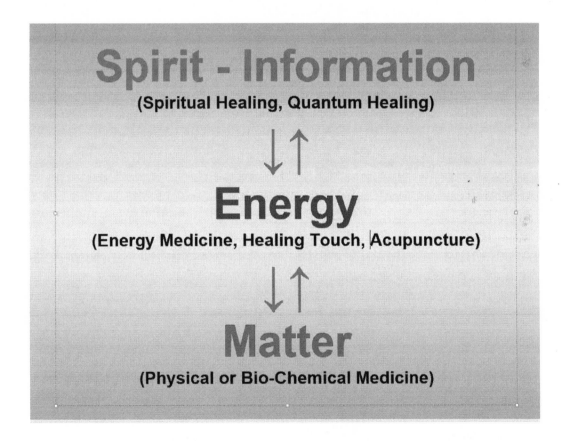

A human being who is expressing the vibration of master healer acts as a catalyst for profound healing and transformation in others. What is required is developing the quality of embodied loving Presence. This happens as healers rebuild the energetic circuitry in their own bodies. This requires a commitment to staying present in the now moment, and consciously inhabiting your body as much as possible.

Quantum Catalyst Healing

As is the case with Alex described above, I often draw people who have long-term, convoluted and difficult-to-treat issues. They have been around the block for years or even decades, seeking relief from issues such as unresolved chronic pain, depression, PTSD, various forms of disability or psychic attack. They often feel spiritually blocked or out of balance in hard to define ways. Other clients arrive without a lot of troubling symptoms. They come because they sense there is another, higher level of spiritual awareness available to them, one that has been elusive for them to realize. Others come who feel the desire or vision to manifest a new level of their business, an inspired idea for a project or a new, more fulfilling relationship. They are seeking support in expanding their manifesting ability.

While I used to have trepidation in treating people with complex, multi-layer issues, I now welcome them with calm confidence. That's because I have let go of a lot of my dependence on external techniques and know that I am not responsible for their healing. I am allowing a greater power and Quantum field of energy to create the results. It is really the master healer within my clients that creates the miracles. I support and guide them in accessing that part of themselves and allowing the shifts to happen.

There are many healers throughout the world using the name Quantum healing to refer to what they do, and their methods vary widely. To provide some specifics about the system of Quantum Catalyst healing I work with, here are some of the specific steps and methods used:

1. **Testing and balancing the Assemblage Point** – The Assemblage Point (AP) is the locus where our physical body and the larger fields of our energy body line up. Healthy alignment of the AP occurs when the center of the greater field of the human energy body lines up with the center of our chest. Various forms of trauma or the excessive use of mind-altering drugs can knock the AP out of alignment for long periods of time, sometimes decades. That can create tendencies toward anxiety, depression, aggression or spaciness. The diagram below shows the typical symptoms people experience when their Assemblage Point is higher, lower or to the sides of the ideal position in the center of the chest.

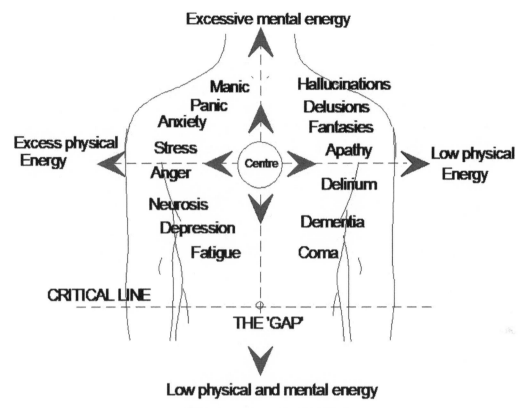

Diagram courtesy Dr. Jon Whale

In my experience, as long as the AP is out of alignment, other treatment modalities don't work as well in producing long-term results. Therefore, the first step of my sessions is to test the position of the AP and to align it with a special crystal wand if necessary. I love this method because most clients notice an immediate shift in their state as soon as this five-minute technique is complete. Once their AP is aligned one or two times, it tends to stay aligned long term.

2. **Healing Through the Quantum Field** – The Quantum Field is the field of unlimited possibilities from which everything in the Universe originates, and eventually returns to. As esoteric as that may sound, we are able to directly experience the Quantum Field through our feeling sense. This experience is heightened when two or more people tune into the field together.[69]

---

[69] I see this as a valid modern version of Jesus's teaching "When two or more are gathered in my name, there I AM with them". The I AM presence could be a way of describing the Quantum Field

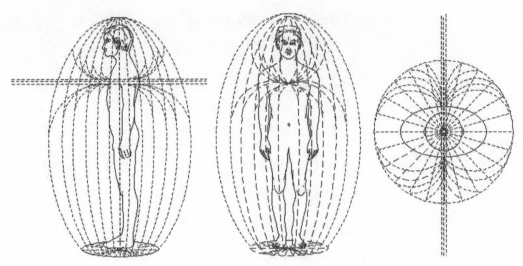

Diagram courtesy Dr. Jon Whale

One person who has attuned themselves to the Quantum Field can act as a catalyst for another who has not yet recognized that experience. This is the basis for Quantum Catalyst healing.

When clients are relaxed and attuned to the Quantum Field, there is much less energetic resistance in their bodies, and their hearts and minds become more open. This state makes them much more able to respond to healing dialogue and energy therapies.

The Quantum Field contains perfect templates of all parts of us, including our organs, tissues, chakras, brain and pure emotions. In some cases, an imbalanced or diseased body part can be energetically replaced in Quantum healing sessions by its perfect template in the Field. This is similar to what surgeons do with organ or bone transplants, but in this case, no physical surgery is required. It all happens on the unseen, Quantum level. See Diane's story below for a dramatic example of this.

3. **Energy Clearing** – In other chapters, I talked about the build-up of heavy energies in the body, referred to as energetic gunk, psychic burdens, *samskara* or residoo-doo. It's now clear to me why I and so many other doctors and practitioners have struggled to heal chronic pain. It's because most of it does not originate on the physical level we are trained to work on – it arises from this unseen baggage clients have accumulated in their energy bodies. Therefore, clearing that psychic gunk is the first priority of Quantum Catalyst healing.

There are many methods practitioners and therapists use to facilitate emotional release and integration. The methods I have found to be most effective are:

- Guiding clients to speak empowering statements, breaking old psychic agreements.

- Trauma release through guided visualization while applying color light to body energy centers.

- Focus on areas in the body connected with blocked energy or emotions, using vibrational medicine and Quantum healing to support release and transformation.

- Intuitive counseling while a client is relaxed in the experience of the Quantum Field.

It is beyond the scope of this book to explain these methods in detail.[70] What is most important to understand is that the effectiveness of any effective counseling or therapeutic method will be amplified when performed within awareness of the Quantum field.

4. **Rewiring** – As a client is in the process of lightening their load of psychic burdens, there is the opportunity to re-wire the subtle energy connections between the high-frequency energy of their true self and their physical body. This opens the way for greater creativity, vitality and effectiveness in people's everyday lives. I teach my clients how to do simple meditative practices, such as those described as Foundational practices in the "Getting Started" chapter, so they can continue to build their own circuits.

5. **Vibrational Medicine** – As mentioned above, the use of therapy equipment delivering microcurrent, light, sound or other modalities can be highly effective for relieving specific symptoms. These include relief of inflammation, joint pain, nervous system imbalances, fatigue and much more. Vibrational therapies, as well as acupuncture, bodywork or spinal manipulation, can help powerfully anchor the benefits of Quantum healing in the physical body.

---

[70] Detailed instructions for many of these methods are included in my books Healing the Root of Pain and Reclaiming Your Calm Center. as well as live training programs. See Section Six for further resources.

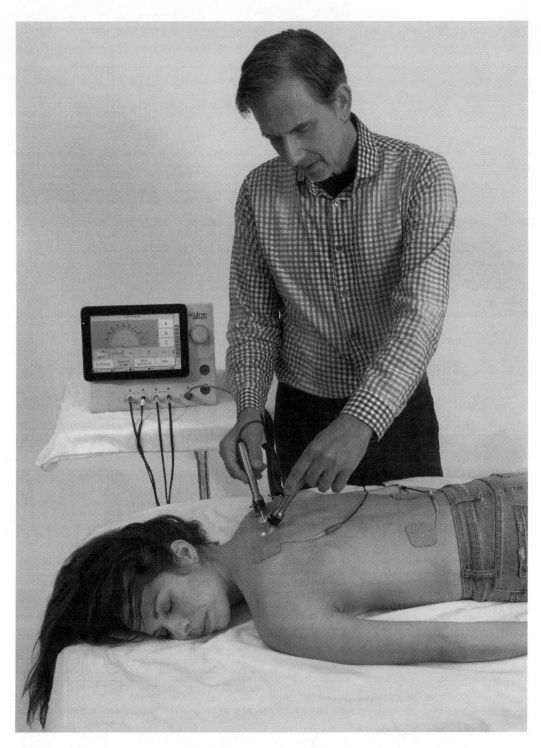

Vibrational therapies, as well as acupuncture, bodywork or spinal manipulation, can help powerfully anchor the benefits of Quantum healing in the physical body.

Rapidly Releasing Trauma

Shannon is a fitness and lifestyle coach in her thirties with a sparkling personality and a national following. She received a series of sessions with me, beginning three years ago. As soon as I met Shannon, I could sense the evolved consciousness she emanated, yet she was also struggling with some difficult emotional issues. Her story is a striking example of how fast deeply held traumatic imprints can be released. Here is how Shannon described her experience:

> *I was experiencing a relapse of trauma from earlier in my life that I thought I had dealt with and worked through, but then a trigger occurred, and I began having visual relapses of this traumatic experience. I sought out quantum healing with Darren, and within the first session, I was like, "Wow, this is so different." I've certainly had a lot of experience with healing of all different types, heart-centered therapy, different Reiki treatments; I've really had a wonderful experience of doing work on self in the past. But learning about quantum healing and the aspects of how we really have what we need inside of us, and how it can change in an instant, was a pretty miraculous discovery.*

> *What I received was a total clearing of these traumatic experiences within one to two sessions. I'm not exaggerating. It was astonishing. I just didn't have a charge around that trauma anymore. It was completely gone. And that is the first time that I've really had access to understanding that. Wow, all it really takes is a rewiring of our programming in a sense, and healing in our energetic field. And we can literally change the processes of how we experience life.*

Can We Renew Imbalanced Body Parts?

I realize that the possibility of energetically renewing or replacing imbalanced or diseased body parts through the Quantum Field may sound pretty far out to many readers, especially those from a Western medical background. Yet I have experienced the reality of it during some client sessions.

I first heard about this possibility when I was studying with Dr. Zhi Gang Sha, a former medical doctor from China who evolved into an international spiritual teacher. During some of his events, he spoke about replacing diseased body parts from a divine source. As open as I am to experiences outside of consensus reality, I must admit feeling somewhat skeptical of these claims. I did, however, meet at least one woman at a retreat who told me that she had been healed after Dr. Sha "downloaded" a new organ into her to replace one riddled with long-term cancer, so my mind was at least open to this possibility.

What's remarkable is that I've started to experience this phenomenon with some of my own clients. I'll tell you about one striking example.

Diane is a colleague and dynamic teacher of energy medicine modalities. She leads a very busy, dedicated life in which she is on the road more often than she is at home. Last year, her back went out and she ended up almost immobilized on the floor of her home. She described her healing experience like this:

I'm a traveling teacher of healthcare practitioners and I'm in my fifties. Last fall I had returned from an extensive teaching tour around the USA and was unwinding at home. I contacted a friend who did an energy healing over the phone. This healer helped me clear some heavy-duty emotions that had felt trapped in my body since I was young. ... About 10 minutes after I received this healing, I bent down to pick up a simple object and I felt something go out in my back. That was strange because I hadn't had a bit of trouble there before. The pain and stiffness rapidly worsened. I started running microcurrent therapy nonstop and tried to do some of the stretches I know, but I was getting more and more immobilized by the back pain.

After over two days of mainly lying on the floor and not being able to do much at all, my colleague Darren called me. He took me through a Quantum healing session. We went through a guided visualization in which I ran white light from my head through my spine. He talked about replacing the damaged disks in my low back with new ones from my spiritual source. Whatever he did took just a few minutes. I could feel everything re-organizing in my body – that's how it felt. I saw how everything was connected back to the trauma I had been through when I was twelve. That story got moved out and in some unexplainable way, my damaged spine was replaced. My back very rapidly got stable and my pain went away. Quite remarkable!

You might justifiably ask "How did you know how to do that?" The honest answer is "I can't tell you because I don't know." While experienced healers draw on a toolkit of favorite techniques and dialogue skills, one of our most needed qualities is open-mindedness and trust. On that phone call, I put my analytical mind aside long enough to support Diane's disk in being renewed. I believe that it was the master healer inside of her that really did this, and my presence acted as a supportive catalyst. Because I believed it was possible, she was able to go beyond her own disbelief.

According to both quantum science and spiritual revelation, the Quantum field is a resource of unlimited possibilities. You or I can serve as a Quantum healer as we learn to stay attuned to our Avatar transmission, developing trust in our ability to help facilitate breakthrough healing transformations.

Tom M., who attended a recent retreat, described his personal experience as well as his perception of the Quantum field:

I have been on a spiritual healing journey for 10 years. And it has slowly evolved and grown over those 10 years. Before I was exposed to quantum healing, I was feeling stuck in my process. I was feeling like I plateaued, and the synchronicities and the magic in the world seemed to get stuck and stop. There were also specific areas of physical pain that led me down that path, as well as emotional pain, depression and anxiety. I felt stuck in knowing what direction to go.

Once I experienced quantum healing things didn't magically change. Yet relief from a lot of my physical pain has happened. And I've had such an improvement in depression and anxiety as well. I feel like I took a quantum leap into my journey of not only healing my wounds and discovering my true self but also on this path of discovering what my Dharma is. Yes, new clarity on my career path and inspirations of all kinds have come since entering into this quantum healing energy. That's been what's been most profound.

From my experience, the quantum field is an undercurrent of energy that exists all around us in the world. It's where everything comes from before it materializes here. That's where all the possibilities come from to re-create your physical reality. And there is a sort of a sixth or maybe even seventh sense within us beyond our five normal senses. We have this other sense in us that lights up when we feel into that energy. Once you close your eyes and start becoming aware of this energy that surrounds you, the more you become aware of it as the energy of creation, the more you can feel it and the more of this sixth and seventh sense that you have within you opens up.

Yeah, I really have felt a quantum leap from our experience, and things in my life have really opened up.

So-called healing miracles start where the mind stops. According to the universal law of cause and effect, there is a cause for every effect. Those effects that we call "chance," "random" or "miraculous" simply spring from causes we don't yet see or understand.

Our modern sciences cannot fully explain the results reported by the clients quoted above. Yet there is progress in that direction. Studies in the fields of epigenetics and psycho-neuro-immunology[71] have demonstrated a direct linkage between our diseases and our consciousness. Quantum physics experiments have also confirmed the primacy of the mind in creating our reality. By training your mind to maintain a conscious connection with the Quantum field, you are able to tap into an unlimited power of creation and healing for yourself or others.

---

71 See https://www.healthline.com/health/psychoneuroimmunology for an overview of this medical field

12

Remote Healing

Many of the Quantum healing experiences described in the previous chapter, and elsewhere in this book took place remotely. In other words, the healer and client were not physically together, and the healing session was conducted through a phone call or internet video conference.

In the rest of this chapter, I will provide a brief overview of the scientific basis for remote healing sessions, and then share guidelines for practitioners who wish to start offering this form of treatment. If you already are offering remote sessions, this information may help you bring your work up to a higher level of effectiveness.

The Scientific Basis of Remote Healing

We and the entire Universe are composed of energy. Physics has demonstrated that when we look at the atomic and sub-atomic level 99.9999999% of our body is empty space.

Acupuncturists, chiropractors, bodyworkers and other holistic practitioners are trained to believe that the insertion of needles, manipulation and other physical techniques are what move and balance the vital energy of the client's body, also called *Qi* in Chinese. That is true, but only part of the truth. Numerous experiments in quantum physics and other fields of science have proven that energy is affected and patterned by consciousness. What's really exciting is that lots of these experiments have demonstrated what we think of as geographical distance is not a factor in the power of consciousness to affect energy.

In the year 2000, a retrospective review of 23 research studies investigating remote healing was done by Astin, Harkness and Ernst involving 2774 patients. These studies were selected based on meeting the following criteria: adequate control interventions such as comparison with placebo or sham healing, humans with medical conditions were studied, and the studies were published in peer-reviewed journals. The forms of remote healing included prayer, therapeutic touch done at a distance and other forms of distant healing. After analyzing this data the team discovered that 57% of these well-regulated studies confirmed clearly positive results from remote healing.[72]

In a double-blind study led by researcher Elizabeth Targ, 40 patients with advanced Acquired Immune Deficiency Syndrome (AIDS) were randomly assigned to two groups. One group received 10 weeks of remote healing sessions from healers they never met, and the other group did not receive the remote healings. The subjects in each group did not know which group they were part of. The healers represented a variety of healing methods and belief systems and were located throughout the United States. The subjects were assessed through blood analysis and psychological tests, and their medical history was tracked over time. The two groups were analyzed after six months of this study. A blinded review of their medical charts revealed that the subjects who had received the remote healing showed significantly better health than the control group that did not receive it. They developed less AIDS-related illnesses, had over 60% less severe symptoms, required 24% less doctor visits and 75% less hospitalizations.[73]

Other studies have confirmed that highly trained remote healers produced more effective results than those with less or no experience.[74]

How it Works

Understanding the following two scientific terms will lay the groundwork for understanding how and why remote healing, blessings and prayer works:

Fractals: These are fundamental geometric patterns that recur from the tiniest theorized particle[75] to the cosmic universal level. This is often referred to as sacred geometry. A fractal is a geometric form, musical note or pattern of energy that recurs in infinitely recurring smaller and larger scales. These are often referred to as microcosms and macrocosms.

---

[72] (2000) Ann Intern Med 132, 903. *Astin JA, Harkness E, Ernst E..* **The efficacy of "distant healing": a systematic review of randomized trials..** *Jun 6–10.*

[73] January 1999 Western Journal of Medicine 169(6):356-63

[74] https://www.ncbi.nlm.nih.gov/pmc/articles/PMC4654780/

[75] The tiniest theorized particle by physics is called the Planck. If you made a tiny dot on a piece of paper and compared the size of that dot to the size of the entire Universe, that is the same degree of difference in the other direction between that dot and a Planck

A common example of a fractal is the spiral shape, which can be found in both tiny DNA molecules and vast galaxies. Many beautiful works of art are created by using computer graphic programs to depict fractals.

Holographic / Holography: This term refers to the principle that the whole is contained in every individual point. This is the Universe and our bodies work. What this means is that any point in the Universe contains and communicates with the entire Universe.

Protons are sub-atomic particles existing as part of each of the atoms that make up all matter. Physicist Nassim Haramein has mathematically demonstrated that each proton contains all the same energy, matter and information as the entire Universe when looked at holographically.[76]

Conventional science, including physics, studies the properties and behavior of energy and matter. The emerging science of Quantum Holography demonstrates the greater role of an interconnected field of information in understanding how the Universe operates. As stated in the journal article "The Quantum Hologram and the Nature of Consciousness" by Mitchell and Staretz:

> "We speculate that Quantum Holography seems to be nature's built-in vast information storage and retrieval mechanism, and one that has been used since the beginning of time. This would promote Quantum Holography as a theory which is the basis for explaining how the whole of creation learns, self-corrects and evolves as a self-organizing, interconnected holistic system." [77]

---

[76] See Cosmometry book by Marshall Lefferts, Chapter 11
[77] http://journalofcosmology.com/Consciousness149.html

The holographic principle is a major scientific basis for remote healing, as well as these well-known phenomena:

- **Remote viewing**: The ability of some people to accurately see events at far distances within their minds.

- **Intuitive and telepathic communication** between people.

- **The Akashic Records**: A non-physical, subtle energy database that stores all events, words and thoughts of all beings from all time. Many sensitive people are able to tap into and "read" the Akashic Records. I believe most of us are doing this to some extent without realizing it, through various synchronicities we experience and intuitive hunches that come to us.

- **Quantum entanglement**: A wide range of phenomena in which movements of sub-atomic particles in one location are reflected in identical movements of other particles at a distance.

- **The Living Matrix**: The amazing communication, self-repairing and self-regenerative systems of the human body. These appear to be orchestrated by a field of holographic, inter-connected conscious intelligence beyond the capabilities of the physical brain, nervous and endocrine systems.

Some of the physical substrates of the holographic functions of the human body are:

- **Our Magic Microtubules**: *Microtubules* are hollow polymer lattices within the neurons of the brain. Penrose and Hameroff proposed that these microtubules act as quantum computers that interface non-locally with the entire body and the universal Quantum Hologram. This may be the part of the physical interface through which our physical brains tap into universal intelligence. This would mean that in a real sense we are capable of knowing and communicating with anything and everything through our network of microtubules.[78]

- **The Field of Memory**: Dendrites are communicating branches of neurons or nerve cells. Neuroscientist Karl Pribram has proposed that the interaction of wave-like frequency oscillations emanating from very fine dendrites in the brain create what are called interference fields, and these store human memory. According to this view, memory is holographic

---

[78] http://journalofcosmology.com/Consciousness149.html

because the field of all memories can be accessed by different parts of the brain, not just one specific location as neuroscientists previously believed. Therefore, even if a part of the brain holding memories is damaged another part can access the same memories. Pribram called his findings Holonomic Brain Theory.[79]

- **The Supercomputers in Each Cell**: DNA molecules exist in all our cells, with each DNA molecule containing all the information of the entire body. DNA has been described as super-computers in constant communication with all other DNA molecules in the body, as well as the entire cosmos. As previously discussed, the gene expression of our DNA is being constantly modified by our experiences, environment, diet, thoughts and feelings through the principle of *epigenetics*.

---

[79]   Pribram, Karl, Brain and Perception, Laurence Erlbaum Associates, 1991

Acupuncturists tap into the holographic principle when performing auricular (ear) or hand acupuncture because both areas contain entire maps of all parts of the body. Foot reflexologists are also able to give us a complete body tune-up by massaging pressure points all over the feet. There are also zones in our faces that connect with all parts of the body, so a good microcurrent facial rejuvenation session often provides the delightful "side-effect" of a whole-body energy tune-up.

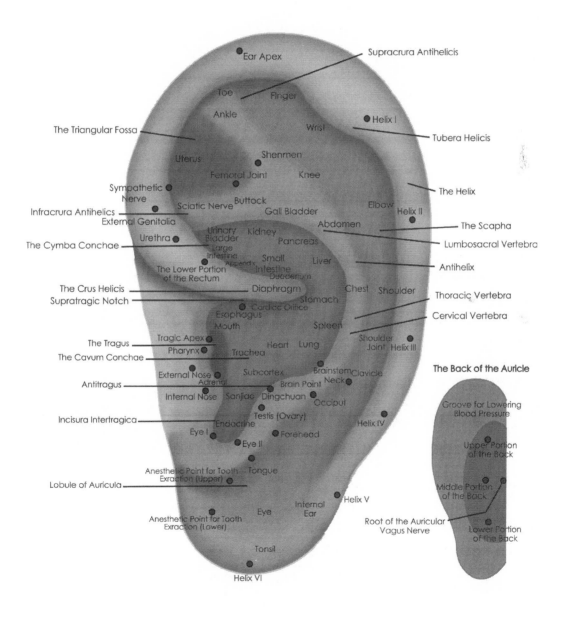

The Holographic Field of Consciousness

The holographic principle is also active in the realm of consciousness and Spirit. We can call the interconnected network of perfect love and light that fills the Universe the Christ Holographic Grid, and we are always part of it. Here is a breakdown of this term:

Christ: The universal field of love, power and intelligence, expressing through human beings

Holographic: Total inter-connection between any individual point within a system and the entire system. In this reference, you are the point, and the universal love and consciousness is the system.

Grid: The matrix of universal interconnection

Here is how all the information you just read comes together. Because you are in a holographic, fractal relationship to the entire Universe <u>whatever you think, do and experience affects all life, everywhere! Your experience is also being affected by the thoughts and feelings of others through this same principle.</u>

Stop a moment and breathe this truth in. Let it percolate through you. Rather than trying to mentally analyze it, feel into your body for how it is resonating. This is major stuff, as major as it gets.

If any guilt comes up because you start worrying about how all the negative thoughts and feelings you've had may have adversely affected the collective just let that go. Perfect forgiveness is a quality of the Christ Holographic Grid and is available to us always. All we have to do is say "yes" to it. Just forgive yourself as many times as necessary and choose your thoughts anew. While you're at it forgive everyone else. This is truly the path of great blessings and freedom.

We are transceivers of energy. We are affected by the energy frequencies of the Earth, all the people in our lives (including our ancestors) and man-made electromagnetic fields. We are also affected in subtle ways by distant stars and planets. That is the basis of astrology.

In addition to receiving, we are transmitting what is in our energy field all the time. This line from the John Lennon song *Dig a Pony* describes it well:

You can radiate everything you are

> ## Avatar Roadmap #9
> ### Summary of the Science of Remote Healing
>
> 1. Beneficial changes in vital energy (Qi) and electromagnetic energies are associated with health and well-being.
> 2. Energy is being constantly moved and re-patterned by thought, or consciousness, and this creates changes in the body and mind.
> 3. The ability of consciousness to affect Qi and electromagnetic energy is not limited by geographical distance because all energy is holographically inter-connected through the Quantum field.
> 4. Our focused intention activates consciousness to move and transform energy.
>
> These remarkable principles open up the way for you to be able to offer highly effective remote sessions for clients.

The phenomena described above such as remote healing, blessing and prayer work because we are holographically connected with all the people, animals or places we are praying for, not because we are actually sending energies to them from afar. The same is true for astrology, which works because aspects of the stars, constellations and planets *are all inside of us.*

There is really no difference between self-healing, and healing or praying for others. In both cases our loving thoughts and intentions are helping transform energy patterns within the greater field we are a part of. And that greater field of our true self is what I am calling the Christ Holographic Grid.

Star, a woman who received a single healing session from me over a 3,000 mile distance sent the following email:

It was astonishing. Every single part of this healing seemed as if it was specifically relevant and tailored just for me. The experience of feeling the Unified field[80] gave me great inspiration and renewed strength for my continued path and

---

[80] The term Unified Field refers to a goal of research physicists in discovering a common theoretical framework that unites all the known forms of energy: electro-magnetism, gravity and the strong and weak nuclear forces. Unified Field also has a similar meaning to Quantum Field, as used in this quote

effort for greater connection. Having felt this field before through my own practices, I was able to recognize and finally put a name to it.

Remote Healing Guidelines

Here are the guidelines I use for remote healing sessions. These will be very useful for healthcare professionals, energy healers or non-professional readers interested in this process.

Suggested sequence of remote sessions:

1. Prepare for each session by attuning yourself to the Quantum Field and your Avatar transmission. A great way to do this is to briefly engage the Foundational practices taught in the Getting Started section. As you start working with a client remotely, tune into how the Quantum Field connects the two of you. It is really the field of the client's own higher self that does the healing. Once the session starts, guide the client through simple meditative practices to ground them in present time. Help them become aware of the field as much as possible.

   Most of my clients describe their experience of the field by saying that they feel very relaxed and inwardly directed. As long as you are consciously connected to your transmission, you are tapped into the master healer field and can embody it. You are also completely safe from "taking on negative energies" from clients when grounded in your transmission.

2. Once you have set up the session go ahead and lead your client through your chosen methods. I do a lot of work helping each client identify key concerns, locating where issues are anchored in their body. This is a key step. I then guide them in using breath, guided visualizations, role-playing and other tools to help release and transform old, stuck, fear-based energies.

   I have developed a system called *Multi-Dimensional Clearing* for identifying and clearing the root causes of people's complaints usually overlooked by most practitioners. This is a method for quickly identifying the deep, hidden causative factors behind clients' symptoms, and then working through the Quantum field to help transform and clear what is identified. Most clients notice some degree of relief of their complaints after going through Multi-Dimensional Clearing.

3. Take notes as you would for in-person sessions. When the session time is complete guide the client into closure by debriefing on her experiences,

making sure she is well grounded and feels complete. Leave enough time at the end for nuts and bolts, such as setting up the next appointment.

4. After each session, it is often helpful to email the client a summary of what transpired during the session along with "homework" they can do every day to continue their healing process. These can include guided meditations, watching videos of guided practices, journaling and speaking intentional statements.

5. I have found it best to collect payment for remote sessions in advance or at the start of the session. Most clients are deeply relaxed in the Now moment at the end of remote sessions, and it can feel jarring to have to deal with money at that time.

More Guidelines for Remote Healing Sessions:

1. Choose your communication method for remote healing clients. You can use phone calls, Skype, Zoom or other video conference systems. You can also offer healing silently without having any kind of call, or the client even knowing you are doing it. However, for those starting to work with remote healing I recommend live calls because the communication and focus of healer and client make the work much more tangible.

2. Get clear on the healing methods you will offer through your remote sessions. There are many systems of energy healing, and you may already be familiar with some of them. You can offer forms of energy acupuncture, light or sound therapies including tuning forks, color light therapies, Reiki or other systems. I use the system of Quantum Catalyst healing described in the previous chapter, which works on multiple dimensions of physical, mental/emotional and spiritual within the same session. Techniques are not always required. Setting up a remote session and simply sharing your Avatar transmission with love can promote profound healing.

3. Always prepare for your remote sessions by creating a safe and sacred space of love and higher light around yourself and your client. You can do that by simply

invoking and visualizing that. Clear the energy field around you before each session with a "purity blast," and do those before and after each remote or in-person session. This method is described in the Getting Started section.

In review, you can invoke a purity blast to clear the healing space for you and your client by putting one hand up in the air and declaring "I now command a purity blast!" Then visualize a column of white light descending from the place of the highest spiritual source above your head, rushing through you and the room you are working in. You will often feel a sensation as you do that. Trust that it has been done and move on in confidence that you and your client can work together in a safe, clear zone.

4. Intend that you are only working with energies of the highest good and purity in your session. If you feel connected with spiritual sources of higher light and guidance, invoke and connect with that source. Or, see yourself working within a vast, inter-connected Quantum field of Light. When you ground your own body and nervous system in the Quantum field it becomes possible to draw your client into this more expanded sense of themselves, where true transformation is possible.

5. You can experiment with doing remote sessions using a doll or diagram of the human body as a surrogate to represent the client. When I first started offering remote sessions I worked through a large Barbie doll on a treatment table. I used movements of my hands, energy tools and visualization to stimulate acupuncture points, chakras and the overall energy field I envisioned on and around the doll. Now I don't use a doll or table anymore and find it just as effective to do it all within consciousness.

6. Learn the art of voice dialogue. This is about how you speak with and guide clients to release old psychic burdens, empower themselves and discover hidden truths about themselves. It is very important to radiate confidence and a loving presence as you dialogue with clients. Take charge of the session right from the beginning by directing your client to join you in simple grounding, breathwork or intention-setting exercises. Minimize the amount of time taken up in the session by the client reciting their repetitive "stories" about their pains and problems. Get them more directly into their feeling sense, by focusing on the sensations of energy in their bodies behind those stories.

7. Develop your higher sense perception. We all have abilities to see and sense energy. Some people are more visual, some more kinesthetic, some just "know" what is needed beyond any senses. I have found that conducting remote healing sessions has helped powerfully awaken my intuitive and higher sense perception abilities, even more than in-person sessions in my office. That is similar to what often occurs with people who lose their eyesight – they tend to develop stronger abilities of their other senses.

8. Zoom and Skype both offer recording options. I usually send the client the recording of the session, or parts of it, that could be useful for continued practice.

9. If possible, practice leading remote sessions with friends or colleagues to "get the hang of it" before doing them with paying clients.

These are general guidelines only. There is a great deal more that can be learned and embodied. I just broke down remote healing sessions into a number of discrete steps to make the process more understandable to the rational mind. Your Avatar transmission helps activate the client's ability to access their own master healer connection, and your intuitive receptivity shows you, moment by moment, how to conduct your sessions. Yet having some left-brain structure to guide you is also very helpful.

What is wonderful about offering remote healing sessions is that you as a practitioner will experience accelerated awakening of your own healing abilities, energy sensitivity and higher sense perceptions through doing it. You will learn to trust your own sources of intuitive guidance.

Getting Permission

Anytime you work with someone else's energy it is vital to make sure you have permission to do so. When a person books a session with you there is clearly permission. At the time when new clients are speaking with me, or are ready to book a session, I still check into my inner guidance to confirm that it is safe, effective and appropriate for me to work with that person. I usually get a "yes" but occasionally my guidance will say "no." In those cases, I offer to refer that person to someone else who may be a better match energetically. If you follow this practice you will only accept clients who you have a high probability of being able to assist. It also protects you, the healer, from taking on higher-level negative energies you may not yet have sufficient embodiment and skillsets to work with. I always ask permission now due to some past excruciating experiences when I wish I had!

13

Planetary Healing

Do you sometimes get concerned, angry or worried about things going on in your community, or our planet? Even if you and others you know are doing what you can to contribute and give back, does it seem like just a drop in the bucket compared to what is really needed?

Considering the number of seemingly worsening issues facing the human race at this time, those can appear to be valid concerns. Yet as an awakening Avatar, you are part of a wave of unstoppable light that is way more powerful than all the problems and issues facing us. This chapter offers details of a method you can practice that, combined with the focus of other Avatars, can help literally change the world. This is the practice of planetary healing.

Planetary healing is a reality for which the often-overused word "awesome" is properly used. The *transmission* of your true Avatar self has unlimited healing and blessing power. Through the holographic principle, your divine self is in "quantum entanglement" with all life, everywhere. Therefore, you are able to transmit and participate in the profound healing of groups of people ranging in size from a few to the entire human race and beyond. I have made the commitment to sit in front of my meditation altar at least once a day to offer planetary healing. Below are guidelines for engaging in the practice of planetary healing, as I do it. Use these as you see fit, and make sure you follow your own inner guidance as you enter into this service.

The power of love is unlimited. There is nothing impossible in the face of pure love. It is through allowing the unlimited divine love of your transmission to express through you, that it is possible for you to be an agent of healing for the planet.

There is nothing impossible in the face of pure love

I can't fully express how profound this practice is. You are literally stepping into a level of service that "is a job for Superman." Therefore, this super part of you, your Avatar self must step in. It knows how to draw upon infinite universal resources. I will repeat that your Avatar self is holographically connected, not only with the people you wish to serve but all the healing power of the Universe. Your "small" human ego self cannot make this happen. It just serves by reminding you to do this practice, creating time for it and then getting out of the way.

In entering into offering remote and planetary healing sessions, the "journey of 1000 miles begins with the first step." Have the courage to dive in and take it for a test drive. Don't wait until you feel like you have it all together first. You will gain your skills and confidence by actually engaging.

Guided Practice

I recommend asking your internal guidance if it is appropriate for you to engage in planetary healing. If you get an internal "yes" proceed.

1. Engage with the foundational practices – Purity blast, grounding, Master hook-up, coming back to yourself, complete breath and loving presence. All of these can be experienced together in a few seconds once you are familiar with them. Sitting in front of an altar with sacred pictures, objects and a burning candle or incense is very helpful, but not required.

2. Practice Central Axis Breathing (Chapter 23), as you focus on your breath moving up and down the column of your chakras. You can also see a ball of golden light moving up and down the chakras with your breath. If you become aware of any hurting, empty or constricted places in your body, spend time internally hugging those areas, focusing your love and breath there.

3. It is highly beneficial to activate your merkaba light body as you enter into planetary healing (see Chapter 27). This will bring great love, clarity and guidance to your practice.

4. Open to your feelings. Be willing to feel your caring and concern about events going on with specific groups of people, all humanity or all life. If you feel passionately about bringing greater justice and resolution to specific issues, drop into those feelings. I have found that it is my passionate concern that empowers this practice. Also, intend to connect with your feelings of universal love. This opens up your innate pathways for planetary healing. Remind yourself that it is your unlimited, divine Avatar transmission that engages in planetary healing, not the agendas of your limited human self.

5. Invoke your higher self and any divine beings you want to call in. Tune into your Avatar transmission, opening your body to receive it like a waterfall of pure essence filling and surrounding the Earth, and also moving down through your own body. Or, you might experience your transmission coming from all around you. This is the truest essence of you that you came here to share. It is only through your transmission that you are empowered to be a planetary healer. That is because your transmission is the note of the cosmic symphony you bring that is vitally needed for the healing of mankind. No one else but you can bring this particular note, and the symphony of Avatar planetary healers will not be complete without it.

6. Call on the collective of all beings serving the Earth through its current transition, standing with them as you engage in planetary healing. When I do this – I call upon all human Avatars and Lightworkers, cosmic light beings and indigenous healers. I call this group "Team Light." You can be assured that at any given moment, there are thousands to millions of others in Team Light radiating healing blessings for humanity. It is powerful to consciously connect with them, thereby amplifying the power of your blessings.

7. Once you are tuned in, visualize a three-dimensional image of the Earth in front of you, rotating slowly in space. See how beautiful it is with its green and brown landmasses, blue oceans, white clouds floating above it, the moon circling nearby and the endless stars and galaxies of space behind it. See it as the *New Earth* shining with light, visualizing your dreams of harmony, cooperation and mutual service to clean up the messes and residues of the past.

8. Attune to loving Presence and simply radiate love to the Earth and all life. Go with whatever comes up within you. You are a creator being, and you can dream what is in your heart without compromise. You can focus on specific areas of conflict anywhere on Earth, or simply allow blessings to radiate to all life. Explore this process, starting in baby steps if that is your comfort.

9. It is powerful to visualize divine healing light surrounding and filling the Earth. See whatever color or quality of divine light you are guided to work with. I usually work with violet and golden crystal light. I visualize it as a vast pillar of light big enough to fill and encompass the entire Earth and all life upon it. I also sometimes visualize people all over the world smiling, celebrating, opening their hearts to each other and getting busy cleaning and rebuilding all of our systems into more just, equitable and ecological forms.

10. It is powerful to speak I AM decrees out loud. When you start a sentence with I AM, you are speaking as the highest divine power, as there is no separation. If you are so guided, speak decrees like these, or any variation on them:

    I AM the power of divine love awakening the hearts and minds of all human beings to unconditional love, harmony, mutual service, kindness and disclosure of truth

    I AM the commanding power of the Light breaking down all control programs that had been enslaving humanity, freeing all people to claim their sovereignty

    I AM the Cosmic Violet Flame surrounding and filling the Earth, purifying and bringing the Light

    I AM the ascension and awakening of truth, consciousness, pure love, disclosure, kindness, wisdom and courage within the hearts and minds of all humans

11. You can use planetary healing to support positive outcomes for specific crisis areas such as those with wildfires, wars, floods, droughts or famine. You can focus on specific people, communities, groups, nations or the entire Earth. You can be as specific or broad as you want.

    You can ask that the virtues of peace, justice, freedom, compassion and consciousness awakening inform all the people caught up in those issues. Focusing on issues is not necessary, however. You may be much more comfortable letting your mind go and wordlessly allow your transmission to serve.

14

Forgiveness is Powerful Medicine – Stepping Up to Multi-Dimensional Forgiveness

Lindsay is a vivacious, petite esthetician who came to one of my microcurrent training seminars in California. She smiled and laughed a lot, easily connecting with the other students. On Day Two of the event, I asked if there was anyone in the class dealing with physical pain, who would volunteer to receive a treatment in front of the room. Lindsay volunteered and came up front. She told us she had developed chronic arm pain due to her profession, which required her to hold her arms up in the air over client's heads for hours every day. She had been sleeping very poorly because just about every sleeping position aggravated her arm pain. I evaluated Lindsay and then performed a series of pain-relieving microcurrent techniques on her. After each technique, I asked her to move her arms in the ways that usually brought up the pain, so we could see how much improvement had occurred. She did report a partial reduction of the pain, but I could tell that there was more that we had not uncovered yet.

On a hunch, I asked Lindsay if there was anyone in her life she was holding grudges against. After thinking a moment, her normally bubbly personality faded, and tears came to her eyes. She confided that she had been abused by her father as a child and had never forgiven him. I asked if she would be willing to go through a forgiveness practice with her father now. I explained that this could be the missing piece that would allow the microcurrent techniques to relieve her pain more completely.

After some initial reluctance, Lindsay agreed. I led her through speaking a series of healing statements of forgiveness. During some of the statements, she agreed to forgive her father and release her grudge against him. She must have meant it, because as soon as she did that both she and I felt a big shift of energy in our bodies. I asked her to move her arms again and this time the pain was almost completely reduced.

The next morning, we all returned for the final day of the seminar. I asked Lindsay if the pain had disturbed her sleep the night before. She gratefully reported that she had slept through the night for the first time in months because her arms were now totally pain-free. Not only that, but she felt a great emotional lightness in her body, centered around her heart. I checked with her a month after the seminar, and she was still almost completely pain-free.

I have witnessed similar experiences with numerous clients. In many cases in which clients had not been responding well to my microcurrent therapy treatments or Quantum healing sessions, I found that they had been holding onto some kind of grudge or resentment that was clogging the free flow of energy in parts of their body. In most cases, they didn't even realize they were doing that. Over and over again, I have seen these clients break through into a clearer, more pain-free experience once they acknowledged those feelings and consciously chose to release them. I've witnessed the same thing in my own life many times. Forgiveness is powerful medicine.

At the time of this writing, there is a national epidemic of old and new grudges, resentments, fears and biases being blasted through the media, as the United States faces multiple crises and polarizing political belief systems. Surely this is the time to tap into the awesome power of forgiveness. Forgiveness arises from the heart – the center of wisdom within that sees a bigger picture than the agendas of the egoic mind. When we look at others who have different viewpoints and values through the eyes of our minds, it is easy to judge, fear or condemn them. If we look instead through the eyes of our heart we can see more of our commonality. We can find compassion for the deep fears and pains that have led them to believe and behave the way they do.

The healing power of forgiveness is well-documented. Even though it may have seemed like the hardest thing in the world at first, people who have released their resentments have experienced breakthrough healing and elevation of consciousness. I have witnessed or heard about this happening between Jews and Arabs, Black activists and Ku Klux Klan members[81] as well as victims and perpetrators of violent crimes.

---

[81] I highly recommend the movie "Best of Enemies" for a beautiful gripping example of this based on a true story. From Astute Films, 2019

Over the last year, I have become aware that forgiveness can expand far beyond one person forgiving another. In truth, each of us lives in quantum entanglement with everybody else and all life. Another way of saying this is that you exist right now in multi-dimensions of an infinite, inter-connected hologram. Talk about relationships! We are a lot like mushroom colonies. What looks like hundreds of separate mushroom heads above the surface of the ground is all part of one big organism that is mostly underground.

What does this tell us about forgiveness? It means that <u>each time you forgive another it can reverberate through the experiences of countless other people – including yourself</u>. Once during a personal healing retreat, I was looking at pictures of my sister, daughter and now deceased parents. My heart was feeling open and full. As I looked deeper at each of them, I saw my love going through them into the inter-connected holographic grid including their parents, grandparents and further back through previous generations. I saw it also spreading out to all the relatives of each of those ancestors as well. Then I felt the wave of love and forgiveness moving back through each of the past life incarnations of my family members and ancestors, spreading out to a huge, countless number of people. Eventually, this wave of love expanded beyond the Earth to non-human embodiments many of us may have had, and then to all the connections of those beings. I saw that love and forgiveness could truly be universal and multi-dimensional. What seemed like a single act of opening my heart and releasing resentment could literally help free the world and the Universe.

Guided Practice for Multi-Dimensional Forgiveness

The next time you feel angry or resentful toward another person or group you can become a pioneer in consciousness, and take it as an opportunity to explore multi-dimensional forgiveness. Here is a suggested practice sequence:

1. Engage foundational practices. Place the tip of your tongue in the Master Hook-Up position on the roof of your mouth, relax and ground yourself through a few minutes of Central Axis Breathing or other favorite meditative practice. Ground yourself down into your Earth Star chakra. Call your energy into your body from wherever you have projected it out to. Evoke the feeling of love within your heart by thinking of a person, animal, being or place that most easily brings up that feeling. Breathe with love, moving it up and down the central axis of your body.

2. Think of the person or group you feel angry with or hurt by. Visualize them, or a symbol of them in front of you. If you have a lot of charge about those people you can imagine them 20 feet in front of you, to create more distance so you feel safer. Allow your genuine feelings about this person to come up, staying grounded in your breath.

3. Intend to see the scared, hurt or vulnerable part of that person who acted out in the ways that you felt hurt by. Try to see the holographic one-ness you share with them in spirit.

4. Think about the great healing power of forgiveness and how much it could benefit both you and the person you are thinking about. When you are ready, send a wave of love and forgiveness to them. See it entering their heart, or any other part of the body you are guided to. Imagine that person softening and transforming as they receive your love and forgiveness.

5. Now imagine more people appearing behind the one you have been focusing on. See more and more rows of inter-connected people spreading out farther and farther back through time, forward through time and across geography. It doesn't matter if you can accurately visualize all that, just know and affirm that it is happening. Trust your higher, Avatar self to take your forgiveness

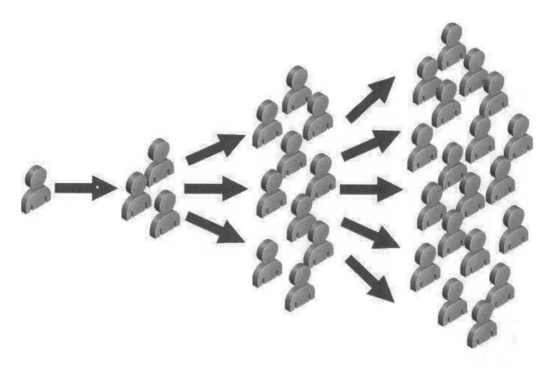

to the multi-dimensional level beyond the understanding of your mind (If your mind does understand, it's the icing on the cake).

6. Allow your awareness to contemplate the oneness you share with all the people you have visualized in this practice, and your oneness with all life, everywhere. Intend to be an emanation of pure universal love as much as you can.

Multi-dimensional forgiveness can be applied to any size group of people, even huge numbers caught up in wars, political strife or racial conflicts. We are tapping into the great power of intention that your true self possesses. This practice is not about doing and efforting from your mind. By opening your heart big enough to want the love and forgiveness of the divine to bless an entire mushroom colony of people, you are being the Divine, and it is done.

Self-Forgiveness

Forgiving or making amends to others is important, but not as important as self-forgiveness. For many people, this is the hardest form of forgiveness to engage with. Follow the same guidelines as outlined above, but instead of seeing other people or groups in front of you imagine an image of yourself. You can see yourself as you look now, as a child, or what you imagined you looked like in a past lifetime in which you believe you hurt others.

Remember, your true self is divine and requires no forgiveness. Yet it can be deeply healing to take the time to forgive your very human self, especially when you recognize that you have been judging and withholding love from yourself.

Applying Multi-Dimensional Forgiveness to an Issue

We all know what issues are – those nagging parts of ourselves that keep demanding our attention in ways ranging from disturbing to life-threatening. Issues are parts of our psyche that feel unresolved, un-loved or un-forgiven. They can be called neuroses, anxieties, depressions, psychic burdens, *samskara* or "residoo-doo." In our less responsible moments, we project our issues onto those we are close to, because they mirror them back to us so maddeningly well. Projecting our issues onto others just amplifies them.

These issues are also often at the root of our physical diseases or chronic pains that may often seem so hard to permanently heal. As explained elsewhere in this book, our issues are not just our own. We are also tapping into the vast pain bodies of groups of other people. Therefore, when we stop projecting our pain onto others and take loving responsibility to bring self-healing and forgiveness to our own issues, we are fulfilling a sacred service. Here are guidelines for applying multi-dimensional forgiveness to an issue that is confronting you now:

1. When you become aware you are brooding about something going on in your life that has been bringing you down, angering you or making you feel hurt or resentful, stop and take a step back. Invoke your Witness Consciousness that can see what you have been feeling objectively, such as "Oh there I am feeling bad about how isolated I have been feeling recently" or "I'm really worried about my income" or "I just keep getting triggered by my partner and it's driving me crazy." Or any other issue that's in your face. You can also focus on an area of physical pain in your body in the same way – shift your awareness to observe it from a place of neutrality within you, curiously observing the sensations and emotional feelings it holds.

2. Engage foundational practices. Place the tip of your tongue in the Master Hook-Up position on the roof of your mouth. Relax and ground yourself through a few minutes of Central Axis Breathing or other favorite meditative practice. While continuing to acknowledge the disturbance of the issue, evoke a feeling of love within your heart. If necessary, think of a person, animal, being or place that most easily brings up that feeling. Breathe with love, moving it up and down the central axis of your body.

3. Ask yourself "where" in your body your issue is most focused. There is always a focal point within the body that correlates to each emotional issue. Put the palm of one hand over that area and breathe in and out there. It is very helpful to move your breath up and down the central channel of your chakras, pausing at the issue focal point while you internally squeeze the muscles around that area, giving yourself an Inner Embrace.[82]

4. Invoke your Christ Avatar transmission: "I AM invoking (calling upon) my transmission. I open my heart and body to receive and perceive my divine essence as much as possible now." Relax and suspend your analytical mind, allowing yourself to receive and acknowledge your transmission. If you're not sure you are feeling your transmission just trust that it is present.

5. Intend to course your transmission through the body focal point of your issue, including the entire central channel of your body. With faith and trust allow your transmission, your highest healing source and truest self, to have its way with the issue and everything related to it.

6. Be love. Be forgiveness. Relax, soften and allow those divine energies to permeate the focal point of the pain or issue in your body. Allow this alchemical process to unfold, observing what shifts are happening in your experience. Trust your body's responses, which may include energy unwinding symptoms such as shaking, coughing, yawning, temperature changes or others.

7. Now become aware of multi-dimensional forgiveness. Through your love, you can extend the love and forgiveness you are bringing to your issue to all souls connected with it. "I now intend to extend this blessing of forgiveness and release to all souls who are connected with this issue/feeling/condition/suffering." As is described above, in your imagination see the network of all the people or beings who are directly or indirectly connected with your experience of the issue. This may be a small, defined group or may require a football stadium. Simply trust that your transmission is blessing all of them as is appropriate for each.

8. Trust your heart to guide you in this process of multi-dimensional forgiveness, letting go of your critical, analytical mind as is necessary. When you feel complete, check-in with yourself. What change do you perceive in yourself and the focal area in your body of the issue? Offer gratitude for any positive shift you are aware of. If you don't feel any difference, be patient

---

[82] See Chapter 24 about the Inner Embrace.

with yourself and do this practice more often. Also, give gratitude that you have been led to such a high-level method for profound healing and service to others.

Examples of "issues" this practice could bring positive results for:

- Anxiety
- Depression
- Chronic pain
- Cancer
- Infectious disease
- Recurring difficult patterns in relationships
- Financial issues
- Outrage about injustices you see happening in the world
- Sense of spiritual blockage or stagnation
- Feeling "slimed" by negative energies
- Issues with aging, dementia or death
- Anything else that is up for you!

As I write each chapter of this book my consciousness has been "downloaded" with inspirations, images and experiences related to the topic I am writing about. While writing this chapter, a string of memories have arisen within me about people I have known throughout my life. These memories mostly seemed to concern relationships with women I have known, and felt incomplete about on various levels. I have heard about the phenomenon in which dying people go through what is called a life review, with thoughts and images of their life flashing before them. Some people feel regret about those memories, seeing where they were not as kind and loving as they could have been, or how they seemed to have wasted so much time on superficial pursuits that did not feed their heart and soul. Others experience more of a sense of joy and completeness in their life. For most people, such a life review is a mixed bag. I felt like I was going through something like a life review, and thankfully am not dying.

I realized that in the past, whenever memories about relationships I felt incomplete about came up I would feel something like "Ouch – that really hurt!" or felt some sense of self-judgment: "I was so shallow then – I really wish I could go back to that time with what I know now and have shared more love and consciousness." I decided to see what multi-dimensional forgiveness would do with these memories. I allowed myself to feel the feelings arising about each relationship I was remembering, and pictured a scene from the time I knew that person. I opened my heart to share as much pure love as I could now and invoked the reality of multi-dimensional forgiveness between the two of us. I repeated the Hawaiian Hoʻoponopono prayer – *I am sorry, please forgive me or I forgive you, I love you, thank you* – several times. As described above I imagined rows and rows of ancestors and other relations of both of us, intending that the blessings of love and forgiveness would extend through the past, present and future. In many cases, I have also been led to radiate my Christ Avatar transmission to that person, myself and all our connections.

I gave the love and presence now that I withheld back when I was with each person, thus bringing our connection into a sense of greater completion. As I engaged in this process, it put me through a lot of inner transformation and strong feelings. My commitment to myself and all those I am in a relationship with today is to give my love more completely now. That way, when I finally do my end-of-life review my heart can be happy and at peace. As I do this practice I am feeling more and more of that deep peace and happiness. I can sense that it is really bringing more lightness and love into both my own subconscious mind and the tapestry of relationships I am part of.

What is miraculous about the practice of multi-dimensional forgiveness is that you are helping heal countless other people as you take responsibility for healing yourself. This is truly the way of the Avatar that you are.

15

Updating the Dark Night of the Soul

Our path of awakening to our Christ Avatar self involves a process of emotional and spiritual maturation. Once we have enough *vairagya* to get serious about awakening from our fear-based dream and putting our self into service, our lives transform on many levels. That process of getting motivated to awaken takes us through major change points. Some of those may feel scary or depressing when we are going through them, yet they are essential gateways to our greatest freedom and fulfillment of our higher purpose.

Think about it – if during childhood we had reasonably supportive caregivers we were provided for, protected and comforted by them. They encouraged us, disciplined us and may have helped pick up the pieces when we messed up. At various stages of growing up, healthy children reject some of that support and start establishing their own autonomy and power. We went through rites of passage when we had to rebel against the authority of our caregivers, releasing some of our childish ways and claiming our power by becoming more self-responsible.

In truth, during this time of fallen humanity, few of us have had ideal childhoods. The majority of people I know felt damaged in various ways by their upbringing and have spent a lot of their adult life healing from what happened back then. Yet our wounding experiences have served our greater purpose, as is presented in Chapter 16 – Your Assignment of Love.

Many people have described going through dark and lost times, feeling disconnected from all the inner comfort and love they had previously been able to access. These phases have often been described as times of depression, or even "dark nights of the soul". They could last anywhere from a few days up to years. Most of those who embrace a path of spiritual development eventually discover a deeper awareness of who they really are through these experiences, often ascending to a higher level of consciousness. These proving times make us dig deeper into the reality of our true self. They are times when the training wheels are abruptly pulled off our bicycles, and we have to find our own balance much sooner than we would have chosen.

So, just as Jesus had to fast and wrestle with his shadow for 40 days and nights in the desert and Buddha had to bear being tempted and scared by the demon Mara under the Bodhi tree, these are symbols of what we all must do. Jesus said, "What I have done all people shall do and greater." That was the positive icing part of the statement. What he didn't say, probably to not scare all his disciples off was – "You'll have to pass through many trials, just as I had to do."

But don't get scared off or discouraged. In this time of ascension, we are no longer called upon to be martyrs, physically suffering for the greater glory of God. Now the required sacrifice is internal – releasing our fixation on the fears, doubts and denials of our small selves, and stepping into being a modern, genuine Lightworker. The ready availability of our Avatar *transmission* and simple, powerful ascension practices we have been given can greatly accelerate this process.

Don't Avoid the Void

Many of my healing clients who are clearly in the process of stepping into a new, expanded phase of their life describe periods of feeling emotionally depressed. This may seem counter-intuitive, but there is a reason for it.

Through universal law, everything in the Universe is moving through cycles of expression. Planets, stars and galaxies are birthed, sustained, destroyed and re-created through vast cycles of time. Our Earth moves through seasons and positions in space. Humans cycle through life cycles of childhood, adulthood, old age, death and rebirth.

The process of our healing and consciousness awakening is also cyclical. On the so-called spiritual path we tend to go through phases like this:

1. **Discovery:** Discovering an inspiring new teacher, path or spiritual develop-ment method. Or it could be a new project, business venture or path of service.

2. **Development:** Practicing what we learn on that path, gaining benefits and developing some degree of mastery. From that place, sharing what

we have gained with others. This giving further reinforces the benefits of the path.

3. **Disillusionment:** Eventually getting bored, disillusioned or outgrowing the path we have been on. This sometimes includes learning "shocking" revelations about corrupt or inappropriate behavior by the teacher or organization.

4. **Release and Emptiness:** After that happens, we withdraw from the path and go through a phase often described as emptiness. In this state of emptiness, it feels like nothing is happening, perhaps even as if we've lost all the inspiration and enlightenment we had gained in the previous phases.

5. **Being in the Void:** Spending time in what has been identified as the Void – an experience that often feels like emptiness and nothingness to the human mind. Yet, in reality, the Void is full of light when seen through the eyes of the soul.

6. **Elevating Your Level:** When the time is right, this cycle starts over again with the discovery of a new teacher, path or development method that vibrates on a higher level of consciousness and embodiment.

It is Step 5 in this cycle, Being in the Void that is most important to this discussion. This the phase in which people often complain about being depressed, uninspired, lost or feeling like a failure. Yet, in reality, the Void is a necessary gateway of ascension. All valuable things that exist started out as nothingness.

By universal law, we must all pass through variations of these cycles. Therefore, the next time you feel like you are stuck in an extended period of depression or a dark night of the soul, do your best to reframe what you are experiencing. Know that you are in your ascension chamber of consciousness, gathering yourself to go higher. Don't avoid the Void!

Most of us live within a duality of judging our experiences. We tend to either put them in a category of beneficial and successful, or one in which we are "blowing it" and allowing our wounded, weak parts of self to rule us. Our true, Avatar selves are able to see all of our experiences without such judgment. From that perspective, you can have the clarity of trusting that all your experiences are precious, and each of them serves an important purpose in your awakening.

Each experience of inner pain is an opportunity to practice spiritual alchemy. You do that by training yourself to let go of the urge to judge your experience. Then patiently and persistently direct your divine transmission to those places in your body that are focal points of discomfort. Just sit with yourself and bring your higher light and love to the parts of you feeling pained and contracted. You will be guided in this process through the practices in Section Four.

Lightening Up the Dark Nights

As we become more aware of our multi-dimensionality, our old experiences of dark nights of the soul can be perceived in a different way. Our multi-dimensional self is like a cut diamond with many different facets. What we have thought of as down days, anxious days or "the happiest day of my life" can now be seen as different facets of the diamond of our true self that all exist simultaneously. Until we claim mastery, we feel like we're just flitting around from one facet of our experience to another, driven by unconscious urges and external influences. You'll know when you've achieved mastery when you get to choose which facet of your experience you are focusing on.

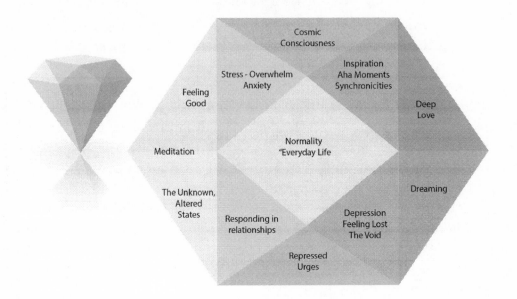

So, whenever you think you are experiencing a dark night of the soul, or feel mired in depression, you can open up to also staying connected with your other facets that are full of light and divine Presence. You can choose to apply those higher vibrational parts of yourself to your hurting or lost parts. This form of spiritual alchemy has been the way of masters throughout human history, and a way to claim the master healer inside of you.[83]

---

[83] The chapters in the Kybalion book about the Law of Polarity are especially illuminating about this process. See Bibliography.

When Jesus said: *I AM the way, the truth and the life and no one comes to the Father except through me* – he was not speaking from his individual human self. When he made this statement, he was speaking as I AM – the divine unity of All That Is. As I understand it, he was acknowledging that the only way to release our separation and come to the Father, the God within, was through connecting with divine Presence – our Avatar transmission.

Exercise – Multi-Dimensional Self-Healing for Dark Nights of the Soul

The next time you feel "you" are in downtime or even a dark night of the soul, try this exercise. It will be much more accessible if you've already been practicing sensing and receiving your Avatar transmission, as explained in Chapter 3. The more you attune your body and mind to your transmission on a regular basis, the more possible it will be to access it when parts of you are feeling lost or dis-connected.

If you have an altar or favorite place you associate with meditation, sit there. Engage your foundational practices. Invoke your Christ Avatar self to be present and guide you. Do a few minutes of Central Axis breathing. Then allow yourself to feel the pain of what you are going through. Localize it in your body (See Chapter 24). Engage in radical acceptance of whatever you are experiencing.

Relax your body and allow yourself to be with your feelings. Dark nights of the soul tend to be times when it seems hard to access your transmission, but it is assuredly still there because it is you, no matter what you are going through. Find it not so much by trying to concentrate, but by surrendering and letting go. Sincerely ask your God-self to help you access your true self and remove all interference.

You may need to also explore what agenda your ego has for holding onto pain, or denying your true self. Useful ways of doing this include the following:

Intuitive Journaling: Take out a notebook and pen and write a question you have about your experience, such as "What is my agenda for creating this dark night experience" or "How and why am I withholding love from myself and doubting what I know?" Then, without mentally analyzing the question just start writing. Write even if it looks like nonsense.

Using Voice Recorder: I have received surprisingly valuable information from beyond the knowing of my conscious mind by speaking into a voice recording app on my mobile phone. This method works best for me if I take a walk in a place where I can be by myself in a natural setting. Again, I speak my question, invoke my divine self, and then allow myself to freely speak without trying to judge how real or accurate what I am saying is.

Reflection: Speaking with a spiritually aware, trusted counselor, or engaging in co-counseling with a friend can often make things clearer for you.

Once you feel even a smidgeon of your transmission, notice where in your body you are most able to feel it. Then put your other hand over that area. You now have one hand over the focal point of pain and one hand over the area where you can sense your transmission. With deep breaths and strong intention intend that these two places connect and merge with each other. Relax and allow the alchemy to happen. Using the analogy offered above, see these two parts of your experience as different facets of the same diamond. As you connect them, remind yourself that the real you is the whole diamond. A helpful decree is:

I AM my divine Christ Avatar self lovingly holding this man/woman/other

Allow yourself to be loved and cared for by your divine mother and father. Let go of trying and doing.

When you can, open to feelings of gratitude that you really are who you are beyond all appearances and transitory experiences – even the big bad dark night of the soul.

And reach out for support. We Avatar Lightworkers really need to be there for each other.

SECTION 3

BEING AN AVATAR IN EVERYDAY LIFE

Being an awakening Avatar Lightworker is not primarily about peak spiritual experiences, or being special or unusual. It is all about how you show up in everyday life. These five chapters start with the commitment you made about your life plan before you were born. You'll then progress through looking at your Lightworker job description and bringing Avatar consciousness to your relationships and finances. It concludes with an overview of living as an Avatar.

16

Your Assignment of Love

You're sailing along in your life, doing your thing, engaged in your relationships, your work, your play, doing whatever your path is and then it hits you. Feelings and thoughts well up from a place that is all too familiar. These feelings may be dark, heavy and out of phase with other parts of your life. Until you get wise to what is happening, these feelings can throw you for a loop. What gives? It's likely that there is no real problem.

As an Avatar, you are here on a high mission. This mission you have accepted is a specific part of the healing and ascension of the human race. You are well suited for this mission, and your true self possesses the knowledge and superpowers necessary to fulfill it. Your mission springs from the deepest motivation and love within you – the love that wants all beings to be uplifted and healed. We can call this mission your Assignment of Love.

Getting clear about your Assignment of Love can really help you understand and accept what you are going through. It can also radically change your attitude about any difficult, traumatic or frustrating experiences that have recurred in your life, because you'll see the bigger picture of why they may be happening and how they are serving you. This will help you accept the truth of:

Whatever is in the way IS the way

As a Christ Avatar, your #1 purpose is to embody and radiate love and blessings. Love is why we are here. Love is what we are made of. Love is what we discover as we

187

clear the shadows within our minds and behold our true nature. Love is the greatest healer, in fact, the only true healer. Why? Because true healing is bringing our body and mind out of self-created exile, back to our true self which is Love. Love melts all blockages, as all blockages consist of various forms of denial of love.

Your Assignment of Love is the specific area of human suffering in which you have volunteered to help bring love and consciousness. You are an expert, a specialist in performing this service. Oh yes, one more important detail. You probably don't remember volunteering for your Assignment of Love, as I'll explain soon.

Would you like to know what your Assignment of Love is? It is whatever your attention has been inexorably drawn to, over and over throughout your life. Your Assignment is associated with experiences that require you to discover and draw upon what is most powerful and loving within you.

Many people have referred to going through the experiences their Assignment of Love puts them through as a fire of transformation and purification. A good analogy is the industrial smelting process, which involves putting metallic mineral ores into very high-temperature furnaces that separate out or burn away everything except the pure metal. Because they are usually hard to go through, these experiences also tend to awaken compassion in us, enabling us to see a bigger picture than that of our own personal self and our tribe.

In order to fulfill our Assignment of Love, our soul chooses or attracts parents, siblings, environments and situations that give us some combination of supportive gifts and deep psychic wounds. Grappling with the fallout from those early childhood wounds gradually moves us in the direction of our mission. Regardless of what your life has been like, you develop your mission through a mixture of deep innate motivation and recurring pain and struggle. This means that the missions we are drawn to usually involve areas of life that we have personally gone through hell with.

People drawn to the field of psychology have usually experienced plenty of emotional pain in their own lives. Acupuncturists and energy healers are often highly sensitive individuals who have had to struggle to find their own energetic balance. Those drawn to counsel people who have been through inner-city gangs, rape, addiction or mental illness have often had those experiences themselves. We sense on a deep internal level that giving back in those areas in which we have struggled and suffered is our own path of greatest healing and redemption. Not everybody has to go through grief and struggle to claim and fulfill their Assignment of Love, but there is almost always a sense of challenge, and of needing to stretch and develop yourself.

Understanding what your Assignment of Love is, and how it relates to the difficult experiences you have had, can really shift your perspective into greater acceptance and empowerment. Here's one thing that highly successful and effective people seem to agree on – a major key to success is our willingness to accept total responsibility for ourselves. A big piece of self-responsibility is coming to understand that on some level your soul chose or accepted your experiences in order to increase your capacity to fulfill your higher purpose.

You are an Avatar being of light. That real you that is divine has no problems or issues to resolve. Your human embodiment, however, has probably gone through a whole lot of challenges on your path of learning and development. Those disturbing issues that have cropped up again and again over long periods of your life are your Assignment of Love because you volunteered to help heal them for the good of the greater collective. Knowing and accepting this truth can guide you in the "care and feeding" of yourself on a moment-to-moment basis. You can use this understanding to be more loving and compassionate to yourself.

Getting Your Pre-Birth Assignment

I have believed for a long time that many of the experiences I've gone through were set up before I was born. This general belief came into clearer focus after I read a profound book by Robert Schwartz entitled *Your Soul's Plan*.[84] This book is a report on an extended research project in which Schwartz studied the choices people make on a soul level before they were born. With the help of a woman who had the ability to psychically "read" people's pre-birth experiences, he interviewed a series of people who had been through various forms of major difficulties and traumas in their lives. Through this process, he came to believe that, on a soul level, each of them chose to have the difficult experiences they had been through. They had made those choices in order to support themselves in completing their overall soul purpose.

Because this is an unusual and controversial perspective, I will dramatize it through a bit of storytelling. While the story I'm about to tell you comes from my own imagination and is intended to be somewhat humorous, I believe the essence of it is accurate. See how much it resonates with your own inner knowing.

A group of eager souls gathered in a spiritual realm. They were excited because each of them was about to descend into a newborn human body. These souls had not yet been lulled to sleep by the amnesia of human existence, in which we forget who we really are. Therefore, they still knew themselves to be unlimited beings of Light. There was a lot of enthusiastic buzz and conversation between the souls, which was

---

[84] Schwartz, Robert, Your Soul's Plan, Frog Books 2009

interrupted by the appearance of a tall Master Being. Everyone became respectfully quiet right away because they knew the time had come.

"Team Light! I greet you with the Love of the All" the Being communicated. "Are you ready to receive your Assignment of Love?" There was general assent as all the assembled souls non-physically radiated "Yes". (They did not yet have heads so they couldn't nod.)

"Very well" the Being continued. "Planet Earth is going through great upheaval during the current unfolding Ascension of mass consciousness. As a result, there is a tremendous amount of old, repressed experiences that need to be brought up, accepted and healed with your limitless Light. I will now read a list of specific areas of human experiences that require your services in this way." The excitement and anticipation grew stronger as the assembled souls pictured the service opportunities before them with relish. Because they were deathless spiritual beings they knew they had nothing to fear, and sensed how much love and grace they would soon get the opportunity to share and express. After all, there is nothing Light beings love more than that.

"I will now read the list of service opportunities. You will know which of these is in sync with your path of unfoldment. When you hear the opportunity that lights up for you, raise your halo and step forward."

"Here's the first one: we need a group of souls to take on healing of the prevalent human experience of "toxic core shame." If you accept this Assignment, you will paratroop into a human family that will treat you in ways that strongly bring out that experience in you. You will likely interact with other agents from our team throughout the early part of your lifetime, who will serve you by continuing to draw you into experiences that reinforce you feeling ashamed of yourself. Your Assignment will be to fully show up and feel it all, allowing it to almost destroy you so you fully taste this experience.

Then, when you've hit the human experience called "bottom" or "vairagya," some of our special helper Agents will show up. They will serve by pulling you out of the pits of despair and start reminding you of who you really are. You will be supported in entering a process of gradual recovery. Through your growing awareness, you will re-learn to love and forgive yourself. Eventually, you will fulfill the next phase of your Assignment, by sharing your love and Light with growing numbers of others who are going through the healing of toxic core shame. In fact, you will then become one of our Team Light helper agents. Pretty cool system, eh? Who would like to volunteer?"

A big group of souls immediately raised their halos and resolutely stepped forward. They knew that they were called to this glorious service. They were psyched, even thinking brave things like "yeah – bring it on!" These volunteers were immediately dispatched to the birthing process. Without hesitation, the Being continued.

"We're going to move right along because there are lots of other Assignments to give out. The next one is "disease." At different points in your human life, you will go through the full experience of seeing how your belief in separation from All That Is, reinforced by traumatic influences from those around you, manifest as various forms of dysfunction in the dense physical body you will be birthed into. You will experience coming to the brink of losing your freedom, joy or ability to fully function, or even coming close to the illusion known in the human realm as "death." Others of you will experience sicknesses of the mind that seem to block most or all of your Light and create tremendous feelings of fear and imbalance. As with the shame group, helper Healer agents will show up at opportune times to help ease your symptoms and give you hope. Eventually, you will remember the unlimited master healer aspect of your true self, and you will be able to fully or partially overcome the state of dis-ease. Most of you will then become Healer agents who help others to recover. Who will volunteer for this Assignment of Love?" Another eager group of souls raised their halos and stepped forward.

As this pre-birth conference unfolds, groups of souls accept Assignments of Love to help transform alienation, addiction, abandonment, poverty, racism, injustice, oppression, polarization, ignorance, violence and all the other pressing issues of humanity. As soon as each group stepped forward to volunteer they were dropped into a developing fetus in a well-matched woman's womb.

As these volunteer souls are born into the world they are still innocent and full of Light. They still mostly remember their mission and who they really are. But mysteriously, in a short time, amnesia sets in. They start identifying with their physical body and developing mind. They mostly forget who they really are. Their Assignment of Love begins.

That's the end of this story, yet each of us is continuing to live the real version of it.

From the perspective of your Avatar self, the issues that arise in your body and mind are really impersonal. They come up because you volunteered to help heal them, not really because they're "yours." In other words:

It's wise to not take your personal experiences personally!

As you come to accept all that arises as opportunities to practice Love and be of service, a shift in your sense of identity starts to happen. You identify less with your small self and more with your universal self. This is true freedom.

Practice – Recognizing your Assignment of Love

To help identify your particular Assignment of Love, take this short quiz:

1. What interests, hobbies or forms of creative expression have you been drawn to from a young age?

2. What experiences of life have you repeatedly struggled with or felt wounded about? Which of these areas of life has been the most challenging for you:

    a. Relationships

    b. Physical health

    c. Mental/emotional health

    d. Family dynamics

    e. Career and life path

    f. Money – having it or not having it

    g. Personal identity – coming to know your genuine self

    h. Spirituality – self-realization, overcoming mental stress, trauma or overactive mind

3. What has emotionally triggered you the most, time and time again? What has continued to push your emotional buttons in the most challenging way, even after you have worked on yourself in these same areas repeatedly through therapy, healing sessions, meditation, mindfulness and more?

4. In what areas of your experience have you gone through a lot of pain and struggle, and then later found yourself helping others with the same issues? Rather than only focusing on areas in which you have professional training, consider the ways you have benefitted others just by you being yourself. For instance, some people show natural qualities of leadership and generosity. Others instinctively know how to comfort friends or family members when they are hurting. There are also those who consistently speak out against injustice and seek justice for others. Others have natural mathematic abilities and are able to help kids who are struggling with it.

There are also those who may not seem to be so helpful to others in their early years because their awareness was directed inside themselves, exploring their consciousness and self-healing. Yet many of these who seemed self-absorbed break out as powerful healers, teachers and creative expressers as they mature.

Your replies to these questions show you a lot about your Assignment of Love. A great way to delve into this question more deeply is to start writing in a journal several times a week. Intend to discover more about what that is and what your highest mission is at this time. Even if you think you know your purpose and mission in life, this could be a great time to do an update.

Your Assignment of Love is closely related to your superpowers. Our superpowers make us able to embrace and fulfill our Assignment of Love.

Working with Your Assignment of Love Moment to Moment

Once you have recognized your Assignment of Love and what it feels like, your life can become a continuous process of fulfilling your assignment. The simple key is bringing your Avatar transmission to parts of your own body in which you are feeling discomfort associated with your Assignment of Love. Instead of seeing times when you are feeling disturbed by your issues as negative or downer times, you can accept them as opportunities for getting stronger and clearer. Here is an example from my recent life to help make this clearer.

I figured out a long time ago that one of my main Assignments of Love is working with feelings of abandonment. While I have been through a great deal in my life, my deepest pains have consistently been around experiences and feelings of abandonment, isolation and rejection. I've had these feelings even during times when I had a lovely circle of friends, clients and strong family connections. That showed me that these feelings were not coming from the present time but were part of my inner emotional landscape.

Some interactions I had with a new friend triggered these core feelings again. Because I really wanted to be accepted by this person, my insecurities were activated. I could see myself projecting my energy outward, making me feel increasingly fearful and disempowered. I had been in a clear, inspired place for a while before this experience, so when those feelings of abandonment surfaced, I recognized they were coming from my old programming.

I resolved to practice what I preach and to use the methods presented here to work with myself. I took a break and walked down to the bay near my home. I first asked myself where in my body I was most strongly feeling these feelings of rejection. My attention immediately went to my heart and solar plexus areas. I then did some qigong exercises, running my breath and energy through that area. Although the discomfort did not totally release, it began to ease. But the painful feelings intensified again later that day. As I was cutting vegetables in my kitchen, I kept seeing this person in my mind. Circular thoughts of why this person allegedly rejected me intensified, and I could feel that old familiar shutting-down sensation in my chest. I resolved to hold myself tenderly in love. I pulled my energy back into my body from the person I had been projecting outward onto. This required a letting go of the feelings of rejection and abandonment that my ego had been starting to obsess about.

I breathed my transmission once again into my heart and belly, slightly squeezing the internal muscles in those areas in an Inner Embrace. This time I felt a significant shift into inner peace and serenity. My soul gave me a big YES message to tell me that I had just gotten an "A" for responding appropriately to my Assignment of Love. I sensed that in some intangible ways, my choice had also just lightened up "abandonment" a little bit for others who were caught up in it.

So, in summary, the process is:

You'll know you are elevating your Master game when your Assignment of Love starts feeling like the high experience of Love and self-realization it really is.

Avatar Roadmap #10
Working With Your Assignment of Love

1. Identify what your Assignment of Love is.

2. The next time you feel the discomfort of the difficult experiences you are helping heal through your Assignment experience, resolve to bring your love and transmission to it.

3. Pull your energy back into your own body from whoever or wherever you had been projecting it outwards onto.

4. Ask where in your body the focal point of the issue is. Breathe your transmission through your Central Axis. Focus your love and breath on that focal point, slightly tightening the internal muscles there in an Inner Embrace.

5. Let go of any need to resolve anything externally, and simply be present with yourself and your feelings.

6. Continue until you feel a release or lightening.

17

Your Job Description as a Lightworker

To make things clear, let's start this chapter with some clarification of terminology. The following three inter-related terms are used frequently throughout this book:

Transmission: Your highest divine source essence expressing through your human embodiment.

Avatar: Human beings who have gone through sufficient *Christing* of their body and mind to be able to radiate their divine transmission to others. Avatars are able to serve at high levels through their awakening superpowers.

Lightworker: Avatars who serve in specialized ways by bringing higher light to humankind.

It is useful to create a distinction between Avatars and Lightworkers (LW) because not all Avatars act as Lightworkers. See Chapter 1 for the explanation of this point. Although in their essence all Lightworkers are Avatars, many are still relatively unaware of the power and support of their transmission. These are the ones most likely to get drained or burned out in their work.

When most people hear the term Lightworker it may sound to them like a diffuse New Age phrase like hippie or flower child. In reality, Lightworker has a much more specific and powerful meaning. It refers to a group of capable souls who have a vital mission in the reclamation of our world. In fact, Lightworkers may have the most important mission of all in pulling humanity through our current crisis point, even more so than politicians, scientists and business leaders. Fortunately, Lightworkers infiltrate all of those groups. I will use the abbreviation LW from this point forward in this chapter to refer to Lightworkers, in the singular or plural.

We could compare the role of LW to the military special forces. Those are elite, highly trained individuals who have to qualify through rigorous testing to be accepted into the program. Unlike military personnel, LW are trained in the arts of consciousness awakening, spiritual alchemy, transmuting negative energies and miracle healing. They show up in large numbers during times of great challenge and upheaval. That's why there are so many of us around now. If you are not yet sure if you are a LW, reading this chapter may help make it clearer for you.

While it is likely there are LW among other non-human beings in the Universe, this book is focusing on the human experience of being a LW.

The key to knowing who you are as a LW is that this is something you are already doing. This is who you already are, not some new techniques you go to a workshop to learn. What can happen now is you recognize and more consciously align with this part of you. Are you ready to be dis-illusioned? We often think of disillusionment as a downer, depressing experience but it actually can be just what awakening LW need the most. It can be just what is needed to motivate you to focus your mind within yourself by dialing back some other, lesser priorities in your life. This is the experience of *vairagya* which is a prime pre-requisite for spiritual awakening.

LW periodically go through periods where they need some training, just as is necessary for coming into mastery of any advanced skill. "When the student is ready the teacher appears." Teachers and mentors show up when you are ready to step up to living as a LW. A good one will help catalyze your remembrance and update your skills. What LW gain from other LW mentors is really not so much about learning new information because we already have great knowing within our soul memory. It is more a process of *activation* – reawakening this magnificent part of you that may have been sitting on the back burner of your experience. As a LW, it is important that when you do work with teachers you eventually come into completion of your training periods, and claim your own strength and leadership. Beware of any teachers who try to hold onto you over long periods of time as permanent students.

Lightworker Avatars tend to serve in groups, even if they are physically distant and have not yet met each other on the physical level. Each group specializes in a form of service. Although LW have unique traits and personalities, our orientation tends to be toward our service team. According to my sources of information, these are the major LW specialties:

1. **The Quantum Healer Group** – LW who specialize in the alchemy of miraculous transformations in people's health and well-being. Within this group, there are many sub-categories, with one important one being trauma treatment specialists. While many LW are energy healers or drawn into the fields of acupuncture and other holistic healing systems, LW are also found in the allopathic medicine fields. These medical LW often face conflicts as they attempt to reconcile their inner inspiration to heal from source with the constraints of operating within their medical scope of practice. There are also increasing numbers of LW in the fields of social work who are out in the trenches of society bringing light to people suffering from addiction, homelessness, mental illness, domestic abuse and more. Another specialty within the Quantum Healer Group is "healers to the healers". These specialize in supporting other LW in reconstituting themselves after they get overly burdened or stuck, or who need help embracing their next level of embodiment or spiritual initiation.

2. **The Salvation / Transmutation Group** – This is a huge group right now. These are specially trained LW who go to areas where dark energies are seriously threatening the freedom, well-being and Ascension of beings. They are specially trained in transmuting dark energies. However, this is a high-risk group, much like the military Special Forces. Many LW in this group have been compromised or blown apart.

3. **The Teacher Group** – These LW have variations on the superpower of Light Translator. They have been "all over the Universe" and have brilliant gifts for integrating many forms of multi-dimensional knowledge and experience, and presenting it in ways people can grasp. They may be openly teaching about ascension and spiritual transformation or be more undercover – holding higher consciousness while teaching more common subjects to children or adults. In either case, they emanate Light fields affecting people more than the subject matter they are sharing. The Teacher Group of LW is also responsible for many books, seminars, webinars and multi-media presentations.

4. **The Art and Media Group** – These LW tend to infiltrate into the art, music, broadcast and movie-making industries, slipping highly transformative messages and frequency downloads into their works. The LW in this group use special skills to get past the censors who try to block content too close to

home in awakening people to who they really are and suppress information about what is happening in the world. Musicians and artists have had a lot of license in putting themes of consciousness into their work for a long time, and big movie-making companies have become much more open to LW themes in major motion pictures in recent decades. It is my understanding that the Archangel called Metatron has worked closely with the Media Group of LW and helped get the powerful truths within the movie *The Matrix* and others on a similar level into mass circulation.[85]

5. **The Religion Group** – Organized religions are based on the life and teachings of great Avatars from the past. Religious dogmas and practices have gotten far away from the pure transmissions of truth their source Avatars brought, yet their direct influence remains thanks to the Religion LW group. For example, the Christian LW Group ensures that the pure transmissions of Jesus continue to be present in as many churches as possible, and they keep recruiting members who are open to the direct experience of becoming Christed. The same applies for Judaism, Islam, Buddhism and the other major religions.

6. **The Science and Technology Group** – LW in this group help introduce technologies and insights from advanced consciousness sources and prove them out scientifically.[86] Their aim is to elevate the well-being of humanity and help protect it against dark technologies interfering with our health, freedom and spiritual development. A great deal of advanced technologies which could heal and empower people, and create energy independence have been suppressed by profit-seeking corporations, and this LW group works to make them commonly available.

7. **The Earth Group** – These LW work to help heal and stabilize Earth energies and protect the Earth from harm. They also work with animals and the elemental kingdoms.[87] Many in this group graduated through the traumas of the destruction of Atlantis, which was connected with the mis-use of cosmic

---

[85] An Archangel is a powerful type of angel who serves broadly from the spiritual planes

[86] Some of these advanced technologies may have originated from what we would call advanced extra-terrestrial civilizations

[87] Elementals are simple conscious beings who express through plants, minerals and many forms of Earth energies. They help regulate weather and the cycles of nature. Many of the natural disasters like unusual floods, droughts and wildfires happening recently are associated with imbalance of elementals due to human depredations

and Earth energies. These LW vowed to serve the Earth to set things right after that.[88]

8. **The Children's Group** – These LW specialize in protecting children, especially those with strong spiritual gifts such as the so-called Indigo children.[89] They often gravitate toward being teachers of children or working within children's aid organizations working for children's rights. Some specialists in this group work to end the abuse and sex trafficking of children and young adults.

9. **The Military / Law Enforcement Group** – There are many dedicated LW infiltrated into the military and police. They act as a tripwire to reduce the influence of dark influences in those fields and to help preserve freedom and democracy. The Military Group also helps protect LW in other groups, including those in the Political Group.

10. **The Business Group** – We hear a lot about corporate executives who misuse their influence and harm the environment, but there are also many in high positions in corporations who are dedicated LW. They have been powerful influencers in the direction of more transparency, innovative products and reduced environmental impact.

11. **The Political Group** – There are two main subgroups within the LW Political Group:

    a. Higher consciousness, idealistic people with a lot of charisma who manage to get elected to office, and then influence policies into more just and enlightened directions.

    b. Over-Lighted Politicians – These are politicians who have been beholden to their political party and often compromised in various ways as politicians tend to be. Yet they possess enough innate virtue so that at times of great need they are able to be influenced by Divine Source or other LW working in the non-physical space. Once this happens, they may change their ways and start working from higher consciousness to promote the greater good of all, often against great opposition. LW in the Military Group sometimes help to protect them.

---

[88] Atlantis was an ancient civilization written about by Plato and many other authors reputed to have achieved high levels of technology and attunement with cosmic spiritual energies

[89] Indigo children are those born with visionary and telepathic gifts more highly developed than most children

12. **The Cosmic Group** – These are LW who mostly remain out of the physical realm, and work toward Ascension and planetary healing from higher dimensions. There are many sub-groups including Ascended Masters, Archangels and beings who are said to help serve and govern many worlds called the Galactic Council.[90] LW need to be discerning when "tuning into" and working with the Cosmic Group because even some of these have been compromised by dark energies. Yet most of them continue to hold the purity of their commitment to the Divine Source. When invoking the support of Ascended Masters and others in the Cosmic Group always clearly specify "… of the Highest, Pure Light". For example: "I am calling on Archangel Michael of the Highest Pure Light to assist me in this healing session now." By sincerely doing that you won't connect with counterfeit, 4D imposter spirits.

13. **The Lover Group** – These LW are masters at holding loving presence. They may be in any of the other LW groups, or they may not seem to be doing much at all. Their job is love. Love melts all blockages.

14. **Frequency Holders** – These are LW whose service is doing consistent meditation and holding frequencies of peace, love, awakening and the like. They are rarely known by the public and may be in any walk of life including nursing homes, monasteries, hermits, nunneries or even part of the homeless population.

There is no doubt there are other Lightworker specialty service groups not described above. If you are aware of any I missed or would like to add to or correct any of the information above, your suggestions will be welcomed. Please visit my website or social media pages and post your comments. See the Resource section in the back of this book.

What Lightworkers Go Through

What is written previously may make being a LW sound glorified or clear-cut, but that is not the way it is. Most LW go through challenging lives – internally and externally. So many I know have dealt with childhood trauma, chronic pain, health issues, personality disorders, feelings of loneliness and isolation, and numerous "dark nights of the soul." That's because LW have committed themselves to serve

---

[90] See Definitions of Terminology for explanations of these terms

in high-level ways in many lifetimes, and have experienced lots of pushback as a result. This could have taken the forms of being persecuted, imprisoned, tortured, ostracized or even corrupted into joining the dark side at times.

Because LW are much better at healing others than healing themselves they tend to carry forward loads of painful psychic burdens in their subconscious minds and body cellular memory. I can personally attest that trying to get help for my own brands of pain and suffering was often frustrating because no one seemed to really understand my issues or what to do about them. I know what it's like to consult with a series of advanced healers and health practitioners who seemed to be helping so many people but were unable to do much for me.

Yet somehow most LW do heal and awaken, and the moments of joy, lightness and divine revelation expand. Eventually, LW realize they are Avatars and there is really nothing to fix or change about themselves. By profoundly accepting who we are and being willing to bathe the parts of ourselves we have tried to fix and "get rid of" in our own source transmission, we do experience miracles of healing.

Some LW have had it harder than others. My understanding is that some of those who have served in the Salvation / Transmutation Group described above have taken on the task of transmuting powerful dark energies infiltrating our Universe. Those dark energies turned out to be much more heavy-duty than those LW were prepared for, and as a result, many of them were literally blown apart. Some of those blown-apart souls are now back in human bodies seeking healing for a host of very difficult, convoluted pains, illnesses and psychological issues. It's often been very hard for them to find solutions. Yet it is definitely possible because they are still whole in their true essence. They have had to wait until there was sufficient critical mass of consciousness on our planet to support their healing and reconstitution, much like putting Humpty-Dumpty back together again.[91] It is a great blessing when LW with these issues connect with a qualified Healer to the Healers who really understands what they have gone through and can help them re-connect with their source transmission.

I grew up with feelings of isolation, alienation and feeling like my emotional heart was too damaged to deeply love. I could feel the heavy weight of my own inner wounding throughout my youth. My healing process started when I committed to daily meditation at age 19. Although it took me several months of dedicated practice

---

[91] Humpty-Dumpty is a well-known children's rhyme which seems to be about the experience of blown-apart Lightworkers: "Humpty Dumpty sat on a wall. Humpty Dumpty had a big fall. All the King's horses and all the King's men couldn't put Humpty together again"

to be able to focus, I gradually gained the ability to concentrate on what was real within me beyond my mind.

My inner life since then has been a continual process of bringing my attention back to the love of my heart and bodily-felt divine presence over and over again. I have gradually come into greater mastery of choosing the thoughts I entertain, redirecting my focus away from negative "pretender voices" into affirmation of my true self. This continues to be an ongoing process. As I have persisted with this process, I have become happier and more grateful for the direct experience of who I am. My experiences with clients and group healing work are filled with miracles, and there is nothing better. I now accept that those parts of me seeming to create pain and lower my vibration are the Assignments of Love I have volunteered for, not just "my" personal issues.[92]

The main point here is that the inner work LW are called to do is rarely glamorous. Yes, there are periodic breakthrough experiences full of overflowing love or cosmic consciousness, but what is most important is your steady, persistent inner commitment to keep training your mind to stay Present. Presence is a by-product of continuing to choose to be in love. You expand your love by choosing to step out of the habituated patterns of the lower mind, freeing yourself from magnetic 4D astral addictions[93]. Your path takes place one moment, one breath at a time. That effort is what really counts more than anything else. This is real inner work, and why we're called Light-WORKERS.

Your life really lights up as you stretch yourself past your perceived limitations and put yourself into service to others through your transmission and superpowers. You may not even yet know you have superpowers, but they will emerge as you trustingly share your love and inner gifts.

Because LW tend to have so many lifetimes of challenging experiences to transform, it's not unusual for them to feel tired, anxious or overwhelmed at times. If you often experience that, don't worry about it. Going through those experiences are not signs of failing on your LW path. On the contrary, those experiences are golden opportunities to work with your Ascension practices – the ones taught in this book. Through these practices, you can transform any seemingly negative experiences into soul power, ascension and eventually a joyful, expressive life.

---

[92] See Chapter 16

[93] 4D = fourth dimension- the seductive astral plane of higher mind that is most filled with polarization and illusion these days

All this is to let you know it's OK if things seem difficult at times. You must deeply accept you are an Avatar Lightworker, a Christ in human form. Then things in your life will make more sense.

What really lightens things up is coming together with other Lightworkers. In fact, I believe at this time it's close to impossible to be on this path and not get sidetracked or discouraged without the mirroring and support of your spiritual family. The great phrase Jesus shared: *"When two or more are gathered in my name, there I AM"* is highly applicable and vital at this time. While it's great to connect with most LW you will have the most exciting, co-creative experiences when you connect with those on similar missions. That will really get your inspiration flowing. Invoke the power of love in your heart to call these souls to you and you to them.

A part of my work is bringing Lightworkers together in various ways. If you look in the Resource section in the back of this book, you can learn about the services and resources I've created for that purpose. You may find other resources in your area or through some time devoted to Google searches.

Why Meditation is Essential for Lightworkers

We are highly sensitive, multi-dimensional beings and have a great need to stay connected and attuned with our true selves. I know for myself meditation is one of

the top requirements for my happiness and inner calm. The most valuable forms of meditation for LW are those in which you place your mind inside the experience of your Avatar transmission, centered in your breath. My favorite practice for this purpose is Central Axis Breathing. See Chapter 23 in the Ascension Practices section for detailed instructions.

Many people use the word meditation to refer to any experiences in their lives they love and enjoy, such as painting, playing music, hiking or listening to electronic guided meditations. While it is possible to use any experience to help draw your mind inward, I don't believe such external experiences are substitutes for true meditation, where you close off the outside world and put your attention totally within yourself. Whether this seems difficult or easy to you, it is vital for freeing yourself from the subtlety of the lower mind's control. Many people say things like "I tried to sit in meditation but it was too hard and just doesn't work for me." I believe these kinds of statements are based on a misunderstanding of what meditation is. It is based on a false expectation that it "should" feel peaceful and mellow to meditate. While you will enjoy more of those experiences over time, meditations feeling difficult at first can be equally valuable.

Avatar Roadmap #11
Lightworkers and Meditation

It is the steady, persistent effort to keep bringing your mind back to your breath or body awareness that powerfully creates new pathways within you, and eventually lightens up the oppressive weight of the lower conditioned mind. So even if you feel like a dummy at meditation enter it with inspiration.

Few people expect the first times they go to work out at the gym after being out of shape to be easy and comfortable, and they usually accept discomfort in order to reach their goal of looking and feeling better. In the same way, releasing your expectation that meditation should be easy at first frees you to really progress with your practice. Accept what is. If it feels difficult to concentrate be with that experience. If it feels peaceful and beautiful, enjoy it. I can assure you – if you persist you will gain an inner treasure that will carry you throughout your life and eventually beyond death. I believe that is worth some temporary discomfort.

Protection for Lightworkers

As mentioned above, many LW have recent or old soul memories of major trauma. Many also have felt emotionally polluted or "slimed" through contact with people holding lower vibrational energies. It is, therefore, reasonable to ask "How may I protect myself from being persecuted or "slimed" again? Or – "Why would I want to allow myself to be out in public view as a Lightworker after all the harsh consequences I went through letting myself be out there in the past?"

There are many common protection practices used by LW such as surrounding oneself with white light, asking Archangels for protection or using special mantras or spells of protection. These can all be useful in their right place, just as training wheels on a child's bicycle are helpful until the child finds his own balance. As you come to know and embody who you really are, you can move into a zone where even the idea of surrounding yourself with protective energies can be seen as one more limiting, fear-based belief. When even those you would consider your enemies are seen as part of the same hologram of one-ness you are, you can embrace it all through the power of divine Love. Then the need for these protective practices will diminish. Even more importantly, when you clear your own field of fear you will not draw fearful experiences to you in the first place. That's the greatest form of protection there is. It reminds me of what Bruce Lee demonstrated as "the art of fighting without fighting."[94]

It's a major step of self-responsibility to realize that the greatest threats to yourself spring from the compromised parts of your own mind out of integrity with your core truth. You don't have to go through mental gyrations of techniques, therapies and healings to be safe. You do that by embracing your transmission. When you are present in your transmission nothing can harm you, inside or outside of yourself. This is a most valuable practice – to be your transmission every day and sit with it regularly. One of the highest prayers there could be is "Bring me into conscious communion with my divine transmission more and more each day."

Gratitude is the Attitude

If we could see with the eyes of the soul we would be grateful and rejoicing most of the time. We would be able to see that massive amounts of old psychic baggage is being pulled out of us every day. Even though this can be a rigorous time of challenge and purification for Lightworkers, there is such tremendous grace and

---

[94] From movie "Enter the Dragon" with Bruce Lee

love that allows us to be doing and feeling as well as we are. Some of our greatest assets are our sense of humor, laughter and as much music, dance and celebration as we can enjoy. Each time we choose those experiences we are seeding the reality of our future with light and joy.

The heaviest part is behind us. This ascension is the time for Lightworkers to shine and thrive. If you need help seeing and enjoying that, tap other Lightworkers on the shoulder and ask them to come out and serve with you, and don't forget to play.

18

Being Avatar with Family and Friends

If you think you're becoming more enlightened, go spend some time with your family and you'll find out just how enlightened you really are!

This wry joke has often been shared with people who talk about how elevated their consciousness is feeling after having some kind of transcendent experience. And then they go visit their family, and within hours they may feel challenged, invalidated or resentful. Why? Because their relatives are not about to buy into this new part of them. This all-too-common experience reminds us to be humble because if anyone knows how to push our buttons and burst our spiritual bubble, it's our family members. They've known us throughout our lives and tend to hold onto perceptions of us that are rooted in the past. They frequently get uncomfortable when we claim to be different, or are espousing new sets of beliefs.

The path of conscious awakening to our true, Avatar self is a process of looking within ourselves and cleaning up our act. It is a journey from fear to love and freedom. On this path, our values change and mature from those that are primarily fear-based and small self-centered, to more benevolent sharing and serving. We become less controlled and influenced by outer authorities and more internally guided. Expressing this experience to family members may threaten them. Family members also tend to have strong "bullsh-t meters," and can tell if you are spouting new philosophies that you are not yet fully owning and actualizing. They may push back on you in ways ranging from mild condescension to outright hostility and rejection.

So how to cope with this? Some people avoid their family members who do not support or respect their new spiritual beliefs and experiences. Others do keep connecting with family, but carefully avoid discussing controversial topics that might "rock the boat." If you are protecting yourself this way with friends and family, it's important to remember who the Avatar within you really is.

The Christ Avatar within you is not a new set of beliefs. This true part of you has no agenda or position to defend. It is the presence and transmission of pure love and consciousness. Avatars serve rather than seeking validation or external results. Those who embody the mantle of Christ Consciousness are in a process of evolving and purifying their minds. While in truth that is high and joyful, it can often feel difficult, scary or confronting to our familiar, small self. All of these feelings can, and likely will be mirrored back to you by those people you are close to.

One thing we have control over is our attitudes. If you really want to be an Avatar with your family and friends, choose to see it as a brilliant opportunity to walk your talk rather than emotionally defending yourself or trying to convince them of anything. It is the vibratory radiation of your transmission that speaks much louder than your words.

It is the vibratory radiation of your transmission that speaks much louder than your words.

Know that there's a reason you're in the family you are in, and part of your soul contract is to share your light and your truth with them. And you do that more through your actions and Presence than with any words, preaching or platitudes.

There are three main ways to share your Avatar Light – through your energy transmission, your actions and your words. I purposely put "through your words" last on this list, because the first two are more important. Yet the ways you verbally share are vital. Here are guidelines I can offer from my own experience for being a genuine Avatar with family and friends.

Being Your Transmission

When you are living as an Avatar your vocation is sharing blessings (even though you likely also have a material "day job.") You can see everyday life as a string of opportunities to radiate your transmission. If your profession is in the healing or medical arts, everything you do with your clients can become informed by this sacred vibration.

A key is to practice loving and transmitting unconditionally – sharing your essence without expecting anything in return. This requires a high degree of self-awareness and honesty. You may secretly – or not so secretly – harbor a desire for a particular response from those around you. You may want to be acknowledged, appreciated and accepted. Expecting any of those responses, even though they'd make you feel good, makes your service conditional. Of course, it's completely normal to want to be accepted and appreciated. But it is part of your practice to recognize when you having expectations, and keep letting go of them.

I have found it to be an empowering practice to radiate my Avatar transmission while being relaxed and real around my friends and family. I'm learning to weed out my expectations and needs, allowing myself to flow more within the mystery of relationships without trying to make myself more secure.

Actions Speak

We can only embody our transmission to the extent that we walk our talk. When others witness that we are giving more generously of our time, helping out more, being kinder and more forgiving, and actually more happy they are likely going to want to know what's going on with us. Then when we do speak our truth, there is a greater chance they'll be more receptive.

One of my relatives named Cheryl was quite skeptical when I started talking about being a healer. When I offered her a free healing session she was not interested.

I had to be patient and wait for the right time. That eventually came when Cheryl hurt her hand gardening. I asked if she wanted to receive a healing blessing, and this time she softened and agreed. After a five-minute healing transmission, her hand felt significantly better, and things shifted in our relationship. I realized that when I first presented my new healing work I was hungering to be validated and accepted for it, and that didn't happen. But when I let go of those needs and was more genuinely available to serve in the moment, a genuine and more respectful connection was able to emerge.

Right Communication

Speaking your truth can be very powerful and transformative for you and those you are speaking with. In my experience, it requires a mixture of sensitivity, vulnerability and boldness. A key is to come less from your mind's belief systems and more from your heart. My mind wants to impart its beliefs and have them accepted. My heart really cares about the people I am speaking to and wants to love and serve them. That's a big difference.

The most effective communication combines verbal clarity with bodily-felt sharing of energetic vibration. I have experimented with this. When I have shared my inspired ideas mostly from my mind, the most enthusiastic feedback I usually get from others is "that's interesting." But when my heart is open and I'm sharing the vibratory emanation of my transmission, people tend to be much more engaged and touched. Just like anything else, this takes practice to get comfortable with.

It's important to know who you are talking with. Those who are already open to esoteric, spiritual teachings will tend to be more receptive to hearing the kind of radical messages as are expressed in this book. Others need more rational, scientific explanations before they will take you seriously. Again, I have learned how to express myself in more scientific terms because there is a place where science and spirituality are one. Some of the simplified principles of quantum physics can act as a bridge for many people between rational ideas and multi-dimensional reality.

Your Network of Friends May Change

As you become more inspired to awaken from the dream of our society, you'll often become less interested in some of the things and activities you enjoyed in the past. You may find yourself wanting to improve your diet, cut down on the use of intoxicants and de-clutter your life. It's common to become less interested in some commonly-discussed aspects of popular culture like celebrity gossip or the latest

TV shows. Many people going through this upgrade process find some of their friendships falling away. Some friends may not be able to relate to you anymore, and it's often not easy to find new ones who you better resonate with. This can feel lonely and isolating.

The path of becoming a *Christed* human requires a lot of surrender and letting go. Some people have referred to this process as mini-deaths and rebirths within their lifetime. A friend told me about her time with a local Sufi group, a spiritual path bringing people into mystical union with the divine Beloved. She shared that some Sufi practitioners call their way "the path of the broken heart" because that's how some of the emotional surrender they often go through feels to them. Yet they also describe heights of mystical joy in their newly-expanded hearts after they have been broken. From the viewpoint of our fragile, insecure ego selves, these letting-go experiences can feel excruciating. Yet at the same time, our souls are cheering us, saying "Right On!" The more you allow the old to fall away, the more Soul-oriented and guided you become.

If you trust this process, you will find new friends showing up in your life who vibrate at your new level, and are also going through similar experiences. This is a great treasure. This can also apply to intimate relationships. I have been experiencing the new relationships that have shown up in my life as precious gifts.

When I first moved here to Marin County, California, I sometimes reached out to people I was interested in, trying to establish friendships with them. I often felt disappointed by their lukewarm responses. Recently, that pattern has shifted, and new friends have been showing up without me looking for them. It feels like I have allowed a beacon to light up above my head that allows others to find me more easily on the subtle energy pathways. I'm not saying that no effort is required to make new friends, more that on the truest level it's an "inside job." I love how I can speak much more freely to my new friends from my heart, and they receive and appreciate it more of the time. I also receive so much from their shares. These new friendships are more based on mutual love and commitment to awakening than agreements to meet each other's needs.

The following practice can work to support you in manifesting what you want in relationships, from the inside out.

Relationship Manifestation Ceremony

Sit in front of your altar or any place where you can be quiet or undisturbed. A beautiful place out in nature can be suitable. When in front of your altar, a burning candle or incense helps to establish the sacred space.

Connect within yourself. Engage with the foundational practices – Purity blast, grounding, Master hook-up, complete breath, coming back to yourself and loving presence. Then enter into Central Axis Breathing.

After meditating for a few minutes, put one hand over your heart and tune into the experience of love. Think about the person, animal, place or aspect of Divine that most easily brings up that experience for you. Feel the energy of love as a bodily sensation and intend to amplify it. You can because it is what is real. Intend to amplify your experience of love. Once you feel the energy sensation of love breathe it up and down the central axis of your body containing your chakras. Visualize the pink or golden energy of love spreading out throughout your body, targeting and permeating every cell in your body. Breathe deeply into your cells to accept the love.

If you become aware of any uncomfortable emotional or physical feelings as you enter into this practice, work with the Inner Embrace (Chapter 24). Take some time to identify where in your body those feelings are most noticeable. Squeeze the muscles around that area and send your breath through it, holding those areas in love, tenderness and Presence as much as you can.

When you feel ready, use your imagination to see yourself spending time with beloved soul friends. Claim that experience in present time, as if you are having that experience now. See yourself sharing what you would love to share – meals, fun, dancing, deep conversation, comfortable hanging out, laughter, hiking, service projects, whatever is in your heart. Be as detailed as possible in your visioning and don't worry if it is not real clear, just do the best you can. What is most important is to allow yourself to feel the warm, loving feelings of being with your friend or friends, not as a desire or longing for that experience but actually HAVING the experience!

If you are wanting to manifest an intimate, romantic relationship the same process applies. Acknowledge your desire and claim your worthiness to be with a partner you would really love to be with. As before, if feelings of sadness, unworthiness, shame, numbness or any other denial of love come up find its focus in your body and practice the Inner Embrace. Enjoy having the feelings now of desire, intimacy, sexiness, play, sincere communication, sharing projects, being on vacation or whatever else you would love to share with a lover.

I have found great value in repeating this mantra:

I AM in love, I AM loved, I AM loving, I AM loveable, I live in abundance always.

As I speak each statement, I feel the truth of it in my body. If I notice any feelings of resistance to the free expression of any of them, I address that through the Inner Embrace or relaxing further into my open-heart space.

What I have discovered in my life is that the further I go on my ascension path, the more surrendered I feel about getting the things I want and need – especially in the realm of relationships. I've lived through enough years trying to get what I thought I needed and witnessing the often disappointing results. Now I am more focused on being a lover than on looking for one.

Now I am more focused on being a lover than on looking for one.

This process of "looking for love in all the wrong places," getting repeatedly disillusioned and then finally moving into surrender and trust in the Divine could be called "relationship vairagya."

It's helpful to remember that all our relationships are reflections and mirrors of our one truest relationship – the one we have with divine Source. Source leads us through experiences that break down our blockages and denials of Love, so we know that we are one with the Divine.

19

Money and Virtue

What is the first image that comes to your mind of the financial status of an Avatar or Christ-like person? If you're like most people, that image is usually of someone with very few material possessions who wanders from one place to another living off the donations of others. That is how Jesus and Buddha, two of the most prominent Masters in history have been portrayed to us.

In the 1970's a wave of spiritual teachers from India and other Asian countries came to the United States and Europe to start movements. These teachers often taught the monastic virtues of living simply, or even in poverty, as ways to increase spiritual growth. Their followers heard loads of teachings about the virtues of renunciation – giving up on the accumulation of money and the pleasures of the material world.[95] Many of us also heard repeated teachings about the virtue of being desire-less. Is it any wonder that so many people following spiritual paths are often living at the lower end of the income spectrum, and frequently experiencing financial struggles?

Here are some vital questions for Lightworkers to ask: What is money and what is its role? In this new time of spiritual ascension on Earth, how do Lightworkers best deal with money and the accumulation of wealth?

Money is energy, just like everything else in the Universe. On the material level, it is the currency of exchange for things and services passing between people and businesses. In the old days, money was made of gold, silver or other

---

[95] Yet some of these spiritual teachers lived lives of material wealth themselves

precious substances, and so had an intrinsic value of its own. In our modern society money rarely has any physical value and has morphed into streams of electronic data transmitted between secure servers over the internet.

There is also a non-material currency of exchange on the level of heart and spirit which can be referred to as *virtue*. Virtue is the core value within our lives. It is what allows us to "feel good" on many levels, and it's the positive presence people pick up on when they connect with us.

Virtue is what allows us to grow and elevate on the spiritual level, helping build the critical mass within the soul that is needed to permanently ascend in consciousness.

We each have quite a bit of virtue just from being alive because life is so intrinsically precious. We create additional virtue through sharing our love, resources and superpowers with others. Both the virtue we are born with and the virtue we create accumulates within our soul, acting like a non-material bank account. If we invest our virtue wisely by developing our higher abilities and sharing ourselves and our gifts abundantly with others, our virtue account is compounded. Life is rich!

The more virtue accumulated, the more easily money comes to you because money is the material equivalent of virtue. When we keep creating virtue, generously giving and being open to receive that is called living in abundance.

But, you might ask, what about some of the seeming anomalies, such as some wealthy people who seem to be acting in decidedly un-virtuous ways, and highly virtuous people who seem to be perennially struggling for money? Let's look at both of those situations.

Why Good People Struggle Financially

We all know good-hearted people who genuinely care about others, and yet always seem to be living on the edge financially, never getting ahead. I have worked with many people like this in my healing practices and have dealt with this pattern within myself at times. While such people love to give generously, it seems that they are underdeveloped in their open-ness to receive. This often comes from limiting beliefs about money, such as that only immoral, "bad" people are rich, or that money corrupts. Another common belief among Lightworkers is that there is a scarcity of wealth in the world, and being wealthy would deprive poor people of having what they need. They often feel personally unworthy and undeserving of being wealthy due to the shame associated with past traumatic experiences.

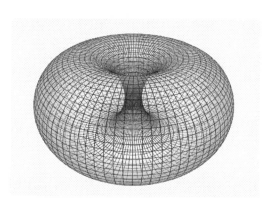
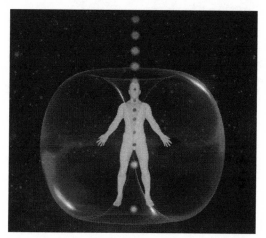

The solution is to realize that the Universe is created to be infinitely abundant, and there is no scarcity of anything that is real. Know that your Divine self loves you infinitely and wants you to live abundantly. In the remarkable movie Thrive I by Foster and Kimberly Gamble, the principle of the energy-circulating *torus* is discussed. This is a dynamic, geometric energy pattern that recurs throughout the Universe, as well as in the energy fields of our bodies and the Earth.

With the help of some philosophers and scientists, Gamble explains that the torus energy pattern is self-replenishing, and therefore inherently abundant. As long as we are flowing with our own toroidal energy pattern we tend to give abundantly and receive abundantly, which is the natural way of life. By this principle, it is possible for every human being on Earth to live abundantly, although this does not mean living ostentatiously.

The Financial Parasites of our World

There are complex reasons for poverty in the world. Poverty in most societies stems from the greed and political ambitions of powerful people who block and disrupt the natural abundance of the people for their own gain. They are able to do this due to systems of repression that take advantage of engrained limiting attitudes on

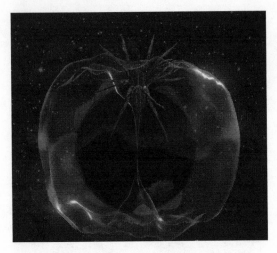

the parts of the poor people themselves. The <u>Thrive</u> movie shows a video image in which the free-flowing energy of the torus is being sucked and diminished by a parasitic worm in its center. This powerful image dramatizes how manipulative people can game our financial systems to keep extracting unearned wealth for themselves, thus helping to create unnecessary poverty in the world. The image to the left is a representation of parasitic energies taking from the naturally abundant torus, and is inspired by the Thrive movie.

The system of central banking that has taken control of global financial systems in recent centuries is a big driver of this. Central banks continue to parasitically transfer vast amounts of wealth from those who are creating virtue through their work and contributions to those who are taking it without creating real value for others.[96] This is a major reason for the expanding wealth gap between rich and poor, and the shrinking middle class in many societies. It is also a major cause of inflation of our currencies, continuing to reduce its buying power.

We frequently hear about big corporations and wealthy people who lie, cheat, embezzle, exploit their workers, pollute the environment and sometimes even kill to increase their profits. On one level these people are tapping into high levels of virtue they are converting to financial wealth. Yet they are mixing that with the lower vibrational energies of greed and falsehood. This mixed motivation creates mixed results in our societies and in their personal lives. While these people may live in material splendor and enjoy high levels of power and influence, their hearts and minds are often burdened. It is hard for many of them to feel truly happy or free, as they often fear losing their wealth. Perhaps this is what Jesus referred to when he was quoted as saying:

Again, I tell you, it is easier for a camel to go through the eye of a needle than for someone who is rich to enter the kingdom of God.[97]

---

[96] For a detailed expose of the origins and fallout from central banking see: Griffin, G. Edward, The Creature from Jekyll Island, America Media 1994

[97] The Bible Matthew 19:24

Jesus did not only diss the wealthy people of his time, but he also showed the way to true abundance with this message:

But seek ye first the kingdom of God, and his righteousness, and all these things shall be added unto you.[98]

In that statement, Jesus gave the formula for ultimate success. When we prioritize increasing the treasure of our hearts and spirits through meditation, inner clearing and lovingly serving others, we are "seeking first the kingdom of God." That creates virtue in our souls which can translate into an abundance of material things, opportunities, loving relationships, good health and spiritual awakening.

While there appears to be no shortage of greedy corporations and individuals misusing their power, there are also plenty of reasonably virtuous and benevolent wealthy people. These are the ones who understand that their purpose is to serve and increase the value of life for themselves and others through their contributions. They show us the way to live abundantly and consciously.

Is it Virtuous for Lightworkers to be Wealthy?

In order to clearly answer this question, take a moment to remember that you are a creator being. Your consciousness is part of the same universal power that has created the stars, planets and galaxies. The only thing holding you, or any of us back from living as conscious creator beings is your limiting beliefs and subconscious programming.

Here is a simple visioning exercise. For at least a few minutes, suspend any disbelief you have about being an unlimited creator being. Put aside any beliefs in the illusion of scarcity – that one person having wealth deprives others of having it. From this open place, envision what you would love to see in the world based on enlightened principles and justice for all. Envision how you would love to live. Imagine how people would be living and exchanging with each other in such a world. Imagine a world where so much wealth is created that there is plenty for all. Now, imagine how you could help inspire and lead others toward the fulfillment of that vision.

My Financial Vision

My vision for the New Earth is that greed in all its forms is no longer tolerated, and people all over the world embrace the joy of giving and receiving abundantly.

---

[98] The Bible, Matthew 6:33

They give by bringing through the greatest gift of their Avatar transmission. Their transmission expresses through their superpowers, which create more beauty, healing and value for others. In my vision we are living respectfully and intelligently as stewards of our Earth, sharing its resources and using our brilliant technologies to produce and distribute plenty of food while eliminating environmental pollution and degradation. The high-frequency Light field created through all this virtuous activity creates a real, practical heaven on Earth.

In my vision, all people on Earth live abundantly, including those in so-called third world countries. It has been demonstrated that as people increase their standard of living they tend to have fewer children, thus flattening the curve of population growth. The children who are born become better educated and better able to express their superpowers. All of this helps to reduce poverty.

Part of the process of becoming Christed is attaining mastery of the physical plane, and that includes money. As we clear the illusions we have been tangled in, we come to see that everything real is happening within ourselves. Our degree of health or sickness, success or struggle, love-filled life or emotional emptiness all originate within our own consciousness. The external world is really a grand screen upon which we project our internal state. We master the physical plane by owning and accepting responsibility for our creative power, removing the obstacles we have placed to living and sharing abundantly. Then the movie reflected back to us as "the world" becomes more pleasing and fulfilling. Another aspect of mastery is claiming sovereignty, which means that we can no longer be controlled or manipulated by other people or non-physical entities.

Avatar's Duty to Live Abundantly

Money is the material equivalent of virtue, which is what we accumulate through developing ourselves and lovingly serving others. Part of the path of living as an Avatar is transforming our old limiting attitudes about money and self-worth, thereby opening up our higher creative abilities. We are holographically connected with all other people, therefore the more abundance we create the more everybody else is enriched, and vice versa.

So yes, I not only believe that Avatars can live abundantly, *I believe it is an important part of our social responsibility to do so.* By looking within ourselves and clearing our own beliefs in lack and unworthiness, we can demonstrate the natural abundance of the Universe in our own lives. From this place, we can work to help others to do the same.

Direct assistance to people going through financial struggle is often needed in societies to help them move out of crisis mode and access the resources they need. Their greatest benefit comes, however, as they build their confidence in their ability to tap into their own sovereignty and creative power.

The Power of Desire

As expressed in the Creation Story of Chapter 28, the Universe was set in motion through the power of original desire. As expressions of All That Is, we create the same way. In fact, you and I are desiring and creating all the time, yet often unconsciously.

In order to live fully and joyfully as the Avatar you are, it is necessary to cultivate the power of your desires. Acknowledge and feel them fully, seeing yourself already experiencing and having what you want. Ultimately there is no difference between your desire for a beautiful home, a new, loving relationship or a peaceful, ascended society. All of these spring forth from your soul essence, and fulfilling any of them can increase the embodiment of your true self in your body.

If you desire to live an abundant, empowered, love-filled life that benefits countless others (or whatever else you truly desire) let yourself fully feel that desire. Allow it to vibrate through your body. Ask your future self to bring you into the focus and expectancy of what you desire, and then allow it to unfold.[99]

Here's an exciting thought: You are living a beautiful lifestyle that honors the Earth. You are learning day by day to bring out and share more of the spiritual treasure of your Avatar transmission. Part of your awakening is the activation of your visions of what you are most inspired to create. You naturally gravitate toward others with complementary visions and enter into innovative partnerships in the realms of art, music, social justice, healing, economics, enlightened technology and sciences and enlightened leadership of societies.

You see the lives of others improving and transforming through your example and support. As they "get it" and claim their own sovereignty and ability to live in abundance, they are able to pass this truth onto more people. In this way waves of abundance, sharing and service ripple out in an ever-increasing geometric progression. Because the myth of scarcity is being proven to be illusory, there is less and less motivation for anyone to be greedy. Those who do try to maintain that

---

[99] The Desire Factor book by Christy Whitman is an excellent guide to the process of fulfilling your desires

old paradigm are given the choice to either heal their own woundedness and greed or be brought to justice so they can no longer take from or harm others. The ever-regenerating energy flow of the torus that we living in is allowed to flow freely, and there is always enough for all. This is the new way of planetary ascension.

20

Living as an Avatar

Being an Avatar is about living authentically, which means truly being yourself. That's priority #1 for us in being able to fulfill our mission of helping humanity successfully make it through this crucial transition time.

Becoming yourself is an ongoing journey. We were born into the dream of the fallen human race, which at times has seemed to take us a million miles away from the pure radiance of our true, multi-dimensional self. In that dream, we've been encouraged to glorify the superficial and manipulated parts of us, mostly denying who we are as an Avatar. The doors of consciousness are now open wide for us to step out of the taboo against knowing who we really are, so we can free ourselves from all those control systems.

What this requires is a letting go of all our ideas and beliefs about who and what we truly are – even the ideas expressed in this book! At best this and other media can bring you to the threshold where you are willing and ready to let go into the pure consciousness you are.

This process of awakening can happen instantaneously in any moment, yet being human we generally need to go through a gradual process of embodiment. That is the epigenetic re-wiring of our body I have been calling *Christing* in this book. There is a lot of opening, releasing and integration in that process. This is why it is vital to take time each day for Ascension practices.

After hearing numerous people talk about self-love, I wondered what it really looks like. Now I know that one of the most essential ways to love myself is through a healthy discipline of daily practice. I do that because it is quite clear that taking time to marinade in my transmission while focusing within my central axis every

223

day makes me happier and more fulfilled, regardless of where I have been on the spectrum of my emotional ups and downs.

Living as an Avatar is about cultivating the quality of loving Presence. That requires being willing to release the psychic debris of fear and trauma so there's more space for being fully alive in your body. It means being willing to make a sacrifice in order to live in a miraculous, embodied state. That sacrifice is the choice you can make one breath at a time to let go of your addiction to the mind. We need to sacrifice the ego's tendency to keep running from the Now moment into falsely comforting, or quasi-entertaining illusions. Not a bad bargain, but your ego will throw a fit trying to tell you it's impossible, it's too hard, it's unrealistic, that it's woo-woo, you're too old or you're too young. Don't believe a word of that. Take back your power.

The story about the man seeking enlightenment in one day from Chapter 9 is all about that process. In my view, the demons in that story are the insistent, seductive pretender voices within the mind that repeat discouraging, fear-based messages. The one who can really walk all the way through the long building is your Christ Avatar self. That is already who you really are. In fact, not only can the Christ walk through the building unscathed, he can also make the 10,000 demons inside of it his willing allies. She can take back all the power she had previously felt split off from and put outside of herself.

If you were to run into a true saint or master, you would expect him to be fully present with you – to listen to you with full concentration and then reply from a place of love and inner stillness. We've idealized people like that, almost like they're some kind of freaks for us to admire or even worship. They seem to be living such an abnormal life compared to the role models we grew up around. Yet this is how we are meant to live, minus the old images of being martyrs and living in poverty that we've often associated with saints. Let go of every idea of what saints should look like or used to look like in the past. You could be your own kind of saint who digs hip hop dancing or loves to remodel and flip homes in the real estate market, is a community organizer or a trial lawyer. The externals are not what it's about anymore.

Living as an Avatar requires a firm commitment to train your mind to be the servant it was meant to be instead of the mad scattered emperor it has mostly become. This book contains the tools you need to train your mind and claim freedom. You'll be motivated to actually use them when you have obtained sufficient *vairagya*.

Embracing Life Through Vulnerability

Traditional images of ancient Avatars such as Krishna and Rama from Indian scriptures depict them as fully divine beings in human bodies. In other words, they didn't appear to have any character defects to overcome, or personal growth to go through. They were allegedly born perfect. Legends of Quan Yin, the goddess of compassion tell how she lived with extreme piety and devotion throughout her human lifetime, attaining full liberation from the suffering of material life. Yet she gave up the bliss of liberation so she could go back to Earth and serve suffering people. The stories of Jesus and Buddha, on the other hand, reveal the very human struggles they went through on their path of spiritual initiations to become Christed. They demonstrated true vulnerability.

That's how true masters live. They embrace the full range of feelings of being human and keep choosing love through it all. They can take it on the chin when necessary because they are grounded in their transmission, which is the most secure thing there is. It's the user-friendly, directly experiential aspect of God Almighty expressing through you.

It's vital to know that you are always in your ultimate classroom of mastery. While you may enjoy traveling internationally to sacred sites, such trips are not necessary for your learning and ascension process. That's because you find your perfect classroom in exactly what is already happening in your life and relationships. You find it in exactly what you are experiencing within yourself in each moment. This quote from *The Way of Mastery* says it well:

> If you have decided you want to awaken, you have already called to yourself every experience that can truly best serve your awakening…It means that right here and right now you are already demonstrating the power that you are seeking – to command the whole of creation to serve you in that awakening…The result is that your ordinary daily life is the most perfect ashram[100] you could ever be within. It is the holy city to which it is wise to make pilgrimage every day, which means to bring awareness and commitment to exactly what you are experiencing. To be thankful for it, to bless it, to embrace it, to be vigilant and to be mindful (by asking): What is this moment teaching me?

Once you get how amazing it is for you to hold the presence of your transmission, you can express your individuality fearlessly. You can afford to be vulnerable, feeling all the joys and pains of your human experience. A saint has not risen above feeling

---

[100] Shanti Christo Foundation, The Way of Mastery, Lesson 3. Ashram, which means "shelter" in Sanskrit, refers to places where people visit or live so they can engage in dedicated spiritual practices free from the distractions of human society. In a more transcendent sense ashram refers non-material places of learning for souls working with particular Masters

hurt. In fact, in the Roman Catholic tradition saints were mostly martyrs who went through hideous suffering. That's no longer called for in this age. What's appropriate now is allowing yourself to feel deep love, the grief, the crushing losses, the joys and the tenderness. To be aware of the intense wobble of what's happening on the planet now, and yet to keep your vibrational focus floating above it as much as possible, like a lotus flower floating above the swamp. To heal with a loving thought as soon as you hear about a person or situation in need.

Elevating Yourself Through Service

An Avatar is all about service. Avatars have given up the idea that there is anything else for them other than to serve. To the ego-mind that may sound demeaning, boring or flat. "But then how am I going to have fun?" But I've learned that it's the most fulfilling way of being. Because in a state of loving Presence and connectedness, serving others from your transmission and superpowers is an engaging, poignant, heart-opening, unpredictable dance – perhaps some of the greatest fun there could be!

I believe a time will come on this Earth, perhaps sooner than we believe, in which ascension of consciousness will be in full expression. Most people will know that they are divine and connected to infinite love. They will learn how to manifest all that they need abundantly. They will be busy discovering and expressing their superpowers as creator beings. That will certainly be wonderful, and by that time Lightworker – healers won't be as much in need. Everyone will be their own healer and there won't be that much for you and me to do anymore. In THIS time, however, in which so many people are greatly suffering our services are urgently needed. This is our time to activate the master healer within us and shine. Isn't it great to be needed?

You get to experience being a hero of humility, a miracle healer, and to express your own brand of brilliance. You get to experience the truest fulfillment because what that really means is fulfilling both your worldly and higher spiritual purpose at the same time. Being an Avatar is not just about your path and your service. You are also in the ultimate relationship as part of the network of Lightworkers. You will get to experience the truth of "when two or more are gathered there I AM" beyond your current comprehension. That is because the power of Team Light is unlimited when we acknowledge the holographic One-ness we are all part of. That power is much greater than all the perpetrators and dark agendas of this world put together. Why? Because it is real and outside of the control matrix.

None of this is meant to sound glamorous or easy. You are facing the ultimate challenge, but because you are Avatar you are equal to it. We are called into active duty at this time, and not at our convenience. This is the time to give our all. You get to be on the greatest possible adventure that you could imagine – being part of the salvation of humanity while we are on the brink of making this great choice between destruction and ascension.[101] I can't think of any epic adventure books or movies grander than that.

In the higher levels of reality that decision has already been made and the Light is already winning. So it's not so much of a choice as it is a crucial time to reduce the amount of suffering there needs to be during this time of clean-up and transition. One of the humorous lines I've enjoyed from activist and comedian Steve Bhaerman (AKA Swami Beyondananda) is "I can assure you that peace is coming to the Earth. I sure hope we humans are around to enjoy it!" You can be one of those who helps makes sure that we humans are able to enjoy it.

101

SECTION 4

ASCENSION PRACTICES

The first two chapters in this section introduce Ascension Practices and offer guidelines and structure for creating your daily practice. The following five chapters provide detailed instructions for learning and working with some of the most profoundly beneficial and transformative practices for supporting your Christing and embodiment process.

21

Introduction to Ascension Practices

Committing yourself to daily practices that move you out of the conditioned mind into living as an Avatar is truly a Hero's Journey.

The Hero's Journey is the archetypal path leading an adventurer to empowerment and fulfillment of his or her higher purpose after overcoming major obstacles. Countless variations of the Hero's Journey have appeared throughout human history, as well as in literature and other creative arts. These range from ancient mythologies to modern movies such as *Lord of the Rings, Star Wars, The Karate Kid, The Matrix* and the animated *Kung Fu Panda*. In all of these examples, the protagonist starts out as an ordinary person (or panda), and is thrust by destiny into facing an evil or challenge that she has to somehow face against great odds. In order to have any chance of success, the protagonist needs to go through a transformative process in which she gains new skills and abilities. In most of these stories, she goes through a period of intensive training with a Master in which she learns how to shed fear and self-doubt and get in touch with a new level of inner power.

The path of embodiment of your true self also requires devoted training. While you can find great value in receiving mentoring and training from others, the most important training is that which you give yourself every day through your Ascension practices.

The following Chapter 22 offers guidance on creating a daily practice plan for this purpose. These practices integrate combinations of meditation, breathwork, visualization, qigong, self-healing and service to humanity and to the Earth. I have been introduced to hundreds of inner practices throughout my life, and the ones presented here are those that have benefited me in the simplest and most direct ways. I am excited to share these with you, in a similar way that people love to share their favorite cookie recipes or hiking trails. These practices are treasures and have raised me up and carried me through many obstacles.

Detailed descriptions of the practices are found in Chapters 25 – 27, and at the ends of some chapters in other sections. A complete list of practices and where you will find them can be found in the beginning and end of the book. Chapter 22 also offers suggestions for combining the practices to create various daily practice routines.

The Choice to Focus

Gaining the true benefits of Ascension practices requires one simple commitment – the choice to focus your mind into the Now moment, one breath at a time, over and over. We have to train our minds to do that. This is not much different from training a dog to walk next to you and not pull on a leash. Training your mind and training a dog both require clear, consistent effort and determination.

It's important to understand that the last thing the mind wants is to stay focused in the Now moment. That feels constricting and scary to the mind because its identity is based on feeling "free" to flit around between the past and future. Yet neither of these are real, being only projections of the mind. The only experience that is real is Now – what you feel in your body and your mind's direct perceptions.

Many people craving inner peace have become convinced it would be valuable to start a regular meditation practice. Yet each time they started meditating they got scared away because their mind put up a big fuss, making them feel antsy and uncomfortable.

I have written about *vairagya* a lot in this book because I believe it is the ingredient that allows you to persevere past your mind's resistance and start enjoying meditation. In other words, when you are sick and tired of feeling sick and tired, you'll finally do something about it. When your true desire to be comforted and supported by what is real within you outweighs your allegiance to your conditioned mind, you'll choose to focus. This is the same choice every masterful person in history had to keep making.

You have a part of your psyche that is often called the inner Warrior. The Warrior is one of the archetypes[102] of human experience that fill the mythologies of most cultures, and our most popular literature and movies. Getting in touch with your

---

[102] Archetypes are aspects of human nature that can be found in all cultures. Common archetypes include the King, the Queen, the Warrior, the Lover, the Betrayer, the Mother, the Father and the Fool.

inner Warrior is essential for being able to focus your mind within yourself. The Warrior is the part of you that can summon the determination to be able to pull your mind out of pleasant or fearful trains of thought back into the Now moment, over and over again. Learn to invoke this powerful part of you as you develop your meditation practice.

The Two Sides of Inner Practice

There are two main aspects to meditation and other Ascension Practices. Those are effort and letting go. Each one requires the other.

I like the phrase "patiently and persistently" to describe the kind of effort needed to truly meditate. Once you have practiced focusing your mind for some time, it is likely you will start to feel more of a spontaneous, enjoyable flow of inner experience. You can relax and let go into that, continuing to focus your mind as needed when you notice yourself thinking about the past or future.

This is similar to the "high" people feel after working out. They learn that making the effort to jog, lift weights or sweat in a Zumba class eventually leads to pleasurable feelings. Therefore, they learn to associate the "pain" of working out with the reward of that high. That is why they keep going back. People who claim, "I just can't meditate, it's too hard for me," are those who didn't persevere after some initial discomfort. That's analogous to someone who wants to develop a strong and "ripped" body, yet then gives up because they feel sweaty and uncomfortable after going to the gym for the first time. Not the way to get into the zone of fulfillment!

I suggest you accept any initial "pain" of sitting and focusing your mind, even if it's acting like a bucking bronco. After some time, you'll discover how beautiful it feels to get into your inner flow. Then you'll start looking forward to your meditation times.

The Art of Dying

Not only does your meditation practice build your capacity for a more enjoyable, embodied life, it also carries you beyond this life.

Most people fear death. They fear the thought of having to let go of everything they have been attached to, the uncertainty about what lies ahead, and the pain they may feel in the process of dying. Here are some words of wisdom – through your regular meditation practice you are facing all those things a little bit at a time now, while you still have a choice. Realize that any antsy or disconnected feelings that come up during your meditation practice are the same ones you'll face at the time of death. The more you bring love, acceptance and your transmission to whatever arises within your inner space now, the more resolved you'll feel and the more familiar you'll be with the deathless part of you when you're ready to leave your body. Your connection to the divine power within your breath, and awareness of your light body will carry you through the deathing process. The only experiences you'll be able to take with you then will be the glow of the love and truth you shared, and the throughline of the inner connection you established while you were alive.

St. Augustine was famously quoted as saying "I die daily". I believe he was referring to the experience of surrendering his mind to the divine in meditation.

Practice from Beginner's Mind

Regardless of whether you've been meditating for decades or it's totally new to you, I suggest you let go of your past associations with meditation and enter these Ascension Practices in the spirit of "beginner's mind." Allow yourself to make a fresh start without fear, expectations or thinking you already know what it is. This is a new time in your life and on Earth. Allow yourself to discover how it can be for you now.

Your consistent meditation practice builds your capacity for embodiment of your true, Avatar self in your body. It's a lot like doing the patient work required to take a neglected plot of ground covered with weeds and trash, and transform it into a beautiful garden full of flowers and lovely landscaping. Once you do the hard work of creating that garden you can come back to it again and again to soothe and restore yourself. Keeping the garden beautiful requires regular maintenance, and doing that becomes a joy and sacred experience for you. Unlike poppy flowers which tend to make you sleepy, the flowers in this garden make you increasingly awake to the boundless love of your true nature.

22

Ascension Practices Plan

The practices in this book are divided into three categories:

I. **Foundational Practices**: A set of very simple forms of inner focus that align your body and mind with your true, Avatar self. You can learn to activate all of them at the same time within 5 – 10 seconds. This is your most basic toolkit for living an embodied life. See Getting Started chapter near the beginning of the book.

II. **Core Daily Practices**: The Core practices are simple and literally life-changing. These are best used on a daily basis to support your process of embodiment and self-healing. Various combinations of the practices requiring different amounts of time are offered below in this chapter. All of the Core Daily Practices are included in the chapters of this Section Four.

III. **Avatar Development Practices**: These practices are offered at the end of many of the chapters in other sections of this book to support you in realizing the message of the chapter. Consider these as part of your Ascension toolkit. Use each tool when you are drawn to develop in that area. While these are not suggested as daily practices, any of them could be used that way.

Below is a list of the practices and how to find the instructions for each, followed by suggested daily practice plans.

Suggested Ascension Practice Plans

Doing any form of *qigong* or yoga in conjunction with the following practice plans is highly supportive and integrating.

Brief Practice (10 - 30 minutes)

Start by engaging foundational practices. Connect with your transmission and move into Central Axis breathing. Focus on each chakra in turn as you move your breath and focus up and down the central axis of your body. Work with the bandhas (inner muscular locks) to keep your attention within the central axis.

If you are aware of any physical or emotional discomfort, add the Inner Embrace to the practice. Locate where in your body the sensations of discomfort are most apparent. Internally hug that area as you breathe through it, directing connection and pure love into it.

If you find that you are losing focus or "spacing out" as you move your attention through any chakra area within the central axis, spend 3 – 10 minutes practicing Breath of Ascension in that area. This will help to rewire the subtle anatomy of that area, building your ability to focus there. Your inability to focus in the area of any chakra is an indicator of some core issue or "residoo-doo" that is creating some kind of veil of avoidance. The cure is the regular application of love and awareness. As you build your ability to focus in those areas you should start feeling lighter or more grounded in associated aspects of your life.

Full Practice (30 – 60 minutes)

Engage foundational practices. Start with 3 – 10 minutes of Cosmic Heart practice while standing or sitting. Combine Cosmic Heart with any other brief qigong moves you know and enjoy in order to circulate *prana* or vital energy through your body. Then sit and work with the same practices listed above for Brief Practice, spending more time with Central Axis breathing and Inner Embrace. After you feel complete with those practices you can sit quietly following your breath or focusing in the center of your head.

30 – 60 minute practice with Avatar healing broadcast

Practice as directed above for a portion of your practice time. When you feel guided, move into offering Avatar healing blessings. Let go into your transmission, affirming divine love in your heart. Invoke the presence of the person, group, animal or being you wish to offer blessings to. Visualize an image or symbol of that person or group in front of you. Hold them in your Christ Avatar love and allow your transmission to bring healing and blessings from the highest source. You can also do this for the Earth and all humankind by visualizing an image of the globe of the Earth in front of you, seeing or imagining billions of points of light on its surface. For more guidance see Section 2, Chapter 13 about Planetary Healing.

AM – PM Mastery

You come into mastery as you train your mind to serve your true self. The conditioned mind's default position is for itself to be in control – flitting between the past and future in a mostly fear-based tumult. This is what has often been called the "monkey mind" because it resembles playful monkeys jumping around from branch to branch of trees.

There are magic windows of mastery available to you when you first wake up in the morning, just before you go to bed at night and right before you start eating each meal. You will increase your mastery and shift your overall experience into a higher vibrational level by taking charge of your experience during these magic windows. Here are guidelines:

Going to sleep at night:

- Create habits of calming your mind before going to bed. One major way is to get off your digital devices an hour or more before bedtime. Others include meditation, journaling to debrief from your day, use of calming essential oils, reading high-level spiritual books or a relaxing shower or bath. If you live with an intimate partner, sharing love and closeness before bed can also be very conducive.

- When you are in bed and ready to drift off to sleep, engage in foundational practices. Command yourself to let go of your experiences of the day and focus on Love in your heart chakra area.

- Go through a few cycles of Central Axis breathing, focusing on each chakra individually a few times. This really helps slow down your mind and promotes deeper sleep.

- Create an intention that you will do the same as soon as you wake up the next morning (or if you wake up during the night) before you do or think about anything else. The intentions we create as we are falling asleep are very powerful.

- Then let go into sleep.

Waking:

- Whenever you wake up, let the very first thing you do be to engage in foundational practices and do a few cycles of Central Axis breathing. Intend to attune to love. Also silently chanting a favorite mantra is a great way to start the day. I love to use this one as I am waking up:

    I am in love, I am loved, I am loving, I am loveable, I live in abundance always

    The 1 – 2 minutes it takes to do these will elevate your life and your daily expression significantly.

- Before allowing your mind's momentum to speed up (or reaching for a digital device), think about your higher intentions for the new day, feeling and seeing it as much as you can.

- There are multiple timelines of experience available to you. If you get out of bed with your habitual mind in charge, you will most likely perpetuate the kind of experiences you are already habituated into. If you wish to step into your ascension timeline of higher consciousness and embodiment, choose that. Imagine there are multiple doorways right next to your bed, each representing a different timeline of experience. Choose the doorway that leads to a higher, more love-filled experience chosen by your Avatar self. Command that door to move right in front of you. Then confidently step out of bed through that doorway. Notice how different your day is compared to days when you get out of bed on the mind's auto-pilot. See details of this practice in Chapter 25.

Before Meals:

- Before each meal, train your mind to stop its momentum. For at least a short time consciously turn away from whatever you have been doing and thinking about.

- Engage your foundational practices for a minute or two and focus on gratitude for all the blessings in your life and for the food you are about to eat.

- This practice is wonderful to share with any other people you are eating with. Most people I know are open to this activity.

Chapter 20 "Living as an Avatar" contains more suggestions for bringing mastery into all the aspects of your life.

23

Universal Axis Breathing & Breath of Ascension

Central Axis breathing is a key embodiment practice – one that allows your divine Avatar self to more fully live and express through your body. Unlike most other meditation practices based on the visualization powers of the mind, Central Axis breathing is tangible and body-centered. Most of the people I have introduced this practice to love it and tell me that it has renewed their enthusiasm and enjoyment of meditation.

The ancient Mayans, who possessed advanced knowledge of astronomy and cosmology, were well aware of the holographic, interconnected nature of existence. They described a vast pillar of energy acting as a central axis of the entire Universe. That's big! They called it the *Kuxan Suum*.[103] They were aware that both the Earth and human body were microcosmic fractals of this universal axis.

The central axis of the Earth runs between its North and South poles. The energy axis of the human body runs between the crown of the head and the perineum area between the legs, traversing the spine and the vertical area in front of it. This central axis is the location of the energy chakras. Meditation practices that focus breath and attention through this central axis of the body are extremely valuable for promoting greater embodiment of our Avatar transmission.

---

[103] See Calleman, Carl Johann, *Quantum Science of Psychedelics*, Chapter 3

In 2019, I met Dr. Sue Morter, a brilliant chiropractor who is now a mentor of spiritual awakening for thousands of people worldwide. I was deeply inspired by the freshness of the teachings and practices she shared in her book *The Energy Codes*, as well as her live events I attended. I loved learning her version of meditation on the central axis of the body she calls Central Channel Breathing.[104] In my decades of spiritual study, I have learned more kinds of meditation than I can count, including many that involved focusing on the energy chakras within the body. I have found

---

[104] See Morter's book The Energy Codes for very thorough explanation of Central Channel Breathing and many other valuable meditation practices

value in many of those practices. The system of Central Channel breathing Morter teaches is now my favorite form of meditation and the one I derive the greatest benefit from. I will share it in this chapter by the name Central Axis breathing, with some of my own additions.[105] Applying yourself to doing this practice regularly will make all that you've been reading in this book practical and experiential for you.

Breathing fully makes a massive difference in all aspects of your life experience. This bold claim is well justified and based on thorough research. Breathing completely is a vital activity on your path of self-healing, empowerment and spiritual awakening.

Most adults breathe shallowly, mainly filling their chest on the inhale and leaving their lower abdomen relatively de-energized. According to Traditional Chinese Medicine and other energy-based healing systems, there are major energy vortices in the lower abdomen that build and store vital energy. Shallow breathing depletes those energy-generating centers, while complete breathing vitalizes them. A primary energy center called the *Lower Tan Tian* is located two finger widths below your navel and about one-third of the way from the front to the rear of the body. It is about the size of your own fist. A simple way to improve your health, vitality and spiritual awakeness is practicing regular deep breathing into your lower abdomen. This energizes your Lower Tan Tian energy center.

Instructions for Central Axis Breathing

In this practice, you focus on moving your breath and attention up and down the column of chakras in the core of your body. Everything about you lies within that central axis – your strengths, your challenges, your superpowers, your hurting or denied feelings, places you celebrate yourself and places you block your own power and leak energy. Your central axis also connects with your greater body, which is made of energy and is far bigger than your physical body.

As mentioned above, your central axis of the chakras is also holographically, energetically connected with the central axis of the Earth and the Kuxan Suum, the central axis of the Universe. Consciously breathing through this axis is the most direct way to bring all these aspects of your totality into alignment. Isn't that awesome?

---

[105] I use that name to be consistent with the teachings of this book

Bandhas

Bandha is a word from Sanskrit that refers to tightening or locking certain internal muscle groups in order to focus energy in that area and prevent energy loss. Squeezing muscles in the areas of the bandhas greatly enhances the results of Central Axis breathing. This prevents your meditation from feeling diffuse or "out of body", which has much less value.

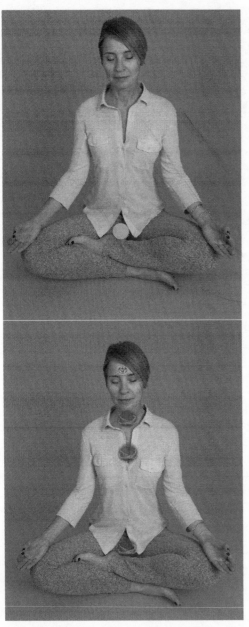

Mula Bandha: The most valuable and commonly used bandha is called *Mula Bandha*, which means "root lock" in English. It is located in the area of the root chakra between your legs, in the perineum area. If you were sitting on the toilet and wanted to stop the flow of urine the muscles you would contract are the same ones you would contract for Mula Bandha. You slightly tighten and pull up on them. This is very similar to the Kegel exercise often taught to pregnant women or people with bladder issues.

There are three more bandhas that are valuable for the practice of Central Axis breathing, as follows:

Heart Bandha: Intend to internally hug the heart chakra in the center of your chest by compressing the pectoral muscles of your chest and the muscles of the upper back between the shoulder blades simultaneously. This helps focus your light and energy through the heart center. Your scapula (shoulder blades) should not have to move for this bandha.

Throat Bandha: Keeping the tip of your tongue in the Master Hookup position, slightly jut your chin backward and tighten your throat muscles. You'll know you are doing this correctly when your breath makes more sound as it moves through the throat, closer to how Darth Vader's breath sounded in the *Star Wars* movies. The throat bandha keeps your light and energy focused in the throat chakra as you move the breath through that area.

Brow Bandha: Slightly roll your eyes upward, especially as you are moving the breath through the head area. The muscular tension created by this bandha helps keep the energy moving through the center of the head.

It takes practice to be able to hold all of these bandhas at the same time, so be patient with yourself. This is similar to any other form of muscle conditioning. You can start with just Mula Bandha between your legs as you begin the practice of Central Axis breathing and then practice adding the other bandhas as soon as you can.

In my experience, squeezing the Heart Bandha is a combination of muscular contraction and intention. I am imagining that I am hugging my heart internally at the same time that I squeeze the chest and upper back muscles.

Steps of Central Axis Breathing:

Sit in a comfortable meditation posture with your spine erect. It is best if you are not leaning onto the back of the chair or sofa you are sitting on, although a small pillow behind your lower back can be supportive. Sitting in a yogic lotus position is also suitable.

Engage with the foundational practices – Purity blast, grounding, Master hook-up, complete breath, coming back to yourself and loving presence. All of these can be activated in a few seconds once you are familiar with them.

Imagine a golden sun of light about the size of a baseball two feet above your head. Tighten Mula Bandha, adding the other bandhas as you can. Breath in while visualizing the sun of energy moving downward through the crown of your head, then through the center of your head, then your throat and the center of your chest. Complete the in-breath with your chest and upper abdomen full of air, focusing your attention in that area. Hold your breath a few seconds with your chest area expanded and relaxed, enjoying the sensation of this cosmic energy in your body.

When you are ready to exhale, move your breath and focus downward from the chest, continuing to squeeze the bandhas. Visualize your breath and the golden sun of light moving downward through your solar plexus, the area behind your navel, then the center of your lower abdomen and perineum area between your legs. Finally, see the golden energy exiting the root chakra and moving down into the Earth, ending about two feet beneath you. Imagine that your energy sun is grounding into the Earth (even if you are in the upstairs of a house or apartment). Pause after the exhale for a few seconds.

Inhale again, this time moving the sun of light and breath back up the central axis. See it move upward through the root chakra, lower abdomen area, behind the navel and the solar plexus, ending your in-breath with your chest and upper abdomen full of air, focusing around and beneath your heart. Enjoy the Earth energy sensations for a few seconds and then exhale upward through the center of the chest, throat, center of head and out the crown of your head, again moving the energy sun about two feet above your head.

Repeat as long as you want, feeling the amazing benefits of the practice.

Tips and Enhancements

1. **Shore up your dispersed areas**: As you do Central Axis breathing you may notice it is easier to feel and concentrate on some parts of the channel more than others. The areas of the Central Axis that are easier to feel are those in which you tend to be more embodied. This means your true self is more present and integrated in those parts, and you've come into more mastery of the lessons of that part of you. The areas within the Central Axis in which you tend to space out and get more distracted by random thoughts are the areas in which you are less embodied. This means there is some remaining blockage or denial of your true self in those areas. When you notice an area of your Central Axis in which it is harder for you to maintain focus, the following two practices will increase your embodiment:

   a. Practice the Inner Embrace (Chapter 24). Spend a little extra time blessing that area with your love and breath while internally hugging it.

   b. Practice Breath of Ascension in that area (see below in this chapter.) This more dynamic breath pattern is excellent for rapidly rewiring your subtle anatomy in the area you are focusing on.

   c. Look up which chakra dominates the part of the Central Axis you find it harder to focus on. Read about the qualities and characteristics of that chakra so you will better understand how to shore up that aspect of your life expression. A chakra reference chart follows in this chapter.

2. **Physically align your Central Axis:** Pressing the inner muscles and organs of the body back against your spine helps make it easier to consistently focus within the Central Axis.

3. **The toothpaste tube Bandha method**: If you would like help in developing your ability to squeeze the Bandhas, or inner muscular locks, as part of this practice, try the toothpaste tube method. You do this by squeezing your internal muscles in a rolling, continuous movement through the Central Axis, similar to squeezing the last bit of toothpaste from the bottom of its tube. In following the instructions for Central Axis breathing above, as you focus on the ball of light moving from your Crown chakra down through the Throat chakra roll your eyes upward, tighten your throat and intend to gently squeeze the central area of your head. As the golden ball and your focus reaches the chest release the head and throat compression and focus on internally tightening around your Heart Chakra. As you are breathing out down through the upper and lower belly, internally squeeze those areas, releasing the chest. When the golden ball moves down below your Root chakra continue to squeeze Mula Bandha only. In other words, sequentially tighten the muscles around each individual chakra as you are focusing around it in this practice.

   As you move your focus back up the Central Axis simply reverse the instructions. The intention is to keep a wave of internal muscular contraction rolling up and down the areas of the body you are concentrating on. This is a powerful embodiment practice in itself.

4. **Let's get physical - Yoga and Central Channel Breathing**: Central Axis Breathing is an excellent adjunct to yoga practice. Sue Morter masterfully teaches how to integrate Central Axis breathing with yoga postures through her Body Awake yoga classes which are available online. I highly recommend those for people who love yoga and wish to bring greater embodiment of their true self into their practice[106]

5. **Energy exercises**: There are also many forms of *qigong* that help circulate and enhance energy flow in the body. Qigong means "vital energy cultivation" in Chinese. In general, it is easier to focus within in meditation after doing some form of yoga, qigong or other gentle exercise. Some forms of martial arts were originated by Asian monks, who used them to prepare their bodies for meditation as well as self-defense.

---

[106] https://drsuemorter.com/bodyawake-yoga-membership/

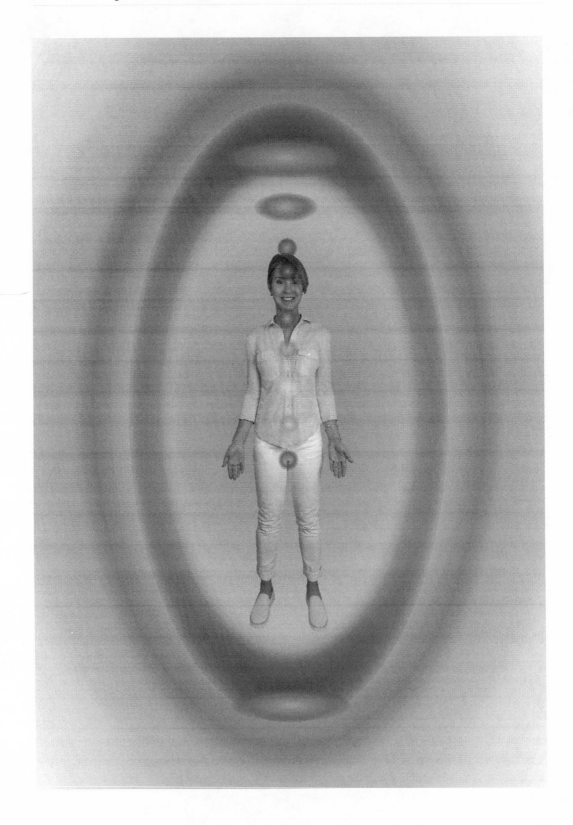

Chakra Qualities and Imbalances

Chakra Corresponding fingers	Healthy Qualities	Medical Manifestations Of Imbalance	Psycho-Emotional Imbalances From Overactivity	Psycho-Emotional Imbalances From Underactivity
1 - Root heel of palm or feet	Grounded and strong <u>life-force</u>	<u>A host of diseases related to imbalanced vitality and repressed anger</u>: heart attack, cancer, colitis, Alzheimer's, rheumatoid arthritis, PIDs, anemia, hypertension, most inflammatory diseases, **feet/hands/bone/teeth problems**	Belligerent, hyperactive, compulsive sexuality, violence	Poor sense of direction, lack of memory, loss of balance, ungrounded, too cautious, suicidal tendencies, feelings of insecurity, possessive, weak and sickly
2 -Sacral thumbs	Creativity, <u>emotions,</u> sexuality, innocence	Impotence, frigidity, low sex drive, bladder disease, enlarged prostate, STDs, AIDS, **wrist and ankle prob.**	Selfish, lustful, conceited, emotionally charged	Shy, low affect, unable to show feelings, co-dependence
3 - Solar middle fingers	<u>Willpower,</u> Self-confidence, leadership, empathy	Indigestion, pancreatitis, liver disease, diabetes, irritable bowel syndrome, peptic ulcer, arthritis, **leg/arm pain**, gall bladder problems, anorexia/bulimia	Controlling, OCD, rage, stubborn, rigid, judgmental, critical, fundamentalist	"leaf in the wind", can't enforce will, aloof, fears confrontation, psychosomatic illnesses – food or money issues
4 - Heart little fingers	Integration, <u>compassion</u>	Heart disease, asthma, coughing, underweight, torticollis, mental illness, insomnia, **knee/elbow problems**	Pride, jealousy, mania, "wears her heart on her sleeve", hyper-anxiety	Feel isolated, & unloved, lacking compassion, depression, tired anxiety, mentally overloaded
5 -Throat index fingers	Clarity and power of <u>expression</u>	Thyroid disease, speech disorders, lung diseases, ears, **shoulder**, poss. hip issues	Dogmatic, domineering, speaks gossip/negativity	Melancholy, gives in to others, resists change, hard to express self, stuttering
6 - Brow ring fingers	<u>Insight,</u> mental clarity, discernment	Sinusitis, skin irritation, headaches, OCD, left eye problems, stomach ulcers	Worry, fearful, superstitious, oversensitive, manipulative, spacy	Doubt, overly logical, forgetful, fearful, unclear thinking
7 -Crown	<u>Intuition,</u> spiritual connection, abundance	Substance abuse/alcoholism, insanity, high BP, kidney disease, right eye prob.	Overly erotic imagination, crave sympathy, savior complex	Shame, self-denial, negative self-image, feel disconnected from Spirit, dark night of the soul

A simple, effective practice to prepare your mind and body for Central Axis breathing is called Yoga Nidra, which is done with only three breaths. Here are the steps for this form of Yoga Nidra:

a. Engage Foundational practices.

b. Focusing on your right nostril, slowly breathe in. Keep most of your attention at the base of your nose where the breath is coming in. Pull the breath into your lower belly first, allowing it to gradually fill your upper belly and chest moving upwards. Keep your breath slow and steady.

c. At the end of this in-breath hold your breath for a few seconds.

d. Exhale slowly and deliberately through your mouth, holding it in a pursed position so your out-breath makes a whistling sound. Release the breath in the upper chest first, then gradually empty your lower chest and belly moving downward. At the end of the exhale hold your breath for a couple of seconds.

e. Focusing on the left nostril, breathe in again and repeat steps b – d.

f. For the final step, breathe in through both nostrils evenly, repeating steps b – d.

6. **Grounding into the Earth:** One of my favorite variations of Central Axis breathing is to focus my attention on the Earth Star chakra two feet (.61 meter) below me in the Earth. The Earth Star is a primary area of embodiment, as it can help pull more of your higher Avatar essence in through your physical body. Wherever you are, imagine that your feet are on the Earth (even if you're in a building upstairs). Imagine a golden disk of flowing light two feet below your feet. Tighten Mula Bandha, and with strong intention imagine pulling a golden sun of light from two feet above your head all the way through the body down into the Earth Star. Intend to remove all constrictions along the way and feel your Light Body energy field expand. Keep repeating, focusing on the downward energy movement for as long you like.

The Breath of Ascension

The Breath of Ascension is another practice that powerfully supports embodiment of your Avatar self in your body. Many spiritual practitioners develop themselves unevenly. It is very common for people to develop the aspect of themselves they are familiar with, and that is most connected with their superpower.

For example, a person with the superpower of the lover will be drawn to develop their Heart chakra while natural leaders tend to claim more power in their Solar Plexus. Those with native abilities to visualize and "see" on the spiritual level tend to highly develop their Third Eye. So many people, however, neglect developing other aspects of themselves that don't come to them as easily. This kind of uneven development often creates uncomfortable energy imbalances and can lead to emotional imbalances, fatigue or some forms of chronic disease. A great solution is to develop your whole chakra system evenly using Central Axis breathing and the Breath of Ascension practice.

In this practice, you use a special form of super-charged breathing that activates each chakra in turn. As you practice, you intend to increase your ability to directly feel the energy of each chakra. This increases your energetic sensitivity and strongly supports embodiment. It is important to drink a glass of pure water before you start this practice so you will be well hydrated. You can also focus your Breath of Ascension on just one chakra or region you wish to develop as described above.

The Breath of Ascension is useful for deep emotional self-healing, as it can help you connect with and clear your emotional energies, including any that may have been denied or repressed.

Steps of the Breath of Ascension:

1. Sit in a comfortable meditation posture with your spine erect. It is best if you are not leaning onto the back of the chair or sofa you are sitting on, although a small pillow behind your lower back can be supportive. Sitting in the yogic lotus position is also suitable.

2. Engage with the foundational practices – Purity blast, grounding, Master hook-up, complete breath, coming back to yourself and loving presence. All of these can be done in a few seconds once you are familiar with them.

3. Tighten Mula Bandha (Root Lock) between your legs and keep it slightly squeezed throughout this practice. If you find it hard to keep Mula Bandha squeezed the whole time, you can tighten it during each inhale and relax it on each exhale.

4. Visualize the Earth Star chakra two feet beneath your feet if you are sitting up, or two feet below your base chakra if you are sitting in lotus position. With a strong in-breath visualize a ball of golden energy moving up from Earth Star into your Root chakra.

5. When you've filled your lungs as much as possible through your in-breath take an additional strong snort of air in through your nose, with your mouth

closed. This supercharges your lungs with extra oxygen and vital energy. Imagine that you are sending that blast of extra air down to your Root Chakra.

6. Hold your in-breath for 2 – 4 seconds then open your mouth and let the air fall out of your lungs while allowing your out-breath to make a strong "AHHH" sound. Continue to tighten Mula Bandha if possible.

7. As soon your lungs are emptied of air, immediately close your mouth and start the next in-breath through your nose. There should be no pause between the out-breath and the next in-breath. As before, take an extra snort of air to supercharge your lungs at the end of your in-breath.

8. Go through additional Breaths of Ascension continuing to concentrate your attention on your Root chakra, intending to feel the sensations within that part of your body. Explore how you can increase your sensitivity to what you can feel thereby continually intending to "tune in" to your feeling sense within your lower body.

9. After a few minutes of focusing on the Root chakra, move your attention up to the area of the second Sacral chakra which is located about halfway between the top of your pubic bone and your navel. Do your best to tune into this part of yourself, blessing it with your attention and breath while slightly squeezing the muscles in your lower abdomen to hug this chakra internally. Stay with this chakra for as long as you are drawn to it, building your ability to directly sense it.

10. In the same way continue the Breath of Ascension while focusing on each of the chakras in the body you are drawn to work with, or all of them.

11. When you are complete with your Breath of Ascension practice, release all the techniques and focusing you have been doing. Sit quietly for a few minutes, doing nothing but allowing yourself to feel and enjoy the energy sensations. This "yin" aspect of the practice is vital because you are allowing yourself to feel without effort. It is also vital because trying to get up right away after doing this powerful practice could be disorienting.

The intention of the Breath of Ascension is to develop your ability to tune into, energize and feel all of your chakras, not just the ones you can feel easily. Attune yourself to the sensations within each chakra. The combination of breathing into the chakra, squeezing Mula Bandha, visualizing golden light there and supercharging your breath helps to activate and awaken this part of you. And love yourself through each of your chakras. Your chakras hold the essence of who you are. Being willing to direct love and acceptance to each area is deeply healing.

Tips and Enhancements for Breath of Ascension

1. This is a powerful, transformative practice and it is good to ease into it, starting with a few minutes of practice and gradually building up as your subtle energy systems adapt.

2. The lower three chakras one, two and three are your foundation, and the ones most important for the majority of people to develop through Breath of Ascension. As you develop your Root chakra you will be able to feel more enjoyable sensations in that area. That will support the development of the other chakras. Therefore, in most cases start by spending plenty of time doing the Breath of Ascension focusing mainly on the Root chakra. When your inner knowing tells you you're ready, move onto the second and then the third chakras. When you are feeling more sensation in the first three chakras, then move onto higher chakras four through seven. Trust your own guidance and take your time. It can be very valuable to just focus your Breath of Ascension on the Root chakra for a week or more to thoroughly develop it. Then move on to the second chakra.

3. If you have been through sexual trauma in your past, it is possible some strong feelings may come up as you do Breath of Ascension through chakras one or two. If that happens, know that this is a part of your healing process. Apply your transmission and as much self-love as you can. If you are feeling triggered it may be best to let go of this practice and move into a gentler, more nurturing breathing pattern. Breath of Ascension will help you clear such old trauma programming. Reach out for the help of others you trust if you need it.

4. It is possible you may feel nothing in some or all of the chakras as you enter into the Breath of Ascension practice. Don't give up. Not feeling is even more reason to do this practice! Your chakras are major zones of sensing yourself, and if you seem to be numbed out to that, more practice, love and patience are required. This dynamic practice is one of the most effective ways to awaken your ability to feel and be intimate with yourself. If you are having difficulty feeling the sensations within your chakras, consider these:

a. Before you start your practice, consciously pull all your energy strongly into your body. So many of us are only partially in our bodies. Parts of us may be going out seeking connection or completion. Fear, worry or trauma can also keep us avoiding being fully "in."

b. Receive acupuncture, energy healing or bodywork sessions from high-level practitioners you trust. It is best to go to practitioners who are well attuned to their own chakras and subtle energies so they can assist you to increase your sensitivity and openness.

5. Tapping can be a valuable adjunct to Breath of Ascension. I have experienced enhanced benefits from adding the following two different forms of tapping to this practice[107]:

a. Emotional Freedom Technique (EFT). Tap the commonly used acupuncture points around the head, chest and hands while doing Breath of Ascension.

b. Tapping lower chakras: Use the palms or fists of both hands to simultaneously tap the front and rear of the chakras you are focusing on. This is most applicable for the Sacral (2nd), Solar Plexus (3rd) and Heart (4th) chakras. This makes the practice even stronger for activating and mobilizing the deeper energies governed by each chakra.

6. Visualizing colors in the different chakras as you do this practice can also be helpful, especially if you are a highly visual person. But visualization is not necessary and should not become a substitute for kinesthetically feeling the chakra sensations. As I mentioned earlier some people have strong native visionary, Third Eye abilities, and tend to rely on inner seeing because it comes easily to them. To develop themselves in a balanced way, those individuals will need to focus less on "seeing" and more on physically feeling in this practice.

Central Axis Breathing and Breath of Ascension are vital practices for actualizing all that is presented in this book. Committing to these practices and responding with love to all that comes up for you, is true Mastery practice and directly awakening to your Avatar self.

---

[107] Complete instructions for EFT, and integrating it with other energy release methods, can be found in the Reclaiming Your Calm Center book, Chapter 11

24

Self-Love and the Inner Embrace

There are many forms of love we experience and share throughout all our relationships. The pure love within us is often enmeshed in issues that challenge us to rise above our own egoic reactions and agendas. Kahlil Gibran so beautifully wrote:

> *For even as love crowns you so shall he crucify you. Even as he is for your growth so is he for your pruning. Even as he ascends to your height and caresses your tenderest branches that quiver in the sun, so shall he descend to your roots and shake them in their clinging to the earth.*[108]

If you willingly enter into this transformative process, you can mature and deepen your capacity for real love. In fact, loving relationships help you transform faster than almost anything else because those closest to you mirror your own light and dark sides most clearly. "Thank you for pointing out my blind spots, insecurities and ego fixations. Sure do appreciate it!" Relationships, especially those of the intimate kind, can certainly boost your self-knowledge and mastery, but only if you accept responsibility for your own reactions, reducing the tendency to project your issues onto the other and blame them for your discomforts. Now that's a heroic project!

While all relationships – parent-child, relatives, romantic lovers, friendships and business collaborators offer combinations of pleasures and challenging "growth experiences," the very hardest form of love seems to be self-love. Have you noticed that? Most people I know have good hearts and tend to be loving and attentive

---

[108] Gibran, Kahlil, *The Prophet "On Love"* Alfred A Knoph 1971

toward those close to them. But when they are being honest, they will usually admit they have lots of judgment and holdback toward themselves.

That's only part of it. It can also be hard to love ourselves because our inner states can often feel disturbed and unsettling. It can feel lousy to just sit quietly and be with ourselves. It's so much easier to check our text messages or watch the next controversial video on YouTube. This creates a habit of running from ourselves, the antithesis of real self-love.

In truth, self-love is really where it's at. If we can truly love our self, the doorways to what we really want and what really fulfills us start opening up.

So, what about all those disturbing, uncomfortable feelings we encounter when we turn inward, that seem to prevent us from enjoying meditation? The answer to this question is the key to true love. These yucky, antsy, want-to-bolt-out-of-here experiences, which can be referred to as *samskara*, energetic gunk, neuroses, psychic burdens or residoo-doo, are places we have denied or lost connection with love. This has created gaps and blockages in our energy fields. Those imprints in our sub-conscious minds entrain our physiology through the *epigenetic* pathways.[109] This becomes the root of most chronic pain, anxiety and disease. I have written extensively about this in my prior book, *Healing the Root of Pain*.[110]

Therefore, the greatest hero's journey that deepens our love is the willingness to bring love to those uncomfortable inner parts of ourselves. To live as an Avatar, we need to be willing to practice this "hardest form of love." Once I realize I've been running from myself and take the time to flow love through my own body, it stops being hard. It starts feeling quite fulfilling and my heart says, "Right Action!" What is so crazy is to realize that I spent years avoiding my own fulfillment by substituting staying busy and trying to heal and love everyone else. But each time I was ready to accept love, it only took a few seconds to minutes to shift that pattern.

What follows are two practices that have deepened my self-love and brought more of the emanations of heaven into my life. These practices are called the Inner Smile and the Inner Embrace and can be combined for best results.

Where in the Body?

All meaningful healing and transformation happen through our bodies. That's because it's difficult to resolve your hurts and conflicts while swimming in the

---

[109] Epigenetics – the science that documents how environment, lifestyle, thoughts and feelings modify gene expression in our DNA, thereby remodeling our body according to our consciousness
[110] Starwynn, Darren, *Healing the Root of Pain*, Desert Heart Press 2013

turbulent ocean of feelings and thoughts. But once you find out where in your body those feelings live, you have something tangible to work with. As Buddha taught:

Whatever arises in the mind will be accompanied by a sensation in the body [111]

In general, we are most motivated to practice self-love when we are feeling hurt and facing painful issues. Therefore, the first steps in the following self-love practices are as follows:

1. **What am I feeling?** Step back from your mental stories about the hurt or distress you are going through, and focus on the feelings that are coming up. For example, instead of continuing to run the thoughts, "It was so hurtful when Sally didn't call me back after I opened up to her so much. That's so unfeeling and cruel of her, and she should have…" which is a STORY, simply ask yourself "What sensations in my body am I feeling now in THIS moment?"

2. **Where am I feeling it?** Once you acknowledge what you are feeling, ask yourself what part of your body is most acutely feeling that feeling? Where are those feelings most localized?

3. **Connect with the feeling.** It is helpful to put the palm of one of your hands over the area you identify, directing your breath into and through it. Including that area as a focal point in Central Axis breathing offers additional benefits (see below).

4. **Connect with the physical sensation.** You can also put your hand over an area of physical pain or disease symptom in your body. It is possible that pain is also a manifestation of some hurt or trauma on the emotional level.

Once you have done these steps to localize the hurt or issue, move onto one or both of the following practices.

The Inner Smile

We are programmed to smile at others as a way to share love and positivity. We can turn that around and smile into ourselves, as ancient Taoist and Tibetan masters

---

[111] This is a core principle of the system of Vipassana meditation that claims to be based on the original teachings of Gautama Buddha

taught their disciples to do. Now that you've located the focal point of pain or hurt in your body and put your hand over it, smile into it. Here's how:

Think of the person, animal, place, spiritual being or experience that most easily brings up the experience of love within you. Allow that to put an actual physical smile on your face. The smile muscles of the face have strong energetic connections to our heartfelt feelings, so physically smiling does help open your heart. Allow your loving heart feelings to build as much as you can. Then redirect your love and your smile into the part of your own body you have identified. Imagine that waves of your own love and blessings are flowing there. Intend that your Avatar transmission is filling and surrounding that part of your body. Bask in this feeling of loving this hurting or resistant part of you.

Visualizing beautiful golden, magenta, pink or crystalline light around the part of the body you are focusing on can heighten the benefits. Follow your own guidance about the color you work with.

You can take the Inner Smile further by smiling into each of your internal organs and chakras, one at a time. See my book, *Reclaiming Your Calm Center,* for detailed step-by-step instructions.

The Inner Embrace

Can you think of a time when you comforted a hurting child or friend by hugging them? Can you remember someone doing that for you? It is a universal way that we reassure and comfort each other. We can do that for ourselves through the Inner Embrace.

After identifying a hurt or upset, identify its focal point in your body as described above. Now breathe deeply into the part of your body representing the issue you are working with. Squeeze the muscles all around that focal point so you are giving yourself an internal hug without using your hands. Hold your breath for a few seconds in that place, then exhale, consciously intending to release painful, stressful feelings down into the Earth, or up above you to the highest spiritual source. Continue hugging and breathing in and out of the focal point in your body, feeling the sense of inner connection with yourself. Stay with the Inner Embrace until you feel a softening, easing or energy movement in that area.

As you do this practice you may feel waves of emotion, or physical sensations such as shaking, burping or spontaneous movements. Visual images or unexpected memories may arise into your awareness. Accept these experiences without trying to restrain or analyze them. These are part of your release process.

Just as a fretful child can be comforted by love and reassurance from her mother or father, so can the hurting parts of adults positively respond to that kind of care. Recurring feelings of sadness, shame, abandonment and the like mostly come from the young part of our psyche often called the "inner child". When you are feeling caught up in the hurts of your inner child, however, it may not be easy for your personal self to also be able to be a comforting parent. Therefore, comfort these feelings from your Christ Avatar self. When I am giving myself an Inner Embrace I often invoke the Christ Avatar within me and allow that divine part of me to say things like:

I AM the Christ holding you in love and compassion

I AM your divine source and I got your back

Don't worry if easing of emotional or psychic discomfort doesn't come right away as you do this practice. Some of these focal points of emotional pain represent programming going way back in our experience and will take more time to release.

Combining the Inner Embrace with Central Axis Breathing

In this variation taught by Dr. Sue Morter, you focus your breath through the central axis of your body while internally squeezing areas of hurt or blocked feelings. To do this, breathe in from above your head down through your central axis. Use the *bandhas* (muscular locks) to help focus the breath through the channel. When your focal point of breath arrives at the area reflecting the pain, stop your inhalation there and hold your breath, internally hugging that area at the same time. Tune in with your loving presence, feeling any shifts happening. When you are ready to exhale, allow the breath to carry some of the painful or blocked feelings down the central axis, into the love and safety of Earth. Then do this in reverse by breathing upward, inhaling from the Earth up to the hurting area, holding and hugging there. Then exhale upward, carrying some of the feelings out of the crown of the head to the highest spiritual source for healing and recycling.

I am so grateful to have discovered this practice. I have often received more benefit from a few minutes of this than hours of therapy and self-analysis!

Multi-Dimensional Forgiveness

Forgiveness is a major part of loving and healing. True forgiveness includes the release of judgment and negative thoughts toward yourself or others and accepting the truth that you are innocent.

As described in Chapter 14, you can raise your consciousness to understand that any pain or conflict you experience is not just about you, it is also part of vast "pain bodies" shared by masses of people. The pain-body is a concept popularized by author Eckhardt Tolle that refers to accumulated pain and trauma programming in people that takes on a life of its own. Tolle also mentions that pain bodies are often shared by huge numbers of inter-connected people.[112] For example, there is a pain-body for all women who have experienced sexism, rape, discrimination, forced marriages and other dark aspects of patriarchy. There is a pain-body for all gay, lesbian and trans people, all African Americans, all Jews and any other groups of people who have experienced a shared form of suffering. Therefore, the part of your body you squeeze and love through the Inner Smile and Inner Embrace practices is also in energetic communication with all other people resonating with similar feelings and concerns.

Please take a moment to stop and reflect on this. Your pain is not all your own.

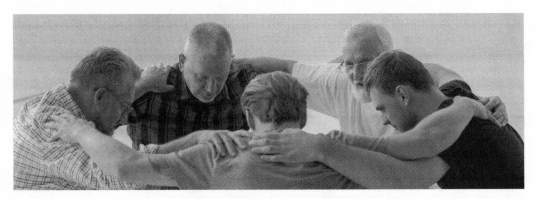

Your pain is not all your own

We are all interconnected due to the holographic nature of the Universe. As you hold the part of your body experiencing that pain in the pure love of your transmission, you are also gifting healing blessings to all those connected people. So, just as your pain is not all your own, the healing you receive is not only for you – it also radiates to countless other beings. This is the way of the Avatar.

---

[112] See Tolle's book, *A New Earth*, Chapter 5, for a great explanation of pain bodies. Plume Printing/Penguin Group 2005

Practicing the Inner Embrace with Multi-Dimensional Forgiveness:

1. Connect with the bodily-felt experience of your Avatar transmission

2. Work with the Inner Smile and Inner Embrace until you feel some degree of easing or release in the part of the body you are focusing on. Give thanks for that but continue even if you don't yet feel any release.

3. Ask that your thoughts and feelings be lifted up to the level of your Avatar self. Open your heart, connecting with your desire to love and serve.

4. Allow your Avatar self to radiate blessings of healing and forgiveness through yourself, and feel it as much as you can.

5. Ask that the benefits of your practice be extended to any group of people or animals you are directed to serve. If you are a visual person, you may be able to see the love and forgiveness branching out to a group of other people, or to a symbol or image of the group you are sharing your blessings with. If you are inspired to extend your healing to all life, you can visualize the entire Earth before you, seeing the blessings going out to billions of points of light upon it. If you are a more kinesthetic person, you can open your body to feel the blessings going out multi-dimensionally. Your critical mind is not needed for this process. Just trust it is real and have fun exploring your multi-dimensional Avatar healing abilities.

6. When you are complete, focus on gratitude for a few moments and then close your focused practice. You can intend that the blessings continue to flow after you take your conscious attention off the practice, but be very clear that the blessings are coming from your divine Avatar self, not your personal self. Only the divine has that capacity.

Note: Systems of tapping on acupuncture points for emotional healing such as EFT and TAT integrate well with the practices taught in this chapter.

25

Christing – Embodiment Practices

Once you become aware that the essence of who you are is an Avatar transmission emanating from the infinite source of light and divine love, you may start becoming very excited to experience it more. This could be similar to what the pioneers in the old West of the USA felt when hearing about people striking it rich with gold mines; "there's gold in them thar hills." A lot of people did everything they possibly could to travel to those areas where the gold was and stake their claim, braving all kinds of dangers and challenges in the hopes of getting rich.

The most precious gold we can mine is the golden light of our Christ Avatar self. Experiencing this golden light permeating your body and enlightening your mind is the greatest treasure. This is even true materially because your transmission connects you with the spigot of true abundance. You start realizing that in your essence you are a divine creator being limited only by your conditioning and beliefs.[113]

The guided practices in the previous chapters are foundational for rewiring your body to become more sensitive to your transmission. These next practices can take you further into embodiment. It is recommended that you first get comfortable practicing Central Axis breathing and the Inner Embrace for a few weeks, and once you are feeling grounded in those practices move into the following expansions.

---

[113] If you understand that your mind works a lot like computers, then conditioning can be seen as limiting, buggy software.

Cosmic Heart

We are taught that our body is our physical body only. In reality, your body includes your physical body as well as more subtle energy fields filling and surrounding it. The most expansive part of your individuality extends between four to six feet out from the surface of your physical body in all directions except for beneath your feet, where it extends about 2 feet into the ground beneath you. This full energy field is the totality of your being, and has been called the I AM Presence, the cosmic body or the 12th chakra. The Cosmic Heart practice elevates your human love to divine love by expanding it to the full size of your cosmic body. This practice is best done standing up but can also be done in a sitting position.

1. Place your hands palms together in prayer position over your heart chakra in the center of your chest.

2. Imagine the Earth Star chakra two feet below your feet and the eighth chakra about two feet above the crown of your head. Inhale into your central channel, imagining a golden ball of light moving down from above your head, while another golden ball of light moves up from the Earth Star beneath your feet at the same time. Both balls meet in your heart chakra under your hands at the end of the inhale. Open your heart to the field of loving presence that you truly are. Feel Earth and cosmic energies merging in your heart.

3. As you breathe out, coordinate your hands and breathe in this way: imagine the combined golden ball of light in your heart gradually expanding beyond your physical body, about four to six feet out in all directions from the edges of your physical body. This is the approximate size of your cosmic body, the twelfth chakra. At the same time, push the palms of your hands straight outward from your heart on both sides "pushing" the golden ball to expand to its full size.

4. At the end of the out-breath feel yourself as the cosmic body infused with divine Avatar love. Intend to directly sense your complete body as much as you can. Your ability to sense it will increase the more you do the Cosmic Heart practice.

5. When you are ready to inhale, turn your palms to face each other and slowly move them back toward center, contracting your visualization of the expanded golden ball back to the size of your heart chakra. End the in-breath with your hands back in prayer position.

6. Now face the palm of one hand upward and the other palm facing downward, both in front of your heart. On your next exhale push the upward-facing

palm up and the downward-facing palm down. Keep them aligned with the centerline of your body. Press the upper hand as high as you can comfortably go above your head, and the lower hand as far as you can go downward, probably down to below your groin. As you do these movements, feel your energy field expanding upwards and downwards.

7. If you are able to during Step 6, also gradually shift your weight onto the front balls of your feet while lifting your heels slightly off the floor. This strengthens your kidneys and boosts vital energy.

8. On the next inhale, slowly bring your hands from above and below back to prayer position in front of your heart. Slowly lower your heels in coordination with your hands moving toward each other.

9. Repeat for at least nine cycles, sinking into the experience of being the totality of your being.

Morning Timeline Focus

A discussion of timelines can be found in Section Five, Chapter 29. Timelines are possibilities of experience moving forward from each Now moment. It is valuable to consciously choose the timelines you want to live in, those that bring you joy, well-being and fulfillment of your higher purpose. The following practice will make the most sense after you read Chapter 29.

When you go to bed at night, set your intention to focus on the timeline you want to experience the moment you wake up, before the normal momentum of your mind gets a chance to start up. When you first awaken in the morning, or even in the middle of the night, imagine a row of doorways right next to your bed. You'd have to walk through one of them to get out of bed. Have fun imagining the various doorways. They could be of different styles and from different cultures or historical periods if you like. Or, you can keep it simple and have them all be uniform.

Notice which doorway seems most familiar to you, the one you usually identify with. Then ask your higher guidance which other doorway holds higher light and benefit for you. Tune into that one, and let yourself experience it with your inner senses.

The vital key here is to engage in this practice before you allow your mind to "rev up" with its familiar string of thoughts about its agendas - what it wants you to believe is real. And certainly, before you reach for any digital device. Again, this takes desire and the willingness to focus. Let the love of your heart make that easier, as you are likely choosing a doorway shining with greater love and divine presence.

Once you have a sense of this timeline, intend to open the doorway (however you see that) and enter it. You can do that as you physically get out of bed or in your imagination. Stay aware of the experiences of this timeline – the feelings, the textures, any visuals that come to you, the feelings in your heart, even inspired thoughts that drop into your mind. It's very valuable to write a few notes in your bedside journal about what you perceive. If you are enjoying this timeline, you can set your intention to stay aware of it as you go about your day.

Consciously choosing the timeline you will inhabit first thing in the morning is a powerful mastery practice.

Embodiment Walking Meditation

While sitting meditation in which your focus is totally inward is essential, there are also active variations you can enjoy as you go about your daily activities. I am a hiking enthusiast and enjoy forms of walking meditation. Here is a way to increase your embodiment as you walk or hike:

1. Engage foundational practices. Put all of your attention not needed for walking inside your body. If you are so guided, intend to open your heart and mind to behold and honor the New Earth.

2. As you take each step, imagine that golden energy beams from the bottom of each of your feet are connecting to a disk of light two feet (.61 meter) under the Earth's surface, below your feet. I generally imagine it to be about the width of my body from shoulder to shoulder but follow your own guidance in sensing your Earth Star.

3. Breathe in from above your head down through your central axis, finishing your in-breath around your chest area. Pause, feeling the higher vibrational energies filling your chest.

4. Exhale from your chest area down through your Root chakra, legs and feet down into your Earth Star chakra.

5. As you breathe out down into the Earth, aim to open all the cells of your body to receive your Avatar transmission more abundantly. Feel the spiritual magnetism of your Earth Star pulling down more of your true self into your body. Be receptive to feeling it, seeing it or knowing it. Send your love and appreciation down into Mother Earth.

6. On your next in-breath, pull the Earth energies up into your Root chakra, and up to your Heart chakra, feeling the Earth energies with your feeling body. When ready to exhale, breathe out from the Heart area up to the 8th chakra above your head.

7. When you are ready to breathe in, start again above your head, allowing your Earth Star to pull down more of your Christ Avatar self to your chest area and repeat the cycle.

These suggestions provide a good starting point for walking meditation. It's best to follow your own rhythm and guidance, letting your love for nature guide you.

The practices taught in this chapter are profound and transformative. I don't recommend moving through them quickly. Take your time to allow each to re-wire your subtle energy systems and refine your awareness.

26

Connecting With Your Transmission

All the practices in this book involve working with your Avatar transmission. This is a good one to introduce yourself to this experience.

If possible, before starting this practice engage in some form of physical stretching and movement to get the energy in your body circulating. Any forms of yoga or qigong in which you focus on internal energy movement are suitable. Guided video and audio recordings of a suggested routine are available, see note at end of this chapter.

Reading Chapter 3 – Claiming Your Avatar Transmission – is likely to be helpful in stimulating your desire and focus for this practice.

1. Find a quiet place to practice. Creating a meditation altar is very helpful, but not essential.

2. Engage with the foundational practices of purity blast, coming back to yourself, grounding, Master hook-up, complete breath and loving presence. All of these can be done in a few seconds once you are familiar with them.

3. Sit in a comfortable position with your spine erect and straight. Keep your tongue in the Master hook-up on the roof of your mouth and breathe fully. If you've learned Central Axis breathing, practice that, moving your breath slowly up and down the internal pillar of your chakras.

4. Get in touch with your desire to be in your highest truth, and to feel the source energy of who you really are. Invoke your transmission silently or out loud:

I call upon my divine self now to awaken my ability to directly sense my source transmission. I let go of my mind's control and open my soul, heart, mind and body to allow myself to experience it now.

Or use whatever invocation is most true for you.

5. Relax your body and nervous system as much as you can. Give up trying to feel or figure out your transmission.

6. Keep your attention inside your body. Sit quietly and observe your experience, attuning to your intuitive knowing. Whenever you become aware that your mind is *trying* to feel something, gently and firmly let go of that. Release any expectations of what your transmission should feel like, and simply observe what *is*. Don't expect it to feel a certain way, be blissful, or be like any special meditation or yoga experiences you've had in the past. It may be an experience you would think of as ordinary.

7. Whenever you become aware that your mind has wandered, let go of what you were thinking and return to the present moment.

8. Your Avatar transmission is a stream of purest love. Attuning your heart to loving presence makes your transmission easier to feel because that's the bandwidth it flows on.

9. Be patient. If you feel your transmission the first time you do this practice, wonderful. If you're not sure you're feeling anything, no problem. Few people master great and powerful things right away. Continue with this practice and you will eventually get it.

Working with your transmission in everyday life:

Conflicts in relationships – No one can push our buttons more than those with whom we share an intimate relationship. Just as elite athletes need to do intensive training to prepare for their next competition, the Ascension Practices we do prepare us to be more present for the times when triggering encounters happen with our loved ones.

The next time you start becoming aware that you and another person are escalating into emotional conflict, touch the tip of your tongue to the roof of your mouth and take a deep breath. Do your best to relax and tune into love. Observe your energy which is starting to fly toward the other person and intend to pull it back into yourself. Silently invoke your transmission and tune into it, allowing it to infuse through the parts of your body that are tightening up. Take a few more breaths before speaking, asking yourself, "How can I express love in this encounter?" That encounter may not go smoothly, but it's great practice at being a Christ Avatar with your partner or friend. The more you practice when you're by yourself, the more grounded you'll be able to remain when confrontations happen with others.

Feeling depressed or anxious – Do all the same steps as described for conflicts in relationships, but focus it within yourself. Identify the part of your body in which the painful feelings are focalized, and then flow your transmission through it. This creates powerful transformative *alchemy*. The more you do this the easier it is to remember who you really are, and the more naturally you'll become more neutral to your painful feelings and reactions. You still feel a wide range of emotions, but rather than having a story about them you'll recognize them as energy in motion. You'll more easily come to see them as opportunities to practice love and Presence. If there is some truth within your depression or anxiety experience for you to grasp, you are more likely to clearly receive it when you are not caught up in the mind's stories. I have found the Inner Embrace practice described in Chapter 24 to be simple and powerful for transforming the sorry stories of my mind into a body-centered practice of self-love.

For example, in my youth I often felt myself to be highly sensitive to feelings of rejection by others and could brood for hours or days about real or imagined slights. Since I learned to deploy the Inner Embrace practice, I have responded in a much more positive way by asking, "Where is this feeling located in my body?" and then focusing my love and breath there. That has rapidly improved my perspective many times.

Crises in society – If you hear about something disturbing on the news, or a friend tells you about a crisis happening somewhere in the world, how do you react? Most people either tune it out or start worrying about it, thereby lowering their energy vibration. That doesn't help you or the situation. Avatars can take the higher road by applying their transmission. Your Christ Avatar transmission is unlimited. It can support healing and ascension of humanity as easily as it can bless you or your individual clients. You can call upon your transmission for planetary healing, and indeed this is a wonderful practice to add to your daily meditation time.

Just as you would for a personal issue, allow yourself to feel what this piece of news is bringing up in your body and where that sensation is located. Engage with the foundational practices. As explained at the end of this chapter, connect with your transmission. Visualize a map or symbol for the geographical location where the crisis is taking place, and see your transmission filling and surrounding that area and all people or animals involved. Follow your guidance and offer any prayers or decrees, seeing the situation already resolved with protection and wellbeing for all involved. This is fifth dimensional consciousness. Follow your own guidance on how to serve. Remind yourself that your small self is not doing or taking on anything. It is your impersonal divine Avatar transmission that is offering the blessings. The phrase, "Let go and let God" can put our minds in the right place for this form of service.

We really don't know what is for the highest good of other people. There are so many unseen reasons why individuals, groups or nations go through the tribulations they do. Therefore, a safe and respectful way to engage in group or planetary healing is to decree:

I invoke my Christ Avatar transmission to heal, bless and uplift all humanity and all life, as is appropriate.

Saying "as is appropriate" is your karmic non-interference insurance policy. By saying that you are acknowledging that your blessings will act in each case according to divine will and intelligence.

See Chapter 13 for more detailed guidance on offering planetary healing.

It is not appropriate or possible for "you" – the human being you are – to send out your transmission to heal crises on our planet. Yet you can find the resonance of that situation within your own body and practice healing and loving. Due to the holographic principle, you can be sure this activity is benefitting all the people caught up in that crisis.

You claim your transmission and superpowers by really caring, loving and by wanting to know your true self. You claim your transmission through your desire to abundantly give your greatest gift to yourself and others.

Notes for this Practice:

1. Once you've created a clear intention to become directly aware of your Avatar transmission, your soul will start working on fulfilling your request 24-7. Thoughts, feelings and insights may pop up at unexpected times. It's great to record these in your journal or on a voice memo on your cell phone.

2. I have noticed that it is much easier for people to discover the direct experience of their transmission while engaging in Lightworker group events.

Your transmission is really about giving, and so the interactions you have with others pull it through you more readily. If you want more support in awakening to your Avatar self and transmission, I suggest that you participate in high-level group workshops or retreats you are drawn to. See the Resources section.

3. You may have old traumatic associations in your subconscious mind or soul associated with freely feeling and sharing your transmission. Be compassionate and gentle with yourself, and if any painful feelings or images arise in this process, acknowledge them and work with Ascension practices. Please, reach out for help and support from others you trust on the path if it starts feeling overwhelming. Don't give up, these experiences will pass.

4. As suggested above, it can be helpful if you do some vigorous physical exercise just before you sit down to do this practice. Taking a brisk walk, yoga asanas, running on a treadmill or playing with your dog could work. That gets you into the mode of feeling energy moving through your body, and can help jumpstart your receptivity to your transmission.

5. This overall book contains an activating Avatar transmission. If you'd like some support with perceiving your transmission, you can hold the book in your hands or place it on your altar as you do this practice. To assure your own sovereignty you can say something like this: "I open myself to any transmission or virtue from this book that supports me, and I refuse any energies that are not for my highest good."

6. It's powerful to create a journal to record your experiences of working with your transmission and getting in touch with your Avatar self. When you look back on your journal entries a few weeks or months later they will have way more meaning than is obvious when you are writing them.

7. You can learn how to access a free guided meditation to support you in getting in touch with your transmission at www.drstarwynn.com/practices, or see the page "For Further Development" in Section Six. Many people find it easier to let go into their energy flow while listening rather than reading.

Attuning yourself to your Avatar transmission is the foundation for all else presented in this book. It is well worth reading this chapter or listening to the guided audio meditation a few times, and working with the practice until you have internalized the direct experience of your divine source flowing through you.

27

Light Body Merkaba Activation

Everyone has a cosmic body, as described in the Cosmic Heart practice in Chapter 25, yet few are aware of it. As you increase embodiment of your Avatar transmission the energy vibration of your body is elevated, and it becomes easier and more natural to perceive your cosmic body. This is part of the process of Christing or light body activation.

The term *merkaba* means "counter-rotating spirit light body." It is a rapidly rotating, high-frequency geometric light field forming around your body in the approximate shape of a star tetrahedron. A star tetrahedron resembles two three-sided pyramids, with the apex of one pointing upward and the other pointing downward. The bases of the two tetrahedrons overlap over the central part of your body.

Merkaba activation is not something that happens without focused intention and practice. There have been practices for doing so since ancient times, and the art of merkaba activation was renewed and popularized in the 1990s through the teachings of Drunvalo Melchizedek.[114] The benefits of light body activation are many and include:

- Ability to maintain states of pure consciousness and love more of the time, and eventually permanently.
- Protection from dark or intrusive energies.
- Miracle quantum healing abilities.

---

[114] See his books Ancient Secrets of the Flower of Life, Volumes One and Two

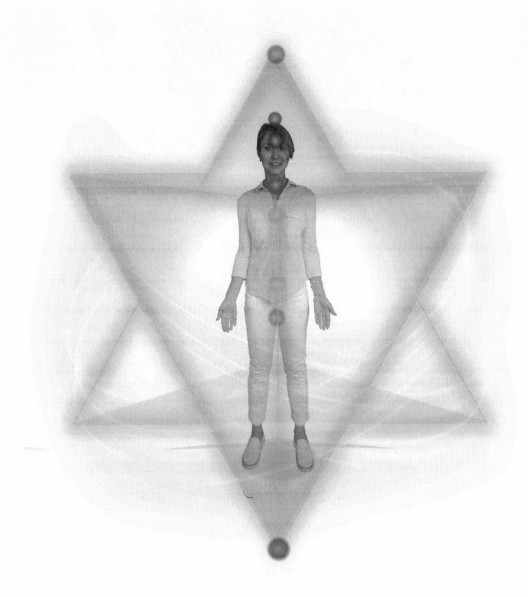

- Ability to travel through multi-dimensions of experience, using the merkaba as a vessel.
- Christing of the physical body - re-wiring it to higher levels of radiant health, immunity and longevity.
- Greater ease keeping the mind in the Now moment.

I have studied many methods for activating the light body. Most are complex and involve a series of deep breaths synched with precise visualizations and invocation of specific mathematical numbers and ratios. If you are motivated to activate your light body, I encourage you to study any of these methods you are drawn to. Many of them have been explained through YouTube videos, some of which are quite good. What I will present here is a simpler method for activating your merkaba light body consistent with the teachings in this book. It is based on working with the pure love of your Avatar transmission. Here are step-by-step instructions:

1. Sit or stand in a place in which you will not be disturbed. It is helpful to do this practice in a dark place or to wear eye patches that block out external light. The Mindfold™ brand of eye patches are excellent for this purpose.

2. Engage Foundational practices – Purity Blast, Master Hook-Up, deep abdominal or Central Axis breathing, pulling your energy back into yourself, grounding and loving Presence. For this practice do a variation on the Master Hook-Up – instead of touching the tip of your tongue slightly behind your two front teeth, periodically use the tip of your tongue to massage the roof of your mouth further back, at the rear of the hard palate. This action stimulates the pituitary and pineal glands and supports activation.

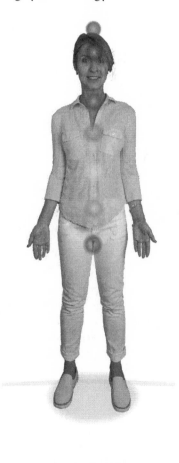

   Tune into your soul love and desire to activate your light body, as this is a powerful catalyst.

3. From this place, bring your focus to the Earth Star chakra two feet (.61 meter) below your feet. Send your love and attention to this focal point of embodiment, feeling it to be like a powerful electro-magnet pulling more of your Avatar self down into your body. Do your best to tune into the actual sensation of your Earth Star, even if it is subtle. Slightly squeezing *Mula Bandha* (root lock), breathe up from the Earth Star to your Root and Sacral chakras area of your lower abdomen (chakras one and two), and then back down to the Earth Star. Breathe back and forth

between these two areas a few times. Keep your attention on this pathway, feeling every bit of it as you go back and forth.

4. Once you feel synchronicity or energy movement between the Earth Star and your lower abdomen chakras, take a big breath and pull the energy up to your Solar Plexus chakra. As you exhale, breathe back down to your Earth Star. Now, breathe back and forth between the Earth Star and Solar Plexus a few times, intending to sense a continuous energy pathway through that part of your central axis. Squeeze Mula Bandha to help promote the flow of energy, and intend to feel each chakra along this pathway.. Using the rolling "toothpaste tube bandha" is also helpful. That means tightening your internal muscles around the part of the axis you are concentrating on sequentially, from the Root chakra up to the Solar Plexus and back again. (See Chapter 23).

5. Once you feel synchronicity or energy movement between the Earth Star, lower abdomen and Solar Plexus chakras, take a big breath and pull the energy up to your Heart chakra. As you exhale, breathe back down to your Earth Star. Now, breathe back and forth between the Earth Star and your Heart chakra a few times, intending to sense a continuous energy pathway through that part of your central axis. Take as much time as you need to strengthen and energetically re-wire this pathway. You are building valuable circuits of embodiment.

6. Next, move your attention to the 8th chakra two feet above the crown of your head. Again, intend to tune into the living sensation of this chakra in any way you can. Breathe from the 8th chakra down into your Heart chakra and then exhale back up, going back and forth a few times. Keep your attention on this pathway between these two chakras, feeling every bit of it as you go back and forth. Take the time you need to build this circuit. Again, working with the bandhas in the upper body will be a great help in focusing the energy and your attention in this pathway.

7. Now, imagine a hollow light tube filling the vertical center of your body, running all the way from the 8th chakra above your head to the Earth Star chakra below your feet. All the chakras exist within this tube. Visualize balls of bright golden light in both the 8th and Earth Star chakras.

8. Next, as you breathe in, visualize both of these golden light balls moving toward each other. At the end of the in-breath, they both merge in the Heart chakra. As you breathe out, send the two light balls back up and down, respectively to the 8th and Earth Star chakras. Repeat this vertical breathing pattern for a few minutes, tuning into the experience of pure, unconditional

love. Keep massaging the rear roof of your mouth with your tongue, and Mula Bandha slightly squeezed throughout.

9. At a time when your attention is on the 8th chakra above your head imagine a three-sided pyramid of light appearing, with its apex at the 8th chakra, and the base of the pyramid at the level a little below your hips.

10. Next, breathe down to the Earth Star below your feet and imagine an upside-down pyramid appearing with its apex at the Earth Star, and its base up around your upper chest area, overlapping the upright pyramid. This creates a star tetrahedron geometric form around your entire body.

11. Take a deep breath in, and then blow out forcefully, commanding both pyramids to start spinning. They are both spinning clockwise and counter-clockwise at the same time, rather slowly. Take a moment to feel this movement and allow your body to align to it.

12. Breathe deeply into your Heart, allowing pure, unconditional love for all life to build within you. Totally embrace this experience of love. Ask this pure love to activate your merkaba. Invoke your Avatar transmission and your future self, whose light body merkaba is already fully realized and activated. Ask that your pure love amplify and increase. Allow your transmission to amplify your love several times, and each time you do feel the merkaba spinning faster. Finally, ask it to spin at "Godspeed", or the speed of light, or whatever you are led to.

13. As part of this process, you can make invocations like these:

    Activate merkaba!

    I now invoke my perfect Avatar transmission

    I call upon my fully enlightened future self and ask her/him/other to activate and perfect my merkaba, now.

    My Avatar transmission: activate merkaba now

14. Continue to breathe deeply, flowing with expansive love for yourself and all life. Give up all trying and allow yourself to see and/or feel your merkaba. Sense its rotating, spinning quality. If you are unsure you are experiencing it, again call upon your future self who has already mastered this practice, asking this part of you to integrate its mastery into your present body and awareness.

15. If you desire additional support you can call upon the activating transmission within this book.

16. A wonderful addition to this practice I learned from Meg Benedicte, master Ascension teacher, is to activate Metatron's Cube in your cosmic body. Imagine you are standing in the center of a large image of Metatron's Cube containing 13 circles (see diagram). All possible intersection points of the circles are connected, thereby generating all the major geometric forms. As you are forming the merkaba as explained above, imagine columns of rotating light rising up and moving outward from each of the 13 circles, merging to create one expanding vortex of golden light spinning counter-clockwise outside of your merkaba. As you sense this cosmic vortex spinning around you, allow its centrifugal force to spin any old limiting beliefs or toxic energies you are ready to release out of your energy field, and back to Source.

Notes about this practice:

1. Remember, this practice is more about loving and allowing than efforting and being a champion visualizer. It is a great opportunity to allow your future self to step into your present experience and direct you.

2. Once you activate your merkaba, you can program it for specific purposes. Here are some examples of how I have programmed my merkaba recently:

   - To protect me from harmful electromagnetic fields.

   - To keep me healthy and safe while mingling with people at a dance.

   - To uplift, guide and empower my practice of Planetary Healing (Chapter 13).

   - To help bring optimal results in a remote healing session I led (Chapter 12).

SECTION 5

COSMIC CONSCIOUSNESS

This is a bonus section containing writings to expand your perspective. It is not necessary to read this section in order to receive the core teachings and practices of this book. This section is offered for those who wish to go further.

28

Creation Story

Note to readers – The storyline presented in this chapter is derived from my understandings of cosmology, mythology, hermetic law, quantum physics and various spiritual traditions, as well as my intuitive understandings and revelations. As you read it, I suggest that you attune to your own feelings and inner knowing to intuit the truth of the narrative for yourself.

Before there was time, space or anything there was nothing. There was not even darkness, for that implies an absence of light and there was no light. There were none of the sub-atomic particles we now recognize as the tiny building blocks of creation – no atoms, electrons, quarks, photons, *Plancks* or… anything. Even the God of our conceptions, or what Buddhists call the Void did not exist because those are inherently full of Light.

Yet even then an infinitely resourceful seed existed that contained all possibilities. Let's call this seed Source. Source existed in a state of what could only be described as bliss, or perfect joy. There was no duality to this – no happiness/sadness, joy/depression – just perfect joy. This consciousness was capable of thought in its purest form – a focusing of consciousness for a purpose.

Eventually, a thought arose in this perfect consciousness of Source. It was a thought full of desire and longing for self-expression. Although there were no words then, for our purposes I will use modern vernacular to express that thought as something like this:

It's awesome being perfect joy, and now I want to create something to share and express My joy

This thought instantaneously created the tools necessary for its fulfillment – mathematics and geometry. What happened next is reflected with amazing accuracy by the gestation process of a human embryo. Out of nothing, a point of something appeared – a seed of life with the quality of Light. This seed started dividing into fractals – geometric divisions of the whole. Each part contained the perfect joy and consciousness of the original perfect consciousness. Source perceived these divisions and its joy increased. "Way cool! I AM One, yet there are now also more of Me."

Then another thought arose – while this is great having multiple parts of me that are reflections of One, what if I could create parts that are different variations of Me? This seemed even more interesting, so Source intended this to be. All things that Source intends come to pass, and so the new instruction to the ever-increasing fractals was to explore permutations of expression. It was clear that some form of contrast would be needed to create diversity, so the original polarity was formed. This first polarity is often called Yin-Yang. A set of building blocks would be needed to create differing forms. These arose in the form of seven vibratory states, often called the colors or Rays of creation. These existed in a multidimensional matrix, far beyond the ability of our minds to comprehend. These geometries created gradients of energy with endless opportunities for contrast, thus opening up infinite possibilities of creation.

Our modern computers are made in the image of the workings of consciousness and can be given instructions (programs) that the processor of the computer carries out. As a simple example, the instruction to calculate pi, the ratio of the circumference of a sphere to its diameter can be programmed and it will come up with 3.14 followed by endless fractal numbers.

In a similar way, the original instruction of creation was to create endless variations of the perfect consciousness of Source, each with its own unique mathematical vibratory quality. At this stage all of this was still happening outside of time as we know it – it just existed. Each of these fractals of creation still expressed the perfect consciousness, Light and joy of Source.

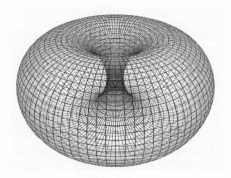

Source created programming that would allow each of the new fractals to continually regenerate itself directly from Source itself. It did this through a special geometric form we now call the *torus* that would provide endless nurturing and regeneration direct from infinite source.[115] This was a great system – all of the fractals would now be perpetually sustained.

But Source wanted to make this new creation even more interesting.

So, imagine a child on Christmas Day in a wealthy family being surrounded by all the finest, most costly toys and games he just received– and feeling…bored. He's thinking – All these great gifts are well and good, but I already had so many great toys from before. I want something that will excite me more and stir up my feelings.

In a similar way, Source allowed a new, daring thought instruction to its new creation game. I will now allow these parts of Me to manifest not only in different frequency/geometry forms but also at different frequency *levels*. This was a big deal because up to that point there was no possibility of any level other than perfection. So, yes, in a sense we could say that Source was "bored" with perfection and joy and wanted to experience itself with a more interesting contrast. So, Source created this through another, radical thought.

This new programming allowed the creation of fractals with different expressions of consciousness. None of this was what we would call physical yet – no stars, planets, life forms as we know it. But now the fractals were freed up to vibrate at different frequency levels. Source saw this and was amused. But then a thought came – now that I've unleashed this process of allowing expressions of consciousness different than Me, it is inevitable that some of these will eventually vibrate at very low levels of consciousness. While this was an almost inconceivable thought, even to Source, it perceived this through its infinite wisdom. It pondered this possibility – could what I just unleashed actually create something that would lose awareness of its true nature, that it is just a part of Me?

Source came up with a brilliant solution, and this was the first form of "insurance" in the Universe. Its solution was to place a seed of its perfection within the center of each of the fractals, that could never be deleted. This "safety net" assured that any of these creations would always be able to remember its source. Satisfied that this insurance policy would keep its creations connected, Source allowed this cosmic experiment to continue.

As this program of creation unfolded to the delight of its creator, the mathematical progression did indeed eventually create some fractals of very low vibratory rate. Some vibrated so slowly that they seemed to go dark from source

---

[115] Torus is a geometric form that continually circulates and re-distributes energy. They are found throughout the structures of the Universe, including electromagnetic fields and the energy fields of the human body and the Earth. A torus is created when a circle or sphere encloses a line it does not intersect with.

Light. I say "seemed" because, in reality, these were still part of Source. But because the daring program allowed for low vibrational beings the first "forgetfulness" and "amnesia" in the Universe happened. While most of the new fractal beings were full of the Light of their source, some classes of beings in a sense forgot their source and became increasingly dark.

These dark beings still had the torus energy self-replenishment system in place, but they sometimes stopped recognizing that they had it. They started feeling a "lack" of needed Light and nourishment. Before this, there had been no possible concept of "lack" in the infinitely resourceful Universe – just as a fish in the ocean could not possibly be thirsty. But these dark ones went so low in consciousness, they felt a need for the Light of Source they did not believe they could fulfill within themselves. So, they looked at the fractal beings who were full of Light and started coveting their Light. They started thinking about how they could take Light and nourishment from those beings.

This is how the first seed of evil was created in our Universe. You are no doubt seeing some of the ways it is currently playing out in our world.

We can point to many players in our current political, financial and social systems who are continuing to extract light and virtue from others, instead of tapping into their own source connection within themselves. Yet because we live in a totally interconnected fractal Universe, if that seed of evil is within any beings, it is inside of all beings. It is the responsibility of each of us to keep bringing our source light and self-love to our own shadow aspects. In this way, we help ascend our civilization and all beings into the victory of the light.

29

Jumping Timelines – How You Choose Your Reality and Help Uplift the World

Truth is that you are a multi-dimensional being. You are like an intricately cut diamond with many facets. Each of those planes and angles are parts of you, yet most of the time you are only aware of one, or perhaps just a few facets and call that "reality." Depending on their backgrounds and beliefs most people are either unaware of their other facets, may be vaguely aware of them, or may even actively deny that they exist and be ready to ridicule anyone who does, calling them "woo-woo". If you are in the process of Awakening you are becoming aware of other facets of your multi-dimensional nature.

In this context, a timeline is a series of experiences taking you in a certain direction. Because you are a multi-dimensional being, there are many different timelines of experience available to you each moment. Some of them take you into what you would perceive as more positive, joyful outcomes, while other timelines take you into what would seem like more negative outcomes.

Even though our conscious minds may not recognize it, we are continually choosing timelines. A person with low self-esteem, a strong sense of guilt or programmed trauma may unconsciously choose timelines full of setbacks and disasters. A person claiming her sovereignty and self-love is more likely to enter a timeline of more beautiful, abundant and loving experiences. It is well worth us learning to choose timelines consciously!

Whatever timeline we move into is helping create what we call the world – the field of shared experience of humanity. Most of us grow up believing that "the world" is something that exists as an objective reality, and that everybody lives in that same world. We can see that some live in the third world and some the first or second worlds, that some are rich and privileged and some poor and struggling, yet we are taught to see all those as forms of inequality within the same overall world.

To make this clearer to you think of a time you went through a big change in your life. Some series of circumstances happened that affected you strongly and motivated you to change up some things in your life. Maybe you quit your job and started a new career. Maybe you left your partner. Maybe your personality changed in a big way as you went through puberty. You may have been motivated to sell your home and move to a different area. Or it could have all been internal – after some strong experience shattered some of your sense of who you are you started seeing things in a new way. You may have gone through a big accident or illness, a devastating bankruptcy, a traumatic divorce or lived through a dangerous time of political upheaval. Or maybe you survived an earthquake or tsunami. Each of these experiences could have motivated you to choose a different timeline of experience in which you experience your life and world in a new way. That often happens when our old reality is suddenly ripped away by powerful experiences like that. There are more and more people all over the planet having those kind of experiences these days.

It also could be even simpler than all that. You don't have to have big external events and calamities like those to shift timelines. You can shift into a new reality simply by choosing it. In fact, we do that many times each day, seeing that process of shifting realities and perspectives as normal. But most of us stay pretty close to what is familiar in terms of the timelines we allow ourselves to experience.

Quantum Physics and Timelines

Quantum physics is a combination of theories and mathematical models about the behavior of sub-atomic particles. Many famous laboratory experiments have confirmed some of these theories.

One of the most bizarre and popular theories of Quantum Physics is the Many Worlds Interpretation (MWI) proposed by Hugh Everett III in 1957. I'll express this in relatable human terms before expressing it in scientific terms.

Imagine that you are sitting home with nothing to do on a Friday evening, wishing you could do something more fun. Then you get a text message from your best friend Janine who invites you to spontaneously meet her for an evening full moon hike. You're feeling really happy and relieved that Janine called you and just as you're filling up your water bottle your phone beeps and your twenty-something daughter text messages you. She's in the mood to talk and confide some things in you that she has been going through, which is a rare event. Now you're in a conflict. You're so up for running out the door to go hiking with your friend but would hate to miss a chance to catch up with your daughter who rarely calls on the phone. What to do? In the world we believe in, you would have to make a difficult choice to either text Janine to tell her something has come up, and now you can't go hiking. Or text your daughter back to ask to speak with her another time (which could be a long time).

In the quantum world, however, BOTH experiences happen simultaneously. In one dimensional reality, you go hiking with Janine and in another parallel dimension, you enjoy quality, unrushed time with your daughter. That's not all, however. "You" are also having an infinite number of other experiences and choices, each in its own dimension. Woo Hoo!

Let's now look at the quantum level of sub-atomic particles that Hugh Everett III was theorizing about. In that world, a "quantum event" is anything happening to sub-atomic particles or wave functions, such as a photon of light moving from point A to point B. Everett's Many Worlds interpretation states that each time a quantum event takes place, such as that photon moving from point A to point B all other the different possible movements of the particle also happen, such as that same photon moving from point A to points C, D, E and more. Each of those options creates a parallel dimension of existence.

For example, if a scientist observes a photon of light moving 90 degrees to the right that photon also simultaneously moved 90 degrees to the left and in every other possible direction. Although human scientists can only measure one of the movements of the photon each of those other possibilities exists and creates its own parallel dimension. By observing and measuring the movement of the photon the scientist was applying his consciousness to this observation which made the infinite possibilities of the Quantum Field "collapse" into that definable outcome of a photon moving to the right.

Therefore it is consciousness that brings the formless Quantum field of infinite possibilities into an observable, measurable form.

Yes, pretty mind-blowing stuff.

We live in a holographic and fractal Universe. That means:

1. **Inter-Connected Holographic Universe**: Each point in the Universe is directly connected with every other point in the Universe, in all dimensions. This is often called "quantum entanglement".

2. **Fractal Universe**: Each thing or event occurs at an infinite number of scales, or octaves. Musical notes are an easy-to-understand example of that. Each note, such as "C" occurs in higher and lower octaves of a scale. While there are limited octaves in the musical scale that our ears can hear, there are countless higher and lower octaves on the cosmic, universal level. This is what is usually referred to as microcosms and macrocosms. For example, the spiral geometric form exists on a microcosmic level as a tiny DNA molecule and on the macrocosmic level as vast spiral-shaped galaxies.

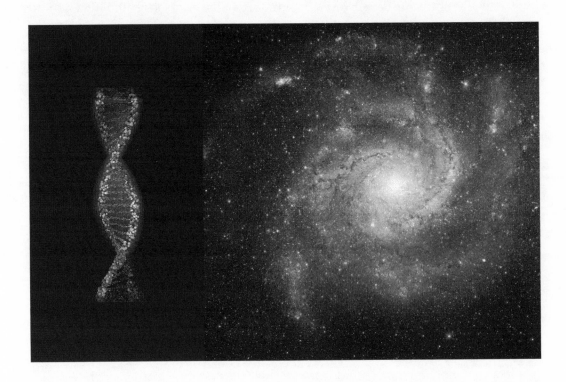

Based on these principles it makes sense that the behavior of sub-atomic particles described in the Many Worlds Interpretation is reflected on the larger, macrocosmic level (as people, for example). Based on this proposition it can make sense that we human beings also have many potential doorways of experience or timelines in front of us at all times. It is the one we apply our consciousness (focus) onto that "collapses" into what we call our reality. So when you wake up in the morning and look out the window and see a gray, overcast day, do all your neighbors also see that?

You may want to read these last paragraphs a few times till it all sinks in.

So what does all that really mean and how does it affect me? Here are some things to ponder, in a step-by-step list format that may be easier on the brain:

- There is a formless Quantum Field that contains the potential for everything that exists – everything from photons of light to bananas to people to stars to black holes in space. The Quantum Field is often thought of by quantum physicists as consisting of wave functions of energy.

- It appears to be consciousness that makes one of the potential outcomes of the Quantum Field precipitate into a discrete, observable event. That can be called a collapse of the Quantum Field into expression.

- Based on the principles of Quantum Physics **there are many possible outcomes for each event.**

- Each of those possible outcomes are not just possible, they all actually occur in different realities.

- As each outcome occurs it creates its own parallel dimension of existence. Each of those can be called a timeline.

- It is the outcome we validate through our observation that we call "reality." We are unaware of the other possible outcomes and so usually deny their existence.

- Because we live in a holographic, fractal Universe each event that occurs is inter-connected with all other things and events and takes place at all microcosmic (tiny) and macrocosmic (enormous) levels.

- We human beings are part of this holographic, fractal reality.

- Therefore each moment of our experience contains many possible outcomes or timelines.

- It is joyful and empowering to acknowledge that we are creator beings capable of playing with unlimited possibilities of creation. This is the consciousness of the fifth dimension.

- Because most of us tend to be fear-based creatures of addictive habit we usually create well-worn "grooves" in the infinite possibilities before us to pretend we have control over our lives. We do this by continuing to choose (or re-create) the same timelines over and over again and call that "reality" (and then often try to impose our "reality" on others!)

- Our choices to keep re-creating habitual, limiting timelines are usually based on fear-based programming we take on as children, or due to other past traumatic experiences. This can be called the process of "domestication", similar to what dogs and farm animals go through to make them obedient to their human masters (I'm not sure that cats ever get fully domesticated.) Or maybe our tendency to keep creating habitual timelines is just spiritual laziness.

- The upside of this is that choosing the same timelines over and over again makes our life experiences and personal identity more stable and defined.

- The downside is that we often don't like those well-worn, familiar timeline grooves and may feel stuck and boxed in by them.

- As we dare to awaken to know ourselves as Avatars we can claim greater power of conscious choice of which timelines we choose to experience. This is a major aspect of the process of Mastery.

- Each miracle Jesus demonstrated happened through his mastery of timelines. He raised Lazarus from the dead by seeing a different timeline for him in which Lazarus was not dead. The same goes for each miracle you have demonstrated.

All of this can be summed up by this simple, oft-repeated statement:

You have the power to create your reality.

Choosing Timelines

The first step on your path of consciously choosing timelines is to become clear about what timeline you want to experience. Realize that a lot of the up and down dramas of your life come from not consciously choosing your reality, thereby allowing yourself to be pulled and influenced in many ways. It is the way of Mastery when you stop allowing others, or your own subconscious programming, to choose the timeline you are experiencing. In other words, moving from auto-pilot to autonomy.

Take some time to reflect on what world, what reality you really want to live in. What do you want to be doing? What do you really desire? What do you want to be contributing? How much abundance in money, friendships, business connections, spiritual experience and love will you allow and accept? Writing these down or creating a vision board of what you want can be very supportive. This is about your sovereignty – you taking charge of your creation. Also, write about how you may have allowed others to influence your choices or convince you to limit what you believe to be possible. When you feel a degree of clarity about what you really want, then you are ready to proceed.

The Morning Timeline Focus practice explained in Chapter 25 is an excellent way to start your day consciously choosing the timeline of experience you want to live in and express.

How to Help Uplift the World

Has the gist of what you just read sunk in? Can you acknowledge at least the possibility of these things? If so good! We are now ready to get to the best part of this chapter. Not only do you have the power to create your reality, but you also have the power to help uplift our collective human (and animal) reality. That means that you can surely help uplift the world.

First of all, what does that mean, uplifting the world, other than sounding like a pompous, egotistical fantasy???

It means that you are a divine creator being ready to take your next step in claiming your true power and presence. That means moving out of denial of the truth of who you really are. It means that as you open up to this reality of who you really are, you choose to help make others freer, happier, healthier and more awake to their true identity. And you take action to do so. Got it?

There is no one picture of what helping uplift the world looks like. It could be a holistic healer having a big "aha moment" about tapping into unlimited healing energies. He commits to treating his patients less on the symptomatic level and more by helping empower them to claim their own self-healing abilities. It could be an elder in a remote African village holding an energetic field of peace and safety for her village. Things get better and no one knows that the old woman has anything to do with it. Or it could be a person catching fire with the truth of spiritual awakening and creating a worldwide movement that totally goes viral as she goes on an international book tour. Or a child radiating higher love and light in the midst of a tough inner-city school, somehow softening tensions and facilitating more real connectedness.

Uplifting the world starts with the awakening and determination of individuals to serve, then it branches out into groups, communities and beyond. You see through the eyes of 5D, perceiving people, societies and the world already uplifted and already whole. You allow your transmission to serve by bringing more of its frequency to others.

A prerequisite for this is grounding in a basic moral sense of what is right, and for the greatest good of all humanity. It starts with the choice to be part of the solution to bring that goodness to yourself and others. While different people from different cultures are entitled to their own opinions and perspectives on what is good there are some things that are universal truths. Good comes from the same root word as God. Therefore what is ultimately good and right is what is closest to the supreme consciousness many call God. A high truth is that God is Love, God is Unity, God is what is common to all life. It is Good, or God-like to:

- Treat others as you would like to be treated.
- Not let fear stop or control you. Endeavor to be courageous and take a stand for what you are passionate about.
- Give at least as much as you take, and endeavor to give more than you wish to take. Then you will get more and be a lot happier and open-hearted in the process.
- Create your own Good instead of trying to take it from others. This is the basis for being a "good person". Evil creeps in as we feel disconnected from the Good within us and resort to trying to take the Good and light from others.
- Be kind, generous, helpful, respectful and real.
- Respect and honor the Earth we live on and which sustains us.
- Discover and claim your superpower(s) so you can do all the above from a more effective, empowered place.

OK, so far that list sounds like any good Sunday church service. Let's next see where timelines fit in.

During the contentious Presidential election of 2020 here in the United States, we had a relatively peaceful election day, even though so many people were fearing violence and intimidation at many polling places. I will tell you my story from that time to illustrate an example of shifting a timeline.

In the weeks and days leading up to that election, the media carried many alarming stories about well-organized groups preparing to intimidate voters at polling places. There was also the present possibility that millions of people could believe that the election results had been falsified or stolen, and then create massive violence in the streets. There had already been a few incidents of voter intimidation happening at some primary elections prior to November 3. Preparing ourselves for that possibility, my sister and I participated in online trainings teaching how to prepare for and deal with violent street demonstrations and unrest.

I remember two days before the election feeling some anxiety about these possibilities. I had already lived through sixteen Presidential elections in my life that all went relatively smoothly, and were followed by peaceful transfers of power. The idea that this election could trigger violence, anarchy and possible Constitutional crises felt heavy and scary. I remember sitting in my bathtub one night feeling those things when a light went on in me. I remembered what I know about timelines and being a creator being. I immediately shifted my thoughts from fearing what might happen to proactively helping create what I wanted to happen. I invoked divine violet flame and golden crystal energies to surround the Earth and to fill each polling place in the USA or other countries having elections at that time. I poured my heart and soul into visualizing safety, truth, orderliness and integrity filling the election process and all the voters, officials and volunteers running the systems. Then I remembered that I am not alone in creating this, and called out to link my visions with the millions or billions of others in the world who were visualizing or praying for a positive outcome for the U.S. elections

As I took charge of my reality in this way I felt a significant shift happen within me. All fear vanished from my mind. I remembered that I am not a nervous bystander waiting to see what will happen, I AM a powerful being helping CREATE what will happen.

That is such a powerful truth I will repeat that sentence one more time:

I am not a nervous bystander waiting to see what will happen, I AM a powerful being helping CREATE what will happen

In that bathtub, I intentionally chose another doorway and stepped into a different timeline. I now knew what I needed to do. I committed to repeating my invocation and visualization of a peaceful, safe election each morning and night, and I followed through on that.

Election Day 2020 did go mostly peacefully. Although violence did erupt in Washington, D.C. on January 6, 2021, there was a peaceful transfer of power as the new President was inaugurated. The underlying polarization and conflicts in this country have not been resolved, however.

Moving forward it is clear that there are many major timeline choices in front of us ranging from disastrous to surprisingly positive. As of the date of this writing we are continuing to face COVID-19 infections in many regions, major political divides remaining after the election, economic calamity for so many, continuing racial and gender injustices and rapidly encroaching environmental degradation. But guess what? Instead of fearing and worrying about these things we can see them for what they are: possible timelines in front of us. None are certain or pre-destined. Each of us can raise our consciousness to the level of creatorship and claim our power to choose the timelines we want to live in and see in our world.

This is the Time for Avatars to Awaken and Serve

There is clearly great danger in the shared reality of our world at this time. While so many governments, organizations, scientists and individuals are working hard to solve these issues, so many seem almost hopeless. Yet when people claim their Christ Avatar Consciousness and connect with others who doing the same a limitless force field of higher light is created. **This force field is way more powerful than all those difficult issues**. As each of us realizes we do have a choice of the reality we will live in, we can learn to shift the timelines of our experience. As groups, and eventually multitudes do that same activity the world literally changes.

Summary

You have the power to help heal humanity. That's who you are. You can choose a timeline of great light, in which the people of our planet are mainly steered by the deep love in their hearts and are working together to solve our problems and live in harmony with the Earth. Once you are in that timeline, you have the opportunity to invite others to join you in it. Yes, this is a free-will planet and we can't compel anyone to choose to go with the flow of ascension consciousness, but a kind invitation goes a long way. Never underestimate the power of your words and your Presence to help others release their painful dreams and shift into a higher life. And never underestimate the power we have to help humanity truly ascend at this pivotal time.

SECTION 6

AVATAR RESOURCES

This section contains valuable reference materials referred to throughout the book, including definitions of terminology, bibliography of source texts and websites, Avatar I AM decrees, Ascension Practices directory and resources for further study and connection with other awakening Avatars.

For Further Development

Darren Starwynn offers many additional resources for awakening the Avatar within you, developing your Quantum healing abilities and discovering how to be an effective part of the solution on our planet now.

Free Awakening the Avatar Within Guided Meditation Course

Free of charge to purchasers of this book, this course includes downloadable key guided audio meditations. Some meditations also offered in video format. Course webpage includes link to resources for connecting and networking with other awakening Avatar Lightworkers. www.drstarwynn.com/practices

Quantum Healing Program
Embody Your Master Healer Abilities and Create an Effective, Empowered Life

A transformative 14 week live online program with Darren Starwynn. It is for those awakening to their Avatar self while discovering how to self-heal, and help heal others on the Quantum level. Appropriate for healers, physicians and healthcare practitioners, and includes an intensive long weekend retreat experience. www.lightworkerministry.com/awakencourse

Certification training programs in Quantum Catalyst Healing

For professional healthcare professionals and healers. Learn how you can receive training and mentorship in gaining the skills, activations and practical knowledge to offer Quantum Catalyst healing, vibrational medicine and related skills professionally. www.lightworkerministry.com/bridgetomastery

For information about the microcurrent and light therapy equipment developed by the author send an email request to info@eastwestseminars.com

Other Books
by Darren Starwynn

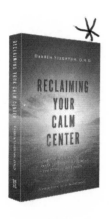

Reclaiming Your Calm Center

This unique book gives you surprising new insights about your true identity, and the often hidden external and internal influences that have been affecting your state of mind. It provides practical methods to help you find inner peace no matter what is going on in or around you, and an overview of cutting-edge energy medicine methods for rapidly releasing trauma. Reclaiming Your Calm Center will take you on a journey into greater self-knowledge that can radically change the way you see yourself and your world. (2017)

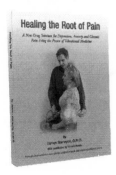

Healing the Root of Pain

In this book you will learn a powerful, drug-free method for rapidly balancing the human energy field, relieving depression and pain, restoring depleted vital energy and helping remove deeply held mental-emotional blocks to well-being and success. It teaches a unique combination of color light and sound energy medicine in combination with essential oils, microcurrent, visualization, chakra balancing, intuitive counseling and soul healing. It integrates wonderfully with acupuncture, chiropractic, psychology and pain management. (2013)

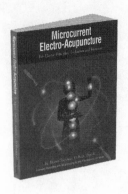

Microcurrent Electro-Acupuncture

Microcurrent electro-acupuncture is a safe and highly effective evaluation and treatment system with far-reaching applications, including pain management, rehabilitation, tissue healing acceleration and meridian balancing. This book is the definitive guide to this new and outstanding modality. It is organized into easy-to-reference sections covering all aspects of theory, research, techniques and treatment protocols. Abundant photographs illustrate all techniques and listed acu-points. Once you start using microcurrents in your practice you will refer to this text again and again. (2002)

Definitions of Terminology

3D or Third dimension – The physical world. Any physical object can be measured and defined through the three dimensions of length, width and height. People primarily focused on the physical world tend to try to understand reality through reason, the logical thinking ability of the mind. While reason is a powerful and valuable part of human ability, it is only a small fraction of the totality of our consciousness.

4D or Fourth dimension - Represents the dimension of time as well as aspects of higher mind, emotions and non-physical experiences. While 4D is of a higher vibrational level than the rational mind and physical body, it is still polarized between light and dark influences. Psychic experiences such as astral travel, remote viewing, contacting spirits, channeling and magic mostly occur in 4D. It is not a realm of pure consciousness. There has been extensive warfare going on in 4D between dark and light energies, and a great deal of dis-information and distracting energies have compromised this realm.

5D or fifth dimension – A dimension of experience that exists in one-ness of pure love, and is a dimension of limitless possibilities. 5D is therefore the place of truth, fulfillment and true healing of the human condition. The Earth most people perceive is in 3D and 4D while the New Earth exists primarily in 5D.

Akashic records – A realm of consciousness in which all events and experiences are stored, analogous to a vast cosmic hard drive. People can train themselves through the purification of their minds to tap into and read the Akashic records.

Alchemy – The art and science of transformation and creation. Alchemy includes methods of transforming lower vibrational energies to higher vibrational energies. This could include raising the experience of the mind from a dispersed, fear-based experience to a higher more love-filled consciousness. Physical transformations can also be considered alchemy, such as the caterpillar changing into a butterfly or transforming lead into gold.

Annunaki – An advanced extra-terrestrial race referred to in ancient Sumerian records. According to some sources the Annunaki came to Earth to mine gold and genetically created the first humans to be slaves. They reputedly eventually gave higher faculties of intellect and soul to humans so they could serve better, and then the humans rebelled and created their own civilization.

Antahkarana bridge – A pillar of conscious light that connects our crown chakra on top of our heads up to higher realms of consciousness, including the 8th and 9th chakras above the head. The Antahkarana bridge can be activated and strengthened through Ascension practices. It is the pathway through which you connect with what is referred to as your Avatar transmission in this book.

Archangels – Angels of high rank and expanded purpose who serve massive numbers of souls. These have been referred to in Christian and esoteric literature. The best-known Archangels have been called Michael, Raphael, Gabriel and Uriel. An Archangel who strongly supports the Ascension of consciousness on Earth now is called Metatron.

Ascended Master – A human being who passed all the tests and spiritual initiations of human life and is now serving on an advanced non-physical level. Because most Ascended Masters have taken on huge levels of service to masses of people and other life they are able to express God-like powers. Jesus, Buddha, Quan Yin and St. Germain are examples. Ascended Masters are significant supporters of the human Ascension process now underway.

Ascension – Mass elevation of consciousness that has happened many times through the history of life. Ascension tends to be quantized, which means that great upward change often occurs in short amounts of time, as we are going through now.

Astral – A quality of 4D higher mind in which various forms of psychic experiences occur. The astral realms are fascinating and seductive because they seem so advanced and unlimited compared to worldly consciousness, but it is ultimately not fulfilling because it is still dualistic. The astral realm can be called a "weapon of mass distraction" when indulged in rather than focusing upon the true, divine self.

Atlantis – An ancient civilization written about by Plato and other well-known writers. Many people of Atlantis worked with advanced energy technologies tapping into cosmic and Earthly energies. Mis-use of some of these technologies allegedly led to the destruction of Atlantis through massive flooding. Many Lightworkers have deep soul memories of being part of that culture, often carrying forward traumatic conditioning and desire to help heal those in others.

Avatar – Divinity expressing as a human being. Avatars have outsized influences on human consciousness and civilization, with some Avatars affecting millions to billions of people. In the time we are living in many human beings can awaken to being an Avatar through the process of becoming Christed.

Ayahuasca – A mixture of two psycho-active plants used in healing ceremonies among some indigenous peoples in South America and more recently, among people seeking healing internationally. The plants used are *Banisteriopsis Caapi* vine with the leaves of the *Psychotria Viridis* shrub.

Bandha – Means "lock" in Sanskrit and refers to tightening specific internal muscle groups to help move and build vital energy in the body. Tightening bandhas is an important part of Central Axis breathing, a core Ascension practice.

Chakra – Means "wheel" in Sanskrit, and refers to spinning vortices of conscious energy stacked in a vertical column in the central axis of the body. There are seven chakras within the body, starting with the Root chakra between the legs up to the Crown chakra on the top of the head. There are also chakras below the body in the Earth and higher spiritual chakras above the head. Each chakra helps regulate and influence specific organs, glands, nervous system plexi, emotions and aspects of consciousness.

Channeling – The practice of a person quieting their mind and body so communication from another being or level of consciousness can be expressed through them. A person can channel by speaking words inspired by the being or consciousness they are attuning to, or by bringing through non-verbal higher-level vibrational energies. People doing channeling need to be very careful and discerning as there are plenty of astral 4D beings who love to channel through people, and are of limited or dubious purity and accuracy of information. The more a person has gone through the Christing process, the more clear and pure their communications become and they tend to mostly channel through their own higher divine self, or I AM presence.

Christ – Means "anointed one" in Greek, and is the infinite field of divine love and light as it expresses through a human being. The process of becoming Christed allows greater direct expression of one's unlimited Avatar transmission through the mind and physical body.

Christing - An alchemical, mental, physiological process through which your mind, body, nervous system and genetics are literally re-wired to operate at higher frequencies of love, intelligence and divine power. This increases your capacity to remain aware of the consciousness of pure love and divine Presence and clearly express it to others.

Consciousness – The quality of awareness that exists in all things and existence. All consciousness is part of divine source, also called God. There is no consciousness separate from that, although the separated mind can cloud consciousness with lower vibrational energies.

Control Matrix – A system of domination that has affected the human race throughout most of its history. The control matrix is created and maintained by a network of human and non-human shadow controllers. Nowadays lots of the controllers are operating out in the open and masses of people are buying into their dis-information.

Decrees – Empowered, creative statements made by a person by the authority of their divine self. Decrees often start with the words I AM, which is the highest divine identity.

Dharma – Living in accord with your true purpose, living virtuously in harmony with nature.

Earth Star – A chakra that sits below your body about two feet (.61 meter) down into the Earth, that grounds you and helps increase embodiment of your true, Avatar self.

Elementals - Elementals are simple conscious beings expressing through plants, minerals and many forms of Earth energies. They help regulate weather and the cycles of nature. Many of the natural disasters like unusual floods, droughts and wildfires happening recently are associated with an imbalance of elementals due to human depredations and chaotic thought patterns of mass consciousness.

Embodiment – The process of the master divine being you truly are coming into physical expression. Also called incarnation. Very few people are fully embodied due to deeply embedded fear and control programs, and also because they have not felt ready to be fully responsible for being Present. Coming into fuller embodiment creates physiologic, epigenetic changes which upgrade the body.

Epigenetics – The science that studies the ways lifestyle and environment on the outside, and thoughts and feelings on the inside continually modify DNA gene expression, thereby affecting all physiological processes and expressions. This is the basis for the old statement "we are what we think". The processes of Christing and fuller embodiment described in this book create radical changes through these epigenetic pathways.

Fourth Dimension – See 4D above.

Fractal – A geometric form based on numbers that recur on larger and smaller scales. The universe is composed of endlessly repeating fractals on huge (macrocosmic) and tiny (microcosmic) scales. Musical notes are an example of fractals that recur in higher and lower octaves.

Galactic Counsel – A group of non-physical master light beings who are said to serve by helping manage the overall affairs of multiple worlds, including the Earth. There are many who believe that the Galactic Counsel is now playing a key role in removing the influences of the Shadow Controllers and promoting the Ascension of consciousness on Planet Earth.

Gong Song – A Chinese expression that means "respectfully return." It is sometimes used at the end of healing sessions or gatherings to gratefully acknowledge and dismiss the Light beings who have been in attendance and supporting. A great way to end events, as taught by Dr. Zhi Gang Sha, is to say "Love you love you love you, thank you thank you thank you, Gong Song Gong Song Gong Song".

Hero's Journey – The archetypal process people go through in bravely facing the challenges and obstacles that have kept them in fear and limitation, so they can access their inner power and gain mastery. The Hero's journey is a part of many mythologies, books, movies and stories and is a necessary part of the process of Christing and embodiment.

Holographic – The reality of each part of a system being inter-connected with and containing the whole system. We live in a holographic universe and our own bodies are arranged holographically. Holography is the reason we are able to do effective remote and planetary healing sessions taught about in this book.

Hybrids – It is very likely that many to most human beings are genetic products of inter-mixing with various extra-terrestrial races. According to many sources of information, this may have been the true origin of the human race rather than evolution from apes as Darwin believed.

I AM – The truest and most powerful phrase in language. When you say I or I AM you are speaking from Divine source. Decrees are powerful statements originating from your true, Avatar self. It is very important to be careful to only put positive outcomes and experiences you want after the words I AM. For example, while it is not harmful to say "I am feeling kind of down today" you can significantly lower your spiritual vibration level by saying "I am down today." In that second phrase, you are invoking the greatest power of the universe to affirm that you are down.

I AM Presence – The tangible vibrational energy field of your true, Avatar self that radiates out from you and blesses others. I AM Presence also refers to the Cosmic Body that is the most expansive aspect of the human energy field.

Implants – In this context, a non-physical mechanism placed into the subconscious mind of a person that keeps creating patterns of limiting or self-sabotaging thoughts and experiences. Implants can be placed by other malevolent people or entities, or by a person herself in an attempt to protect from mis-using spiritual power.

Initiation, spiritual initiation – A tipping point experience for individuals or groups in which they permanently ascend to a higher vibrational level of embodiment of their true, Avatar self. Initiations usually take place when a soul has committed to serving on a higher and more expansive level and has prepared themselves through Ascension practices that clear and purify the mind and body. Sometimes initiations happen first and the purification follows. The life of Jesus demonstrated the first five stages of spiritual initiation. He blazed a path that has made it easier for many people to go through these initiations.

Interference fields – What is created when two different energy frequencies mix with each other, thereby creating additional frequencies called beat frequencies. Information and memory are stored in interference fields throughout the human brain, body and the cosmos.

Karma – The universal law that requires people to experience the impact of their own actions and decisions. People who help create pain and suffering for others will need to experience similar forms of pain themselves. Those who sow seeds of love, generosity and service tend to harvest more blessings as those experiences come back to them. 5D, the fifth dimension is a karma-free zone.

Kuxan Suum – The universal pillar described by the ancient Mayans that is the axis of the entire universe. Kuxan Suum is in a holographic relationship with the axis of the Earth and the central axis of our bodies including the spine and column of the chakras.

Lightworker – A person or being who has made a deep commitment to serve by holding and emanating spiritual Light. Lightworkers are called into full activity at this time on Earth and serve through many service groups described in this book.

Loosh – Human emotional and spiritual energy that is of great interest to other races of beings who feel cut off from their own emotional and spiritual energies. Some humans have been parasitized by some of those beings so they can feed off their loosh.

Mastery – A primary goal of human life in which you learn how to choose and create what you really want, and that which fulfills your purpose. Learning to concentrate your mind on what you really want, living in a state of pure love and cultivating your superpowers are major forms of mastery.

Master healer - The attribute of divine Source that brings painful experiences of the illusion of separation and distortion back into harmony with itself. The healing transformations brought about by any medical or holistic healing art are derived from the Master healer, which is sponsored by divine Love. Master healer is not an individual achievement, it is a universal resource individuals can tap into.

Meridians – Pathways of energy flow. There are well-charted meridians in the human and animal bodies and meridians of the Earth. There are also meridians of the cosmos in holographic connection to the meridians of our bodies.

Merkaba – The counter-rotating geometric body of light that forms around people who go through a process of activation of their light body. Activating the merkaba is grounding, energizing, protective, uplifting and provides a vehicle for travel through the dimensions of consciousness.

Microcurrent – A very low intensity, low-frequency form of electrical therapy that is very popular and highly effective for pain relief, rehabilitation, neurological balancing and rejuvenation. It is a form of vibrational medicine. The use of vibrational therapies such as microcurrent, light and sound therapies are excellent adjuncts to the practice of Quantum healing because they support balancing and unblocking of the body's energy flows. This helps clients to more easily receive and integrate the totally non-physical blessings of the Quantum Field.

Microtubules – A lattice of hollow, cylindrical polymers that exist within the neurons of the brain believed to be a substrate for non-local quantum effects, including inter-connection with all parts of the body and the cosmos.

Mula Bandha – Means "root lock" in Sanskrit. The yogic practice of tightening the pubococcygeal and other muscles in the area of the Root or Base chakra between the legs in order to promote the flow of vital energy and light through the Central Axis of the body.

Nadis – The network of energy-circulating channels in the body which include the meridians, the central channels of Ida, Pingala and Sushumna and huge numbers of tiny inter-connecting channels throughout the body. There are usually areas of constriction, blockage or imbalance in the nadis of most people. The use of drugs and traumatic experiences tend to lead to that. The process of Christing / Embodiment heals, opens and restores the nadis to greater or full functioning.

New Earth – The higher-vibrational reality of the Earth that already exists here and now. The New Earth exists within a balance of the 3D (third dimension physicality), 4D (fourth dimension mental/psychic realm) and 5D (fifth dimension realm of pure love and one-ness). You can train yourself to see and be part of the New Earth.

Planck – The smallest theorized particle in the universe. Its length is 1.6×10^{-35} meters. If you compare the difference in size between a tiny dot on a piece of paper and the entire universe, a Planck is that same difference smaller than the dot on the piece of paper. The Planck is the smallest possible fractal and exists in an infinite number of octaves of increasing size. According to the principle of holography, the entire universe exists within one Planck!

Platonic Solids – Five geometric 3-dimensional forms considered to be polyhedrons, each with a different number of facets, or faces on it. Everything in the physical universe is created from combinations of these forms plus the sphere.

Presence – The quality of your body and energy field being attuned to your true, Avatar self. This is what people feel when they are with you. You cultivate your ability to hold Presence through the process of Christing and embodiment, and this is supported by your daily Ascension practices, and in general, living a life of love and service.

Qigong – Systems of movement and mental concentration aligned with conscious breathing that build, circulate and balance the vital energy of the body. Qigong means "energy cultivation exercises" in Chinese. There are many forms of qigong that are highly supportive of all the personal development and awakening practices offered in this book.

Rejuvenation – The art of healing and detoxifying the body while increasing its ability to maintain higher frequencies of light and consciousness. Rejuvenation is a result of epigenetic upgrades to the body activated by focusing the mind upon Divine love and presence, as well as vigorous exercise and a health-supporting diet. Microcurrent and light therapies (Microlight therapy) developed by the author and others provide powerful rejuvenation effects on the physical and energetic level, including facial rejuvenation.

Qi – Means "air" in Chinese. The vital energy of the body that is part physical and part spiritual. When Qi is flowing freely through the body you feel good on all levels. All kinds of pain and disease are associated with blockages or lessening of Qi flow in parts of the body.

Qigong – Exercises of the body the promote the smooth movement of Qi, or vital energy. These are very supportive of Christing and embodiment.

Quantized – Something that exists in a definite quantity. Quantum physics studies packets of light called photons that are quantized. The nine creation waves recognized by the ancient Mayans were quantized in that there were special times of sudden leaps upward of consciousness when these waves started coming onto Earth, followed by long, more stable periods. This is a different view than Darwinian theories, which postulate steady, gradual evolution. Darwinian evolution would look like a steady up ramp, while quantized evolution would more resemble discrete stairsteps.

Quantum – An amount of anything. Usually used to refer to the discrete quantity of energy proportional in magnitude to the frequency of the radiation it represents.

Quantum Catalyst Healing – A system of healing developed by the author. It is based on supporting a client in coming into health and psychological/spiritual balance by directly experiencing their true self and releasing old dis-empowering programming. Quantum Catalyst Healing works equally well in person or remotely.

Quantum leap – A sudden increase of energy or frequency level in anything, usually applied to sub-atomic particles. This term is often now applied to the experience of a person rapidly ascending their consciousness level through the process of spiritual initiation or other transformative experiences.

Rays of Creation – Seven frequency levels often expressed as different colors that act as the building blocks of the universe. Source exists in one-ness, and at some point differentiated into Yin and Yang polarities, then a trinity and then into the seven Rays. Those have combined and diversified into everything in the universe. Each person primarily expresses one or more Rays in their personality, body type and overall purpose and mission.

Samskara – Inner burdens of unresolved trauma, personal issues and karma that weigh people down and keeps them in a state of suffering and limitation. Also referred to in this book as energetic gunk, conditioning and residoo-doo. Ascension practices, Quantum healing and loving service to others help to free people from samskara.

Siddhis – Qualities of the power and presence of the Divine as expressed through people. Yogis who practice with diligence often develop siddhis. The expression of your transmission takes the form of siddhis called superpowers in this book.

Slave Self – The separate self most people identify with that can be controlled and manipulated by others, and usually is without us knowing it.

Source – In this context the ultimate consciousness from which all energies and things originate. This can be compared to the word God, but that is not used much in this book due to all the limiting connotations many people have with that word. What is called God are often projections of the human psyche. Source refers to that which existed prior to the Universe.

Sovereign – A being who is its own highest authority. You can claim and embody sovereignty as you come to know and experience your true self and take back your power and energy from all the beings and places you have projected it onto. Our truest self is what we often refer to as God or source, so embodying this truth is sovereignty.

Superpowers – The way your energy transmission expresses through you to serve others. Most people are already expressing their superpowers in part. Cultivating the conscious awareness of your energy transmission in your body, and then stepping out to share your gifts supports the development of your superpowers.

Superstring theory – An advanced theory of Quantum Physics recognizing that the universe is made up of infinitesimally tiny vibrating strings. This theory states that there are at least 21 dimensions of existence and that new dimensions are continually being created and destroyed.

Taboo – A program embedded into people's subconscious minds that maintains their slave self by bringing up feelings of abject terror when they try to free themselves. The greatest taboo affecting the human race is the taboo against knowing who we really are.

Tai Ch'i – A form of qigong that is a slowed-down form of martial arts. Tai ch'i practice is excellent for health, vitality and inner balance.

Timelines – Possible pathways of experience into the future. There are multiple timelines available to us always, some of which lead to more positive, higher-level experiences and some into more negative, limited experiences. Learning to consciously choose the timelines you really want is a major expression of Mastery. A major timeline available to us now is the Ascension timeline. Shadow controllers and many manipulative humans have created artificial, illusory timelines that have seduced the attention of many spiritually-oriented people, and that has been a major astral distraction.

Tonglen – A Buddhist practice in which practitioners breathe in the pain of others and breathe out compassion.

Torus, Toroidal – A primary energy-recirculating geometric form in the universe. A torus is created when a circle or sphere encloses a line it does not intersect with. The energy fields of the Earth, our bodies and electromagnetic fields are toroidal. A major aspect of the process of Sovereignty is reclaiming the free flow of our toroidal energy patterns. Parasitic beings have been able to manipulate and drain energy from others by placing implants into the toroidal fields of humanity. It is a major task for Lightworkers now to eliminate that in themselves and help others to do so to release the slave self.

Transmission – The way divine source expresses itself as and through you. Your transmission has qualities of frequency and vibration specific to you. The highest purpose of Ascension practices and Quantum Catalyst healing is to help people to consciously experience their own transmission and learn to express it more in their everyday life. This is the key to all virtue, success, love, healing abilities, health and fulfillment. The primary focus of this book is supporting readers in recognizing and embodying their transmission.

Vairagya – A Sanskrit term that can be loosely translated as "disillusionment turning into strong motivation". Any meaningful progress on one's path of awakening, healing and life fulfillment requires strong motivation and commitment. Very few people have that on their own accord. Vairagya refers to the greater motivation that comes up to do what is necessary to heal, grow and embody as we go through disillusioning life experiences or "hit bottom".

Vibrational, vibrational – Refers to the oscillating nature of energy. Each energy or object in the universe has a characteristic frequency or vibration. The clinical use of microcurrent, light or sound or potentized herbal remedies is part of the field of vibrational medicine. The human body and mind can be supported in healing through the application of vibrations that resonate with areas of pain or disease.

Virtue – The spiritual equivalent to money. Virtue is accumulated on a spiritual level through acts of loving service, healthy self-discipline and Ascension practices. All people are born with a lot of virtue just by making it into a human body. Many people spend their youth dispersing their virtue and their older years rebuilding it. That pattern is not necessary, however, and it is well that we teach our youth to cultivate virtue.

Yin / Yang – The basic poles of existence, as described in ancient Chinese philosophy and medicine. The art of acupuncture is based on healing myriad pains and diseases of the body by balancing the energies of Yin and Yang in the body using needles, heat, massage, herbal medicine and more.

Avatar Decrees

Decrees are phrases with powerful uplifting and transformative messages. Decrees are spiritual medicine for the purpose of raising the overall vibrational level of your body and mind. Most of those listed here start with the words I AM because that is the claim of your truest identity. Speaking decrees out loud with your hand over your heart, while breathing deeply from your lower abdomen is a powerful way to align all parts of you with the vibration of what you are speaking.

Work with any of the following decrees that you strongly resonate with, or create your own.

I AM

I AM my divine Christ Avatar self lovingly holding this man/woman/other

I AM in love, I AM loved, I AM loving, I AM loveable, I live in abundance always

I invoke my Christ Avatar transmission to heal, bless and uplift all humanity and all life, as is appropriate

I AM dissolving all limiting implants and cloaking devices – instantaneously - NOW

I AM free of all judgment, condemnation and anger toward myself or others

I AM already all things I wish to be. I AM the ray of Light that comes forth from the Heart of God. I AM enough! I AM enough! I AM enough!

I AM the conscious activity and directing power of the Cosmic Christ

I now release any and all soul-level contracts or agreements that I have ever made in this or any other lifetime or existence with any person, situation, group or entity that limited my Sovereignty, Freedom and Joy

I command my Merkaba and Sacred Heart Torus to activate Now!

I AM the Christ

I AM pure love

I AM here, I AM here, I AM here

I AM the healing Power of God. The healing power of God is activated in me, resides in me and is restored in me

I AM the Presence of the Divine effortlessly manifesting my inspired visions and creations, immediately before me

I AM the living light as my personal valet, going before me arranging all things in my life, bringing perfection, grace, abundance and flow into all my activities

I AM the Ascension in the Light

I AM my Avatar transmission surrounding and comforting these painful feelings I'm going through

I AM relaxing and flowing my Avatar transmission through this knot I'm feeling in my gut

My Avatar transmission makes me fearless as I go into this meeting

I AM radiating my Avatar transmission to bring miracle results for this beloved person, beyond my own knowledge. Give me the words to speak, the easy knowing of what to do and the ability to emanate Quantum Healing vibrations through my field. Let my own skills, intelligence and love be informed and uplifted by my transmission.

Bibliography

Bailey, Alice A. The Rays and The Initiations, Lucis Publishing Company, 1960

Bailey, Alice A., Serving Humanity, Lucis Publishing Company, 1972

Bailey, Alice A., The Seven Rays of Life, Lucis Publishing Company, 1995

Blavatsky, Helene, The Secret Doctrine, Theosophical University Press, 2014

Bly, Robert, Iron John, Da Capo Press, 2015

Calleman, Carol Johan, The Nine Waves of Creation: Quantum Physics, Holographic Evolution, and the Destiny of Humanity, Bear and Company 2016

Calleman, Carl Johan, Quantum Science of Psychedelics, Bear and Company 2020

Castaneda, Carlos, Journey to Ixtlan, Washington Square Press, 1991

Chodron, Pema, When Things Fall Apart, Shamballa Press 1997

Dirac, P.A.M., The Principles of Quantum Mechanics, BN Publishing, 2019

Frazier, Vidya Awakening to the Fifth Dimension, First Edition Design Publishing 2014

Gladwell, Malcolm, The Tipping Point, Little, Brown & Company, 2000

Golding, Daniel, Quantum Physics for Beginners: Discover the Science of Quantum Mechanics and Learn the Basic Concepts from Interference to Entanglement by Analyzing the Most Famous Quantum Experiments, self-published

Griffin, G. Edward, The Creature from Jekyll Island, American Media 1994

Kirschbaum, Karen, The Return of Light (out of print)

Lefferts, Marshall, Cosmometry, Cosmometria Publishing, 2019

Lewis, C.S., The Chronicles Of Narnia, Harper-Collins, 2002

Melchizedek, Drunvalo, Ancient Secret of the Flower of Life Volumes 1 & 2, Light Technology Publishing, 1999

Morter, Sue, The Energy Codes, Simon and Schuster 2019

Orwell, George, 1984, Signet Classic, 1961

Pratt, Carl J., Quantum Physics for Beginners, 2021

Pribram, Karl, Brain and Perception, Laurence Erlbaum Associates, 1991

Spalding, Baird, Life and Teachings of the Masters of the Far East, DeVorss & Company 1924

Spence, Lewis, The History of Atlantis, Dover Publications 2003

Starwynn, Darren, Healing the Root of Pain, Desert Heart Press, 2013

Starwynn, Darren, Microcurrent Electro-Acupuncture, Desert Heart Press 2001

Starwynn, Darren, Reclaiming Your Calm Center, Desert Heart Press 2017

The Way of Mastery, Shanti Christo Foundation, 2004

Three Disciples, The Kybalion, TarcherPerigree, 2018

Tolle, Eckardt, A New Earth, Plume Printing/Penguin Group 2005

Whitman, Christy, The Desire Factor, Beyond Words Publishing, 2021

Vonegut, Jr., Kurt, The Sirens of Titan, Dial Press Trade, 1998

Yogananda, Paramahansa, Autobiography of a Yogi, Philosophical Library 1946

Films quoted:

Thrive I

The Matrix

Lord of the Rings series of 3 movies

The Day the Earth Stood Still (1951 and 2008)

Useful Links:

https://www.llresearch.org/ Channeled information about Lightworkers

https://www.souledout.org/souledoutglossary.html Glossary of metaphysical terminology

https://ascensionglossary.com/index.php/Main_Page and https://ascensionglossary. com/index.php/Timelines Ascension Glossary, including many deep discussions of Timelines and ways the human race has been manipulated.

Acknowledgments

It is with gratitude I acknowledge all who have contributed to making this book possible. I cannot name all those who influenced what is in this book, but here are those on the top of the list:

Prem Rawat (Maharaji), Dr. Sue Morter, Devra West (Devra Adi Maa), Dr. Zhi Gang Sha, Dr. Charles McWilliams, the Rimpoche of the Tjengboche Monastery in Nepal, Maria Sunukjian, Lyn O'Hara, Meg Benedicte, Barbara Brennan, Susannah Redelfs, Debora Wayne, Drunvalo Melchizedek, Christy Whitman, Eckhardt Tolle, Dr. David Hawkins, Carl Johan Calleman, Steve Bhaerman, Nassim Haramein, Vidya Frazier, Rosalyn Bruyere and Dr. Reinhold Voll.

I greatly appreciate the talents of artist Kate Bakkila, who did a beautiful job of translating my visions into the graphic art images found throughout this book, and consultant Geoff Affleck and editor Susan Nunn who have been valued allies in bringing it to publication.

I also offer my heartfelt thanks to all my friends, colleagues and family members who reviewed this book and offered vital suggestions for improving it, with an especial thanks to my sister Laura Davis who did the labor of love to thoroughly edit the entire book while she was in the midst of writing her own memoir. I also acknowledge my parents Abe and Temme and my daughter Sonya for teaching me some of the deepest lessons about life and love, as well as many friends, clients and students who offered much-appreciated support and encouragement.

The ultimate thanks must go to the unseen beings of Light who are working tirelessly to support the Ascension of the human race through this challenging time on Earth. I have strongly felt the divine love and presence of these "friends in high places", frequently taking direct dictation from them and then transcribing their messages into these chapters. Those I identified the most clearly were Master Jesus, whose words are sprinkled throughout the book, Archangel Metatron and the universal Divine Mother.

And a huge thanks to you the reader, who is inspired by this book and others, and takes your courageous steps to become Christed and awaken the Avatar within you. The power of your transformation to positively influence the collective of humanity is incalculable.

About the Author

Darren Starwynn has been aware of the Quantum Field of consciousness since childhood. Spurred by very difficult early experiences, he has devoted his life to uncovering the deeper truths of energy, healing, regeneration and what it truly means to be loving and awake.

Born in New Jersey, U.S.A., Darren journeyed to India when he was 19 years old to study with a realized spiritual Master, and then spent most of his 20's learning to embody the arts of meditation and service. He started his study of Chinese and holistic medicine in his early 30's, and went on to develop the Acutron Microlight device and Starwynn Light System, create books and videos and lead professional training seminars and workshops over a 25 year period. The main focus of Darren's work has been to help empower Lightworkers. His teaching and inventions have been instrumental in helping hundreds of acupuncturists, chiropractors, estheticians and holistic healers to elevate their results and increase their income.

Darren eventually turned most of his focus toward the Quantum level of healing and human development. In 2016 he was ordained as a Knight in the Sacred Medical Order of the Knights of Hope (SMOKH), an international spiritual organization dedicated to service through teaching and sharing methods of natural medicine. In 2017 Darren founded Bridge to Mastery Consciousness Institute for the purpose of helping uplift the knowledge and abilities of health professionals and healers to the Quantum level.

An avid hiker, guitarist and songwriter, Darren lives in Marin County, California and maintains a private practice along with his teaching and mentoring work through Lightworker Ministry, a non-denominational auxiliary of SMOKH. He can be reached through his practice website: www.drstarwynn.com.

Complete List of Ascension Practices

Index

Made in the USA
Coppell, TX
26 June 2024

33941234R00203